COGNITIVE THERAPY FOR BIPOLAR DISORDER

The Wiley Series in

CLINICAL PSYCHOLOGY

Dominic H. Lam *Steven H. Jones* *Peter Hayward* *Jenifer A. Bright*	Cognitive Therapy for Bipolar Disorder: A Therapist's Guide to Concepts, Methods and Practice

Previous titles published under the series editorship of:

J. Mark G. Williams   *School of Psychology, University*
                          of Wales, Bangor, UK

William Yule *(Editor)*	Post-Traumatic Stress Disorders: Concepts and Therapy
Nicholas Tarrier *Adrian Wells* *Gillian Haddock* *(Editors)*	Treating Complex Cases: The Cognitive Behavioural Therapy Approach
Michael Bruch *Frank W. Bond* *(Editors)*	Beyond Diagnosis: Case Formulation Approaches in CBT
Martin Herbert	Clinical Child Psychology (second edition)
Eric Emerson *Chris Hatton* *Jo Bromley* *Amanda Caine* *(Editors)*	Clinical Psychology and People with Intellectual Disabilities
J. Mark G. Williams *Fraser N. Watts* *Colin MacLeod* *Andrew Mathews*	Cognitive Psychology and Emotional Disorders (second edition)
Phil Mollon	Multiple Selves, Multiple Voices: Working with Trauma, Violation and Dissociation

A list of earlier titles in the series follows the index.

COGNITIVE THERAPY FOR BIPOLAR DISORDER

A Therapist's Guide to Concepts, Methods and Practice

Dominic H. Lam
Institute of Psychiatry, London, UK

Steven H. Jones
Birch Hill Hospital, Rochdale, UK

Peter Hayward
Institute of Psychiatry, London, UK

Jenifer A. Bright
Institute of Psychiatry, London, UK

JOHN WILEY & SONS, LTD

Chichester · New York · Weinheim · Brisbane · Singapore · Toronto

Copyright © 1999 by   John Wiley & Sons Ltd,
Baffins Lane, Chichester,
West Sussex PO19 1UD, England

National 01243 779777
International (+44) 1243 77977
e-mail (for orders and customer service enquiries):
cs-books@wiley.co.uk
Visit our Home Page on http://www.wiley.co.uk
or http://www.wiley.com

Reprinted September 2000

Other Wiley Editorial Offices

John Wiley & Sons, Inc., 605 Third Avenue,
New York NY 10158-0012, USA

WILEY-VCH Verlag GmbH, Pappelallee 3, D-69469 Weinheim, Germany

Jacaranda Wiley Ltd, 33 Park Road, Milton,
Queensland 4064, Australia

John Wiley & Sons (Asia) Pte Ltd, 2 Clementi Loop #02-01,
Jin Xing Distripark, Singapore 129809

John Wiley & Sons (Canada) Ltd, 22 Worcester Road,
Rexdale, Ontario M9W 1L1, Canada

Library of Congress Cataloging-in-Publication Data

Cognitive therapy for bipolar disorder : a therapist's guide to
concepts, methods, practice / Dominic H. Lam ... [et al.].
p.   cm. — (The Wiley series in clinical psychology)
Includes bibliographical references and index.
ISBN 0–471–97939–2 (cased : alk. paper). — ISBN 0–471–97945–7
(pbk. : alk. paper)
1. Manic-depressive illness—Treatment. 2. Cognitive therapy.
I. Lam, Dominic. II. Series
RC516.C64   1999
616.89'50651—dc21   99–20568
CIP

British Library Cataloguing in Publication Data

A catalogue record for this book is available from the British Library

ISBN 0-471-97939-2 (cased)
ISBN 0-471-97945-7 (paper)

Typeset in 10/12pt Palatino by Saxon Graphics Limited, Derby
Printed and bound in Great Britain by Biddles Ltd, Guildford and King's Lynn
This book is printed on acid-free paper responsibly manufactured from sustainable
forestry, in which at least two trees are planted for each one used for paper production.

CONTENTS

ABOUT THE AUTHORS

Dominic Lam received his clinical psychology training and his Ph.D. at the Institute of Psychiatry, University of London. He has published in the psycho-social aspects of mental illness, particularly depression and manic depression. Currently he is a Senior Lecturer in Clinical Psychology at the Institute of Psychiatry and an Honorary Consultant Clinical Psychologist at the Bethlem and Maudsley NHS Trust. His clinical work is based in the Affective Disorders Unit at the Maudsley Hospital.

Steven Jones, works as a Consultant Clinical Psychologist at Birch Hill Hospital in Greater Manchester, where he has been based since 1995. He received clinical training at the Institute of Psychiatry, University of London, where he also undertook doctoral research into information processing in schizophrenia and subsequently worked as a Clinical Lecturer. His research interests are primarily in cognitive psychological approaches to the treatment and understanding of severe mental illness.

Peter Hayward attended Harvard University, and, after teaching secondary school, earned a Ph.D. in Clinical Psychology from Long Island University, New York. He is employed by the Maudsley Hospital and the Institute of Psychiatry, and is interested in psychological approaches to serious mental illness.

Jenifer A. Bright obtained a B.Sc. in Psychology from the University of Wales College of Cardiff and a qualifying M.Sc. in Clinical Psychology from the Institute of Psychiatry. She has obtained further specialist training in cognitive therapy and her clinical and research interests have been in the application of CBT techniques to severe mental illness, particularly manic depression. She is a tutor on the diploma course in CBT at the Institute of Psychiatry.

PREFACE

Psychotherapy for manic depressive patients has been very much neglected. In the past two decades, the treatment for manic depression has been mainly pharmaco-therapy, especially prophylactic treatment. However, recently questions have been raised about the effectiveness of common prophylactic medications such as lithium (Moncrieff, 1995; Solomon et al., 1995). About 20–40% of classic manic depressive patients do not respond to lithium. The evidence of efficacy of carbamazepine and valproate is only tentative and the main findings point to equivalent efficacy to lithium (Solomon et al., 1995). Meanwhile, only one randomised controlled treatment trial of cognitive therapy for manic depression has been reported (Cochran, 1984). In that trial, therapy was not specially designed for manic depressive patients and consisted of six sessions of a cognitive behavioural approach to promote medication compliance.

This book describes our attempts at working with manic depressive patients as a form of prophylactic psychotherapy in conjunction with medication. We hope that a combination of cognitive therapy and medication can provide a desirable effect for manic depressive patients who do not do well with prophylactic medication alone.

The treatment package described in this book contains elements from traditional cognitive therapy for depression (Beck et al., 1979). It also includes elements specifically devised for treating the particular difficulties experienced by individuals with bipolar illness. This is based on the combined work of the authors over several years in developing a treatment approach which is practical and acceptable to clients, whilst also based on current understanding of the psycho-social aspects of bipolar illness. Research findings with this approach are preliminary but an early randomised controlled trial does indicate that significant clinical gains can be made by the appropriate application of the procedures described (Lam, Bright, Jones et al., in press).

This book consists of two parts. Part A aims to provide readers with a basic knowledge about manic depression, treatments available so far, the psycho-social aspects of manic depression and our model for psychological intervention. Part B describes the treatment package. It consists of chapters on the pre-therapy assessment, how to introduce the model to the patient, specific cognitive and behavioural techniques for manic depression, and self-management and coping with prodromes. It also describes the long term issues, the sense of the self, family and social aspects, interpersonal issues in therapy and issues related to services in the context of manic depression.

ACKNOWLEDGEMENT

Throughout this book, we have outlined our therapeutic approach to bipolar illness. This approach grows out of our contact with manic depressive patients, a contact which some of our fellow professionals may not have had. Our approach is of course not unique. It grows in the first instance out of the Cognitive Therapy approach to depression, as expounded by Beck and coworkers (Beck et al., 1979; J. S. Beck, 1995; Blackburn & Davidson, 1990), and it parallels the work done by many other workers in the area of manic depression (Basco & Rush, 1996; Scott, 1996; Newman, unpublished) and to some extent other psychotic illnesses (Kingdon & Turkington, 1994; Fowler et al., 1995). As such, it is an example of what Alford & Beck (1997) have called the 'integrative power' of Cognitive Therapy. We are clearly in debt to many workers in this tradition, and the model of treatment set forth in this book is offered with great humility, in view of the size of our debt to so many fellow workers.

This debt, great though it is, is overshadowed by another debt, to our patients. We have found the manic depressive patients we have met to be charming, exciting, creative and vibrant people. They have also been, at times, difficult, obstreperous and contrary. In light of the difficulties, life events and emotional suffering that they have had to endure, we can only wonder if we would have coped as well as they do. Working with them has been a privilege. If this book encourages other professionals to work with this challenging and rewarding group of people, then we will be well pleased.

ACKNOWLEDGEMENT

Chapter 1

INTRODUCTION TO BIPOLAR DISORDER

This book describes the use of cognitive behavioural therapy in the treatment of manic depression. The terms 'manic depression' and 'bipolar disorder' have been used interchangeably by many people, though the latter is more commonly used in the United States of America and increasingly more frequently in Europe. In this book the two terms will be used interchangeably. In our approach, it is accepted that bipolar disorder is an illness. The diagnostic criteria for bipolar illness are taken from the current *Diagnostic and Statistical Manual* (4th edn) (American Psychiatric Association, 1994b). This identifies that depression, mania, hypomania and mixed affective episodes can exist within a bipolar diagnosis. Bipolar disorder affects a substantial proportion of the adult population and usually strikes in early adulthood. The course of bipolar illness tend to be relatively severe with many people suffering from multiple episodes, which tend towards longer duration as people get older. Recurrence of illness can be associated with multiple factors, which include substance abuse, family and relationship difficulties and persistence of subsyndromal symptoms between episodes. In addition to a pattern of recurrent episodes, there is a substantial risk of completed and attempted suicide associated with bipolar illness. These issues are highlighted in this introductory chapter to indicate the scale and severity of problems with which people with this illness are faced.

An important issue in approaching the treatment of bipolar illness is whether people can identify developing symptoms at relatively early (prodromal) stages. If such prodromes exist and can be identified then opportunities may exist for effective psychological intervention at those points. The ability of patients to detect and in some cases cope with prodromes is therefore discussed in some detail as intervention in this area forms an important part of the therapeutic strategy discussed later in the book.

Cyclothymia, in which people experience less severe manifestations of bipolar symptoms, is associated both with significant psycho-social difficulties and with possible benefits in periods of heightened creativity and increased productivity. Cyclothymia may not lead to full bipolar disorder but there is a substantially increased risk of this, in comparison with general population samples. Thus many current bipolar patients will have experienced cyclothymia and may indeed miss aspects of it when their illness is 'too well controlled' by medication. Meanwhile other bipolar patients will find pharmacological treatments ineffective which would tend to increase the risk of forms of substance abuse for self-medication.

The social costs of bipolar illness are substantial. People tend to break down at what would usually be the beginning or early part of their careers, with very few sustaining their chosen line of work. Difficulties with family relationships are common and rates of divorce are high. Social functioning even between episodes tends to be impaired. These factors create a picture of multiple difficulties present throughout the course of the illness.

This introductory chapter identifies the above issues to highlight the nature, severity, frequency and impact of this illness, which underline the urgency with which more effective treatment approaches, which acknowledge both the psychological and pharmacological aspects of the disorder, need to be identified. It is hoped that the approach described within this book will form one part of this endeavour. The topics covered in this chapter are diagnostic criteria, epidemiology, factors in recurrence of the illness, bipolar prodromes, cyclothymia, and high social costs.

DIAGNOSTIC CRITERIA FOR BIPOLAR DISORDER

Kraepelin (1913) described manic-depressive illness as encompassing the categories then employed of circular psychosis, simple mania and melancholia. This overall category was distinguished from dementia praecox in terms of course and prognosis in particular. Manic-depressive illness was seen to be a disorder of fluctuating course in which periods of normality were interspersed with periods of illness and prognosis was thought to be less bleak than the inevitable ongoing decline in functioning attributed to dementia praecox. Leonhard (1957) distinguished between bipolar and monopolar forms of manic depressive illness, the former identifying patients with a history of mania and the latter those who suffered depression only. The distinction between bipolar and unipolar depression as currently used was introduced into the American Diagnostic and Statistical Manual (3rd edn) (DSM III: American Psychiatric Association, 1980) and has more recently been included in the World Health Organisation Classification of Diseases (ICD-10: WHO, 1993).

DSM-IV Criteria

The current DSM IV (American Psychiatric Association, 1994b) is the diagnostic scheme which has been employed in our research into the role of psychological treatments in bipolar disorder and will therefore be referred to in some detail in this section.

Bipolar illness is characterised as a mood disorder within DSM IV. The criteria specify first the mood episodes which can be included within a diagnosis of bipolar disorder. These include (a) major depressive episode; (b) manic episode; (c) mixed episode and (d) hypomanic episode.

Major Depressive Episode

A major depressive episode is characterised by symptoms of:

(1)   depressed mood most of the day, nearly every day;
(2)   markedly diminished interest in all or most activities, nearly every day;
(3)   significant increase or decrease (when not dieting) in weight;
(4)   sleep disturbances—oversleeping/insomnia;
(5)   psychomotor changes (agitation or retardation);
(6)   low energy level or fatigue;
(7)   feelings of guilt or extreme self-criticism;
(8)   inability to concentrate or make decisions;
(9)   recurrent thoughts of death or suicidal ideation.

At least five of these nine symptoms must be present for a minimum of 2 weeks, always including either depressed mood or loss of interest or pleasure. Symptoms must be of sufficient severity to cause clinically significant distress or impairment in occupational, social or other important areas of functioning.

Manic Episode

In contrast in a manic episode mood is required to be 'abnormally and persistently elevated, expansive or irritable' for a period of at least a week. During this time the following associated symptoms are listed:

(1)   inflated self-esteem/grandiosity;
(2)   decreased need for sleep;
(3)   more talkative than usual, pressure of speech;
(4)   flights of ideas, thoughts racing;

(5)   distractibility;
(6)   increase in goal-directed activity;
(7)   excessive involvement in pleasurable activities that have a high potential for painful consequences;

DSM-IV requires at least three (four if mood is only irritable) of the above symptoms in addition to mood disturbance for a period of at least a week to meet diagnostic criteria. Disturbance again has to be sufficiently severe to cause marked impairment in occupational functioning, usual social activities, or in relationships with others. It may require hospitalisation and may include psychotic features in the symptom presentation.

Mixed Episode

A mixed episode is described as one in which symptom criteria for both manic and major depressive episode (with the exception of the duration criterion) are met nearly every day over a period of a week at least. The disturbance of mood needs to be 'of sufficient severity to cause marked impairment in occupational functioning, in usual social activities or relationships with others'.

Hypomanic Episode

A hypomanic episode has the same symptoms as those of a manic episode except delusions or hallucinations may not be present. Mood disturbance required is for *only 4 days* rather than a full week and has to be 'clearly different from usual undepressed mood' rather than 'abnormal', which suggests less severe disruption of mood. In contrast to mania disruption in social or occupational functioning is not marked, hospitalisation is not required and psychotic features are absent.

Bipolar 1 Disorder

Bipolar 1 disorder requires the presence of at least one manic episode during the person's psychiatric history. A diagnosis of first manic episode also falls within the bipolar I disorder heading. Other variants of bipolar I disorder are:
(1)   most recent episode hypomanic;
(2)   most recent episode manic;
(3)   most recent episode mixed;
(4)   most recent episode depressed; or

(5)   most recent episode unspecified (in this category symptom, but not duration, criteria are met for at least one of the above disorders of mood).

Bipolar II Disorder

Bipolar II disorder describes individuals who experience recurrent major depressive episodes with hypomanic episodes, but without meeting manic episode criteria during their psychiatric history.

Rapid Cycling Specifier

In both bipolar I and II disorders a rapid cycling specifier is added when four or more episodes occur within a given year.

Cyclothymic Disorder

Cyclothymic disorder requires the chronic presence of 'numerous periods' of hypomanic and depressive symptoms over a 2 year period which do not meet full criteria for either mania or a major depressive episode. At no time during the initial 2 year period must criteria for major depression, mania or mixed state be met. Symptom-free intervals during this period must be of no longer than 2 months duration. Mood disturbance must be sufficient to cause clinically significant distress or impairment in social, occupational, or other important areas of functioning. This is differentiated from rapid cycling bipolar disorder by not reaching full symptom criteria for any of the three categories above during the course of the disorder.

Although DSM IV includes this as a separate mood disorder it is clear that there is the potential for diagnostic confusion between this and milder forms of bipolar disorder. Furthermore whilst not included as a personality disorder within DSM IV, cyclothymia is described elsewhere as a personality type; this is discussed further later in the chapter.

EPIDEMIOLOGY

Bipolar disorder affects around 1–1.5% of the adult population. This estimate appears to be consistent in America (Robins et al., 1984: Weissman et al., 1988) and England (Bebbington & Ramana, 1995). Joyce (1984) reported an average age of 23 years for onset of first affective syndrome in 200 bipolar patients, whilst Burke et al. (1990) found onset closer to 19 years old on average. Goodwin & Jamison (1990) estimated from pooled data of 22 studies a mean age of onset of 28.1 years for manic-depressive illness. Reanalysing the data in age-related cohorts indicated that in fact the peak frequency of onset was between 15 and 19 years, with similar levels in the 20–24 years range. Clearly therefore this indicates a disorder which develops usually within early adulthood and can be present in teenage years. Studies are consistent in reporting similar prevalence rates for men and women.

For individuals with this disorder there appears to be a pattern of significant social disability and likely relapse in many cases. Winokur et al. (1969) estimated that 80% of individuals with an initial diagnosis of mania would go on to have further episodes, whilst Tohen et al. (1990a) having followed up 75 bipolar patients from an index mood episode reported that by 5 years approximately 90% had experienced at least one relapse. In spite of this pattern of recurrence, and in contrast with psychotic illnesses such as schizophrenia, there is little evidence of downward social drift associated with bipolar illness. Thus most studies of social class in relationship to bipolar disorder suggest that either there is no association or that rates of disorder predominate in middle and upper social or professional groups (Weissman & Myers, 1978: Coryell et al, 1989). There appears to be no consistent evidence to support elevated prevalence rates according to marital status or to city or rural locations. Fluctuations in onset according to time of year have been reported for affective disorders peaking primarily in spring (March–May) with a subsidiary peak in autumn (September–November) according to Goodwin & Jamison's (1990) review of available studies. The limited data for specifically manic episodes is suggestive of increased prevalence rates in spring or summer months (Myers & Davies, 1978: Carney et al., 1988).

COURSE OF BIPOLAR DISORDER

In a general population study of bipolar I disorder (in this case using DSM-III R criteria—American Psychiatric Association 1987—which are very similar to DSM-IV as previously described) conducted in America it was found that there was a 0.4% lifetime prevalence of this disorder, with a similar 12 month prevalence rate (Kessler et al., 1997). All cases apparently reported at least one other DSM-IIIR disorder and in almost 60% of cases these predated the onset of bipolar illness. This study indicates therefore that many people with bipolar illness may well have additional psychiatric difficulties beyond those associated with this specific diagnosis.

Interestingly this general population study also identified that only 45% of those identified as currently experiencing bipolar illness were in treatment. Whilst this may in part be due to patchy availability of mental health services, so that some people who may have welcomed psychiatric help had difficulty accessing it, it is unlikely that this is a sufficient explanation. Additional factors are likely to include the limitations of currently available pharmacological treatments and limited availability of alternative or additional forms of treatment such as psychotherapy. Thus Prien & Potter (1990) estimated that lithium may be ineffective in up to 40% of cases. This figure implies that a significant proportion of people are receiving treatments which are not significantly beneficial, and this is likely to be associated with both non-compliance with specific interventions and also dropping out of contact with mental health services in general. Those who have done so will tend not to appear in studies of the course of bipolar illness and hence there is some risk that the information currently available is skewed towards those patients who are responsive to and/or compliant with treatment.

Number of Episodes

Early estimates suggested that few patients experienced more than three episodes of mania or depression in total. However, this seems to have been partly based on inappropriate criteria. Exclusion of episodes not requiring hospitalisation led to underestimates of recurrence rates, as did failure to control for extended admissions during which several separate manic and depressive episodes may have occurred. More recently Carlson et al., (1974) followed up 53 bipolar manic depressive patients who, at time of follow-up, which was an average of 14.7 years after illness onset, had experienced an average of 3.7 manic episodes and 2.1 depressions. In another study Zis et al., (1980) found as many as 25% of patients with manic depression had seven or more episodes during the course of their illness. Current estimates suggest that on average a person with a bipolar I diagnosis will suffer 8–12 major depressive episodes and 4–8 manic episodes during their life, when clinical criteria rather than hospitalisation, are used as an episode indicator.

Age of Onset

Although age of onset has been suggested as a factor in likelihood of experiencing further episodes, research has not established a clear pattern here. Thus Zis et al. (1979) reported that probability of recurrence within 24 months rose from 0.2 in patients with age of onset in their 20s to 0.8 in patients with age of onset at 50+. However, contrasting with this are several reports indicating either no such pattern (Winokur et al., 1993: Tohen et al., 1990b) or an increased risk in patients with younger onset (Winokur & Kadrmas, 1989).

Duration of Episodes (Cycle Length)

There is more agreement on decreasing cycle length with increasing number of episodes. Thus Goodwin & Jamison (1990) summarise data which suggest that after first episodes a cycle length of around 40–60 months decreases with following episodes so that following a third episode cycle length is down to 10–30 months. This decrease in cycle length does not continue indefinitely, seeming to reach a constant level around episode 5–7 at between 5 and 10 months, according to their figures. Tohen et al. (1990a) reported that history of previous episodes was an important prospective predictor of time to relapse in a 4 year follow-up study of 75 bipolar manic patients. Those individuals with a history of depression or mania prior to the index episode in the study showed significantly reduced time to manic relapse, and similarly continuation of remission over the study period was associated with an absence of such history prior to the index episode.

Factors in Recurrence of Illness

Recurrence of mood episodes in bipolar illness have been associated with many different factors. Life events have been associated with both the onset and recurrence of illness episodes in bipolar disorder (e.g. Bebbington et al., 1993). This association will be discussed in detail in Chapter 3 and so will not be discussed further here. Tohen et al.'s (1990a) 4 year follow-up study found that, history of previous episodes, depressive symptoms and psychotic symptoms during index episodes were predictive of shorter time to relapse, as was a positive history of alcoholism. Factors associated with relapse include substance abuse, family relationships and subsyndromal symptoms. These are considered in turn below.

Substance Abuse

Another factor in course of bipolar disorder appears to be substance abuse. Sonne et al. (1994) interviewed 44 patients with bipolar illness. They found that current substance users reported twice as many previous hospitalisations and earlier onset of mood problems, and were more likely to be experiencing dysphoric mania and to have comorbid axis I diagnoses. Regier et al. (1990) reported that more than 60% of bipolar I and 50% of bipolar II patients had a substance abuse history. Strakowski et al. (1996) studied 59 patients with a first episode of psychotic mania. It was found that 12 had abused alcohol and 19 had abused drugs prior to hospitalisation for the index episode. Goodwin & Jamison (1990) estimate an overall rate of alcohol abuse and alcoholism of 35% in people with bipolar disorder, based on their review of 20 studies dating from 1921 to 1990, which compares with a rate of between 3 and 5% in the general population. Rates for cocaine use in bipolar patients range from 58% (Estroff et al., 1985) down to 10% (Miller et al., 1989), as compared to a general population rate of around 5%. Rates for opiate use are estimated by Miller et al. (1989) at around 5%. Although direction of causality is not firmly established Regier et al. (1990) report a bias towards affective disorder predating abuse. This possibility of affective state preceding substance use coincides with clinical descriptions of self medication. In particular the use of alcohol and opiates in trying to control agitated dysphoric or depressed states is described. In contrast to this the use of stimulant drugs is not commonly described in low mood, but rather as a means of sustaining hypomanic states or indeed of intensifying the effects of elevated mood states. In these cases then, the substance use would be more accurately described as a symptom of manic behaviour than an effort to 'self-treat'. In both cases however it is important to assess the nature and extent of drug use in relation to the risk of developing patterns of chronic substance use which become driven by addictive processes independently of the mood states which might have first triggered their use.

Family Relationships

Whereas there is an extended literature concerning the impact of family relationships in outcome for schizophrenia, there is less available data on the implications of this for course and outcome in bipolar disorder. Such results as there are suggest that bipolar patients may well be significantly sensitive to domestic atmosphere and that this could be an important variable in terms of both course and outcome. However, Ramana & Bebbington (1995) comment in their review that it is important that properly constructed studies of reasonable size, with clearly defined bipolar populations, are conducted to firmly establish the importance of this factor in the course of bipolar disorder. Issues of family and other social factors are returned to in Chapter 12.

Subsyndromal and Persisting Symptoms

In addition to relapses which require psychiatric attention many patients suffer from subsyndromal symptoms in between episodes. These symptoms, which can cause significant distress and disruption, were observed in 50% of patients in one treatment study (Keller et al. 1992). Gitlin et al. (1995) reported that even for patients who did not relapse over an average follow-up of 4.3 years, 46% continued to report significant levels of affective symptomatology. The presence of such subsyndromal symptoms, as well as causing distress in its own right, would seem likely to predispose patients to greater risk of full 'relapse' during their illness course, although we are not aware of any conclusive research evidence on this point at present. In addition there is a significant minority of patients whose illness persists over extended periods. Winokur et al. (1993) reported that 14% of bipolar patients who were ill at intake to their study remained so 2 years later.

Suicide Risk

Risk of suicide and suicide attempts are significant features of the course of bipolar illness. Goodwin & Jamison (1990) reviewed 30 studies in which rates of suicide of manic-depressive patients ranged from 9 to 60% of the studied sample. The averaged rate in this review was approximately 19%, substantially higher than the figure of 10% reported by Winokur & Tsuang (1975) for completed suicide in bipolar patients followed up over 30 years.

Regier et al. (1988) reported that 25% of bipolar patients make suicide attempts. Goodwin and Jamison (1990) found that rates of attempted suicide in 15 studies reviewed ranged from 20 to 56% in bipolar patients, rates being higher in women than in men. In a more recent study Chen & Dilsaver (1996) reported a lifetime rate of suicide attempts in bipolar disorder of almost 30%, which compared with 16% in unipolar and 4% in 'any other axis I disorder'. Goodwin and Jamison (1990) suggest that it is common for suicidal intent to be communicated in quite a direct way before such attempts are made and that such attempts often follow on from disrupted sleep patterns and following (not so much during) extreme depression. Mixed affective states are also identified as high risk for suicide attempts and completed suicide. Studies therefore seem to be consistent in identifying a disproportionate risk of both attempted and completed suicide in people with bipolar disorder as compared with other psychiatric disorders including major depression. Information on higher risk states within bipolar disorder in conjunction with good outpatient follow up and appropriately responsive treatment delivery would therefore be important in helping to reduce suicide rates within this group.

Summary

The preceding discussion indicates that, as Solomon et al. (1995) have argued, bipolar disorder is far from a disorder with good prognosis, as it has been perceived clinically in the past. Whilst Kraepelin's distinction between manic-depressive psychosis and dementia praecox, with the latter being distinguished at least in part by its more benign course, has been clinically important in many ways, the currently available evidence supports the view that whilst some people with this diagnosis do indeed do very well, for the majority it has a severe impact on most areas of their lives, with substantially increased risk of future episodes, substance abuse and mortality.

PRODROMES

Another issue in the course of bipolar illness is that of prodromes. This use of information related to prodromes in the psychological treatment of bipolar illness is discussed in detail in Chapter 10. This section will therefore confine itself to the following questions:

(1)   Can bipolar patients detect prodromes?
(2)   What are the common prodromes of both mania and depression?
(3)   Are the individual patterns of prodromes idiosyncratic?
(4)   What are the prodromes that are consistently detected by patients?
(5)   How long is the prodromal stage?
(6)   How do patients cope with prodromes?
(7)   What difference does coping make to the course of the illness?

Each of these questions will be discussed in turn.

Can Patients Suffering Manic Depression Detect Prodromes?

Five studies have addressed this issue. The studies on prodromes in bipolar affective disorder were either retrospective studies in which subjects were asked about their past experiences (Molnar et al., 1988; Smith & Tarrier, 1992; Joyce, 1985; Lam & Wong, 1997) or a single longitudinal study in which subjects were seen regularly for assessment (Altman et al., 1992). These studies tended to be small in sample size. Three out of five studies reviewed (Molnar et al., 1988; Smith and Tarrier, 1992 and Altman et al., 1992) had a sample size of around 20. However, despite this small sample size, the finding that bipolar patients can detect prodromes seems robust.

All five studies agree that bipolar patients were able to report prodromes. Interestingly bipolar patients seem to be better at spontaneously reporting manic prodromes than depression prodromes. Lam and Wong (1997) reported that 25% (10/40) of the manic depressive patients could not detect prodromes of depression in their study. Only 7.5% (3/40) of their sample reported that they could not detect prodromes of mania. Similarly in Molnar et al.'s study, 30% (6/20) of patients could not report depression prodromes spontaneously but all 20 patients could report mania prodromes spontaneously. The high proportion of patients who could not detect depression prodromes could be due to the insidious onset of bipolar depression. Some patients even said that depression was like a virus and that you wake up with it. This makes the detection of depression prodromes more difficult.

What are the Common Prodromes Reported by Manic-depressive Patients?

As studies used different instruments for prodromes of bipolar patients, comparison across studies is not straightforward. For example, Joyce (1985) used a semi-structured interview and rated patients' ability to recognise and respond appropriately to early symptoms of relapse on a six-point scale ranging from very poor to very good. There was a problem with inter-rater reliability on this item and no details of what the early symptoms of relapse were reported. Altman et al. (1992) reported that the BPRS-rated conceptual disorganisation was elevated during the four months prior to a depressive episode.

Table 1.1 shows the most common prodromes of mania in Molnar et al.'s (1988), Smith & Tarrier's (1992), and Lam & Wong's (1997) studies. Across the three studies that listed individual prodromes, there was strong agreement about prodromes of mania. With the exception of irritability, the six most often reported prodromes of mania (sleeping less, more goal-directed behaviour, irritability, increased sociability, thoughts start to race and increased optimism) are also among the most frequently reported prodromal symptoms by Smith & Tarrier's (1992) and Molnar et al.'s (1988) studies. Irritability was not one of the most common prodromes reported by Smith & Tarrier and Molnar et al.'s studies. Even so it was reported spontaneously by 33% of Smith & Tarrier's sample.

Table 1.2 shows the common prodromes of depression reported in Molnar et al.'s (1988), Smith & Tarrier's (1992) and Lam & Wong's (1997) studies. Subjects' reports of their prodromes of depression between the three studies, though agreeing less with Molnar et al's and Smith & Tarrier's studies,

Table 1.1   Common prodromes of mania across studies

Molnar el. al. (1988)— spontaneous recall (*n*=20)	Smith & Tarrier (1992)— 40-item checklist (*N* = 20)	Lam & Wong (1997)— spontaneous recall (*n* = 37)
Increased activity (100%)	Emotionally high (100%)	Not interested in sleep or sleeping less (58%)
Elevated mood (90%)	Energetic/very active (87%)	More goal-directed behaviour (56%)
Decreased need for sleep (90%)	Don't need much sleep (80%)	Irritable (25%)
More talkative (85%)	Ideas flowing too fast (80%)	Increased sociability (25%)
Racing thoughts (80%)	More talkative (80%)	Thoughts racing (19%)
Increased self-worth (75%)	Senses seem sharper (80%)	Increased optimism (14%)
Distractibility (65%)	Feels creative (80%)	Over-excited (14%)

Table 1.2   Common depression prodromes across studies

Molnar el. al. (1988) spontaneous recall of prodromes (*n*=14)	Smith & Tarrier (1992) 40-item checklist (*N*=20)	Lam & Wong (1997) spontaneous recall of prodromes (*n*=28)
Depressed mood (86%)	Low in self-confidence (88%)	Loss of interest in people or activity (45%)
Loss of energy (86%)	Can't face normal tasks (82%)	Feeling sad or want to cry (20%)
Concentration difficulties (79%)	Nothing seems enjoyable (82%)	Interrupted sleep (17%)
Morbid thoughts (64%)	Can't get up in the morning (71%)	Not able to put worries or anxiety aside (17%)
Decreased sleep (57%)	Not feeling like seeing people (71%)	Low motivation (14%)
Loss of interest (57%)	Feeling sad (71%)	Low self-esteem (10%)
Weight loss (43%)	Difficulty concentrating (71%)	Negative thinking (10%)

are quite similar. The top four most common prodromes reported spontaneously by the subjects in Lam & Wong's study (loss of interest in activities or people, not able to put worries or anxieties aside, interrupted sleep, feeling sad or want to cry) were also reported by 71–82% of subjects in Smith & Tarrier's study. They were also among the top six most commonly reported prodromal symptoms in Molnar et al's study. However, taken as a whole, there seems to be more diversity in prodromes of depression. Across three studies, subjects reported fewer depression prodromes and there seemed to be diversity in the report of prodromal signs and symptoms of depression.

Are the Individual Patterns of Prodromes Idiosyncratic?

Molnar et al. (1988) reported that bipolar patients had considerable interindividual variability but very little intra-individual variability of prodromes. Smith & Tarrier (1992) also commented on the idiosyncratic 'relapse signature' of the individual patient. Hence there is a consensus that each patient's pattern or combination of signs and symptoms may be unique. Asking for spontaneous reports of prodromes has the advantage of personalising the prodromes in the individual's context. For example, a minority of patients were able to report some idiosyncratic prodromes such as 'people scheming to get rid of me', 'feel more capable and wanting to get involved in other people's problems', 'posters seem more vivid and carry special and subtle messages that normally I would not notice' as clear prodromes of mania. Another patient was able to report 'getting irritated with her husband' and 'not enjoying reading to my children' as prodromes of depression.

What are the Prodromes that are Consistently Detected by Patients?

Lam & Wong, in a paper in preparation, followed up their sample of 40 depressive patients and asked them about prodromes 18 months later. Mania prodromes were reported reliably at both T1 (at recruitment) and at T2 (follow-up 18 months later). Furthermore, patients reported behaviourally orientated mania prodromes more frequently and more reliably: sleep less (55.3% at T1 and 55.3% at T2), more goal-directed behaviour (44.7% at T1 and 55.3% at T2), increased sociability (18.4% at T1 and 21.1% at T2). Mood-orientated mania prodromes and cognitively orientated mania prodromes were reported less frequently and less reliably: thoughts started to race (15.8% at both T1 and T2); increased optimism

(26.3% at T1 and 10.5% at T2), irritability (10.5% at T1 and 13.2% at T2). Similarly, depression prodromes were reported reliably at T1 and T2: loss of interest in activity or people (28.9% at T1 and 36.8% at T2), interrupted sleep (13.2% at T1 and 26.3% at T2) and not able to put aside worries (15.8% at T1 and 18.4% at T2). At both times, patients reported fewer and less frequent depression prodromes. Furthermore, there was no difference in the frequency and reliability of behavioural and cognitive prodromes in depression.

How Long is the Prodromal Stage?

The duration of the manic or depression prodromal stages also varies from individual to individual. Molnar et al. (1988) reported that for his sample the mania prodromes lasted on average 20.5 days. However, the range is enormous: from 1 to 84 days. Similarly, Molnar reported that the average length of depression prodromes was 11 days, ranging from 2 to 31 days. Smith & Tarrier (1992) reported that in their study, the average duration of prodromes of depression was 19 (s.d. 19) days and the average duration of mania prodromes was 29 (s.d. 28) days.

How do Patients Cope with Prodromes?

Only one study, by Lam & Wong (1997), addressed this issue. Joyce (1985) rated how patients 'seek treatment at an early stage of future relapse' but published no details. Lam & Wong (1997) rated independently their subjects' coping on a seven-point scale, ranging from poor to adequate to extremely well. Good inter-rater reliability was reported. The sample was then divided into good (from adequate to extremely well) to poor (below adequate to poor) groups. Table 1.3 shows the coping strategies for prodromes of mania in Lam & Wong's (1997) study. The most common coping strategies for prodromes of mania employed by subjects in the good coping group were 'modifying high activities and restrain themselves', 'engaging in calming activities', 'taking extra time to rest or sleep' and 'seeing a doctor'. In the poor coping group, the most common coping strategies for prodromes of mania were 'continuing to move about and take on more tasks', 'enjoying the feeling of high', 'going out more and spending money', 'finding more to fill out the extra minutes of the day' and 'doing nothing special'. It is interesting to note that the spontaneous coping strategies reported by patients are behavioural.

Table 1.4 shows the coping strategies of depression prodromes from Lam & Wong's (1997) study. The most common ones employed by subjects in

Table 1.3 Subjects' coping with mania prodromes in the good and poor coping group

Coping strategies for mania prodromes	Good coping group ($n = 21$) %	Poor coping group ($n = 15$) %
Modify my excessive behaviour and restrain myself	61.9	0
Engage in calming activities	47.6	13.3
Take extra time to rest and sleep	42.9	0
See a doctor	28.6	6.7
Take extra medication	19.0	6.7
Prioritise and reduce the number of tasks	14.3	0
Take time off work	14.3	0
Continue to move about and take on more	0	26.7
Nothing special	0	26.7
Enjoy the feeling of high	4.8	20.0
Go out more and spend money	0	20.0
Find more to do to fill out extra minute of the day	0	20.0
Drink to keep going	0	13.3
Lose my temper over small things	0	13.3

Table 1.4 Subjects' coping with depression prodromes in the good and poor coping group

Coping strategies for depresson prodromes	Good coping group ($n = 17$) (%)	Poor coping group ($n = 12$) (%)
Get myself organised and keep busy	52.9	0
Get social support and meet people	29.4	0
Distract myself from negative thoughts by doing things	23.5	8.3
Recognise unrealistic thoughts and evaluate if things are worth worrying about	23.5	0
Maintain a routine	17.6	0
Exercise or keep fit	17.6	0
See a doctor	11.8	0
Stay in bed and hope it will go away	5.9	58.3
Do nothing	0	25.0
Take extra drug, e.g. lithium or sleeping pills	5.9	16.7
Avoid social contact	5.9	8.3

the good coping group were 'get myself organised and keep busy', 'get social support and meet people', 'distract from negative thoughts by doing more', 'recognise realistic thoughts and evaluate if things are worth worrying about'. In the poor coping group, subjects' most common coping strategies were to 'stay in bed and hope it would go away', 'do nothing' and 'take extra medication such as lithium or sleeping pills'. Subjects in the good coping group for prodromes of mania reported the spontaneous use of behavioural techniques, for example restraining themselves from excessive behaviour, engaging in calming activities and taking extra time to rest or sleep when they detected prodromes of mania. Similarly, subjects in the good coping group for prodromes of depression used behavioural techniques such as keeping busy. However, some subjects also reported cognitive techniques of distraction from negative thoughts and recognising unrealistic thoughts and evaluating if these thoughts were worth worrying about.

What Difference does Coping Make to the Course of the Illness?

Since the evidence is that bipolar patients can report prodromes, the next question is how recognising and coping with prodromes can affect how patients fare. Only two studies addressed this question. Joyce (1985) found that, in addition to non-compliance with medication, inability to recognise and respond to early symptoms of relapse were important factors in the management of bipolar illness. However, in Joyce's study the rating of response to early symptoms focused mainly on being 'able to seek treatment at an early stage of future relapse'. There was no investigation of patients' natural cognitive or behavioural ways of coping. Furthermore the subscale on 'ability to recognise and to respond to early symptoms' had poor inter-rater reliability. In Lam & Wong's (1997) study there were significantly more high functioning subjects in the good coping group for prodromes of mania. More high functioning subjects were also present in the good coping group for prodromes of depression but the difference just failed to reach statistical significance. Subjects' current levels of depression, coping with prodromes of mania, insight and ability to recognise early warnings for depression made significant contributions independently to their levels of social functioning. Hence subjects' coping with prodromes of mania appears to be an important factor in determining their level of social functioning whereas coping with prodromes of depression was not. The possible explanation is that being in a stage of early mania is much more public and perhaps immediately destructive whereas the early stage of depression can be more private. For those who are less able to cope with their prodromes of mania, the effect on their social functioning can be more detrimental. At their 18-month follow-up (Lam & Wong paper in preparation), how patients coped with mania prodromes and the number of life events patients experienced during the 18 months predicted bipolar relapses during the 18 months. These two variables made a significant contribution in a regression analysis to predict the number of bipolar relapses, with the effect of number of previous episodes, patients' level of depression and mania at recruitment controlled for.

Joyce (1985) reported that most readmissions within a year were due to mania. Clinical experience suggests that early mania symptoms can fuel themselves into a full-blown episode. Gitlin et al. (1995) reported that subjects' social functioning was important as it can in turn affect the duration between episodes. Coupled with Lam & Wong's (1997) finding that coping with prodromes of mania is an important determinant of subjects' level of functioning, it is particularly important to teach bipolar affective disorder patients to tackle prodromes of mania.

Summary

Most patients suffering manic depression can report prodromes. There are significantly more patients who could not spontaneously report depression than those who could not do so for manic prodromes. This is probably due to the fact that the onset of a manic episode is more acute and less insidious. Furthermore, the individual's pattern of prodromes can be very idiosyncratic. However, there are prodromes that are frequently reported for mania (e.g. sleeping less, more goal-directed behaviour, increased sociability, thoughts start to race) and for depression (e.g. loss of interest, not able to put worries aside, interrupted sleep, feeling sad and wanting to cry). Patients also appear to report prodromes reliably over time. Most patients report spontaneous coping during the prodromal stages. There is evidence that how well patients cope with mania prodromes can predict patients' level of social functioning, which in turn predicts less frequent relapses.

CYCLOTHYMIA

Cyclothymia was used as a diagnostic category within the DSM-IIIR criteria. It was very similar to cyclothymic disorder as defined by the DSM-IV criteria, both highlighting the persistent presence of numerous hypomanic and depressive symptoms over at least a 2 year period. Prior to these specific criteria the terms cyclothymia/cyclothymic personality usually implied the presence of manic and depressive symptoms that did not reach sufficient severity to indicate a full psychiatric diagnosis of mania or depression and which had been recurrent usually over many years.

Jamison (1993) has described the association between cyclothymic personality and subsequent onset of manic depressive illness as fundamental. Cyclothymic personality is identified as the presence of a consistent pattern of cyclothymia over a period of many years, which may or may not have received psychiatric treatment. Whilst she recognises that it is possible to have characteristics of cyclothymia without developing manic depression, it is noted that one third of people in this category do just that. This contrasts starkly with a rate of illness of 1% observed in general population samples. In addition to this it is noted that people with milder symptomatology respond similarly to lithium. Also there is some evidence for genetic concordance in that the presence of a cyclothymic individual in a family pedigree substantially increases the likelihood of finding other individuals within that pedigree with bipolar illness.

Akiskal, Khani & Scott-Strauss (1979) describe cyclothymia as presenting initially in early adulthood usually as a personality disorder, with the patient often unaware at first of mood changes. The changes in mood will be of short duration and may usually not meet the full criteria for depression or hypomania. The course of cyclothymia is noted to be biphasic, with alternation of hyper- and hyposomnia, low self-esteem and then overconfidence; mental confusion and apathy and then increased focus and creativity; uneven quality and quantity of work output; introversion and extroversion. The individuals who are cyclothymic can be prone to irritable and angry outbursts of a severity that can distance them from their partner. Sexual behaviour can be episodically promiscuous, with consequent relationship effects. Work patterns can be variable with periods of enthusiasm for particular career paths alternating with changes of direction and altering of plans. There is a significant risk of drug and alcohol abuse, as is observed in bipolar illness itself. This can be associated with the self-medicating of affective symptoms or efforts to enhance positive mood states. A recent study by Rounsaville et al. (1991) studied a group of 298 cocaine abusers and found that in this sample 56% had a current psychiatric illness and 74% had had one at some time in their lives. Although many of these patients had affective and bipolar diagnoses this study reported that drug abuse predated the onset of psychiatric illness. However, the presence of a cyclothymic personality may well have predisposed the individual to both substance abuse and bipolar affective disorder. Hence this may fail to recognise the importance of subsyndromal symptoms in this pattern.

In contrast to the difficulties described above there is also evidence that cyclothymia is associated with significant benefits. Thus both Jamison (1993) and Goodwin and Jamison (1990) report that amongst high achievers in the arts, science and business are many individuals who would meet bipolar criteria. Indeed Jamison described her own bipolar illness in a later book and is quite clear that some of her academic creativity and output was associated in particular with periods of hypomania.

Goodwin and Jamison (1990) list among others: Samuel Taylor Coleridge, Gerard Manley Hopkins, John Ruskin, Robert Schumann, Oliver Cromwell, Winston Churchill and Benito Mussolini, as having had likely bipolar or cyclothymic disorders. Therefore it is important to bear in mind the likelihood that many individuals presenting for treatment will have had these experiences of increased effectiveness and creativity either premorbidly or as part of their illness course. Their concern about successful treatment robbing them of this positive side has to be treated with respect, even if the clinician's views diverge from those of the client. Indeed Jamison reports that many creative individuals have for instance tried to reduce their intake of lithium with a view to achieving a moderately controlled state of hypomania.

Interestingly Jamison also reported on findings from two studies in which artists rated their own creative productivity following lithium. Fifty-seven per cent reported increases in productivity whilst 20% remained the same. However, in spite of this positive outcome, 17% of people reported that they stopped their lithium because of its effects on creativity, hence the importance of assessing its impact in an individualised manner (Marshall, Neumann & Robinson, 1970: Schou, 1979).

HIGH SOCIAL COSTS

Bipolar illness can have multiple impacts across many areas of psychosocial functioning. Education can be interrupted or impaired, career progression halted, jobs lost, marriages put under strain or ended due to the illness itself or behaviour associated with it. Sexual activity patterns can be radically changed during illness leading to effects on interpersonal relationships, which can in themselves be under strain from other effects. Even the ability to live alone or enjoy and profit from non-work activity can be impaired in some people with this diagnosis. Physical health effects can also be observed in some sufferers, sometimes as a consequence of co-morbid substance abuse, as a side effect of chronic drug taking and also as a consequence of reckless behaviour during manic or hypomanic states.

Social Functioning

Bellack et al. (1989) assessed social competence in a group of schizoaffective ($N = 16$), schizophrenic ($N = 58$) and bipolar ($N = 29$) inpatients by means of a structured role play test and interview measures including Weissman and Bothwell's (1976) Social Adjustment Scale II (SAS). It was found that all three groups exhibited significant levels of impairment both on role play and SAS measures. When the schizophrenic group was subdivided into those with a negative syndrome and those without the former group performed worse than all other groups. However, the non-negative syndrome schizophrenics did not differ from either schizoaffective or bipolar patients. Such data indicate that substantial social impairments can be observed within bipolar disorder especially when comparisons between diagnostic groups do not confound diagnostic differences with differences in symptom severity at time of testing.

Romans & McPherson (1992) compared a group of 64 patients with bipolar disorder with a random community sample of 232 women. Social networks for both groups were assessed using the Interview Schedule for Social Interaction (Henderson et al., 1981) which indicates availability and adequacy of both intimate and more diffuse social interactions. Results were that the bipolar patients had lower scores (worse) across all measures of social interaction. These were associated with age, length of illness and number of manic episodes. This pattern was suggestive of greater deterioration in social networks the longer the illness continues, with especial damage to social contact being associated with recurrent manic episodes.

Bauwens et al. (1991) meanwhile investigated social adjustment in remitted bipolar and unipolar patients. Remission was defined as at least six months free of any significant symptoms and at least two months free of probable minor depressive or hypomanic episodes. The measure, used to assess social adjustment was the social adjustment scale of Weissman et al. (1971). Controls had no psychiatric history and were matched for age and sex with the patient groups. Patients, not surprisingly, showed worse overall adjustment than controls in particular in terms of social and leisure activities, with diminished contact with friends the most prominent feature for bipolar patients. Unlike the unipolar patients the number of episodes and current level of residual (subsyndromal) symptoms was associated with social adjustment deficits in the bipolar patients. This suggests that social functioning difficulties are apparent in patients with bipolar disorder even when currently relatively well and in the absence of depression or mania, which suggests a persisting problem which may need to be a target for psychological intervention. Indeed Cannon et al.

(1997) has investigated premorbid social functioning impairment in schizophrenic ($N = 100$) and bipolar ($N = 49$) patients compared to a group of 100 controls subjects with minor medical problems. Their study used maternal interviews to obtain retrospective interview data on Premorbid Social Adjustment Scale scores (Foerster et al., 1991). These indicated that, compared to normal controls, social functioning in bipolar patients deteriorated in adolescence, although school performance was relatively preserved, indicating the possibly long-term nature of social functioning pattern difficulties even prior to the first psychiatric episode.

Work Outcomes

Of 53 bipolar patients with a mean illness duration of 14.7 years followed up by Carlson et al. (1974) 59% were either not working or were working in lower status positions than premorbidly. Gitlin et al. (1995) studied 82 patients with a diagnosis of bipolar disorder over a mean period of 4.3 years. They reported good occupational outcome in only 28% of subjects. Prien & Potter (1990) reported on a US Department of Health Education and Welfare study of 1979 which estimates that an average woman experiencing bipolar disorder with onset at 25 years might expect to lose 14 years of major effective activity (which would relate to both work and family responsibilities).

Family Burden and Marital Issues

Although divorce is not uncommon in general population studies, running at around 20%, in bipolar illness it is disproportionately high. Speer (1992) in a study of 407 patients over the age of 55 years found that the highest rates of divorce were in bipolar (55.6%) and schizophrenic (56.4%) patients; patients being treated for medical conditions not associated with mental health difficulties had a comparison divorce rate of 15.6%. Carlson et al. (1974) reported family interaction difficulties in 56% of bipolar patients in their study. Almost all families rate bipolar illness as imposing a severe burden on the family as a whole. Chakrabati et al. (1992) investigated family burden using the Family Burden Interview (Pai & Kapur, 1981) with relatives of 90 patients meeting DSM-III criteria for major affective disorder. Of the 90 relatives interviewed only 1 denied burden. Of the 29 relatives identifying severe burden, 27 were relatives of patients with bipolar illness; this same rating was given by only 2 of the relatives of major depressive patients. Detailed discussion on family burden and marital issues will be found in Chapter 12.

Summary

Prien & Potter (1990) estimated that, in addition to the decline in effective activity referred to above, bipolar disorder is associated with dying 9 years younger and losing around 12 years of normal health. Gitlin et al. (1995) concluded that even with appropriate pharmacological intervention many patients continued to relapse repeatedly and that significant symptoms were often present even in the absence of relapse. This is therefore clearly an illness which has significant impact on the individual sufferer, often across their life span, and also on family and society, in terms of inability in many sufferers to function at their premorbid levels once the illness has begun its course.

CONCLUSION

This introductory chapter has set out to indicate that bipolar disorder is a severe psychiatric illness which is only partially treated by pharmacological interventions. People with this diagnosis are likely to have significant and persistent difficulties across important areas of social and psychological functioning. Furthermore, elements of the symptoms noted within bipolar disorder are also apparent within the even larger group of people with cyclothymic personality who are themselves at elevated risk of developing this illness. The remainder of this book sets out in more detail the currently available treatment options with respect to bipolar illness and provides information on the strengths and weaknesses of these approaches. These lead on to an introduction to our cognitive therapy approach to the treatment of bipolar disorder. It is emphasised throughout this volume that this form of treatment is seen as adjunctive to appropriate pharmacological interventions rather than being in conflict with a medical approach.

In terms of the general form of the cognitive approach described it draws upon the extensive work on cognitive therapy for depression but includes elements developed specifically for this client group to address coping with manic and hypomanic symptoms and prodromes of both mania and depression with a view to reduction of relapse risk and enhancement of psychological functioning. In a disorder whose effects can be profound both for the individual and those around them it is also felt to be important to include within this approach support for the individual in dealing with the psychological and social consequences of behaviour engaged in during mania.

An important principle throughout this form of treatment is that it is collaborative. Clients work with their therapist through a process of guided discovery to develop more adaptive coping skills. These new skills are not presented didactically and the possible feelings of loss associated with changing behaviour and thought patterns are addressed within this approach. This allows clients, who are usually independently minded individuals, when well to feel satisfied that any changes through therapy are not imposed on them from an external agency, but have developed from a balanced assessment of how best to act for their own greater benefit. It is our view that this type of approach is essential in maintaining engagement with the treatment process itself and that more proscriptive approaches would be likely to be associated with high drop out rates and inefficient therapeutic interventions.

Chapter 2

REVIEW OF CURRENT TREATMENT

Treatment for manic depression in the past three decades has been pre-dominantly pharmcotherapy. Lithium carbonate has been the most common and influential drug of choice. From the late 1960s to 1970s, reports of the efficacy of lithium as a prophylactic agent were very optimistic, to the extent that it has commonly been used as a yardstick in drug trials of newer chemical agents.

One of the implications of the initial reports of the dramatic effects of lithium in the treatment of manic-depressive disorder has been that psy-chotherapy for patients suffering from the disorders has been neglected in the past couple of decades. This is surprising as manic depression is often seen in a diathesis–stress model: there is a strong genetic component and yet stress has been known to trigger an onset. It is commonly regarded as sensible to deal with both the stresses affecting patients and the biological aspects of the illness. Stress does not have to be an acute upsetting life event. It can be a build-up of life's hassles. The way an individual responds can alleviate the stressful situation or exacerbate it.

It has been long observed that mania fuels itself and that chaos can lead to more episodes. This suggests that psychotherapy that targets chaos and reduces maladaptive coping can be usefully employed. Furthermore, the manifestation of the illness is predominately affective, cognitive and behavioural. Psychotherapy has long been used in dealing with these three aspects of the illness. It may help patients to examine extra strategies that help them to deal with their illness and can be seen as the stress side of the equation. However, there is only very tentative evidence for the effi-cacy of any psycho-social intervention. As spelled out in Chapter 4, our model of intervention is to tackle both the diathesis and the stress sides of the model. We do not, however, advocate psychotherapy as a substitute for pharmacotherapy. Medication targets the biological vulnerability while psychotherapy tries to help patients to tackle and adjust to the illness.

Therapists using this manual need not have a medical background.

However, they should have a critical understanding of the current state of drug treatment and the side effects of commonly used drugs in the treatment of manic depression in order to be informed and to have a knowledgeable discussion with patients regarding the role of medication in managing their illness.

Before reviewing the evidence of the extent current treatments help the illness, it is necessary to make the distinction between efficacy and effectiveness of a drug treatment. Efficacy is defined as the performance of the drug under clinical trial conditions. Often the sample in a clinical trial is carefully selected and there is tighter control of serum levels to ensure compliance and adequacy of dosages. Effectiveness is defined as the performance of the drug in normal clinical situations, when the sample may be more heterogeneous and the conditions under which the drug is prescribed are constrained by what the local service can provide. In the case of lithium, the initial reports on the efficacy of clinical trials conducted in the 1960s and 1970s had been very encouraging. Yet from the early 1980s, clinically it has been observed that the effectiveness of lithium as a prophylactic drug for manic depressive disorder may help only a proportion of patients. Both Dickson & Kendell (1986) and Symonds & Williams (1981) reported increasing admission rates to British hospitals for mania, despite increased use of lithium. Some naturalistic studies, for example, Marker & Mander (1989) and Harrow et al. (1990), even reported a failure in detecting good outcomes for patients on lithium compared with those who were not. Questions have been raised about the optimistic estimation of the effectiveness of lithium in normal clinical settings (Solomon et al., 1995; Moncrieff, 1995). In the case of psychotherapy for manic depression, one could argue that the distinction of efficacy and effectiveness also applies. Furthermore, the issue of psychotherapy research is complicated by the issues of the therapist's competence in carrying out the treatment and the therapist's adherence to the treatment model. However, psychotherapy for manic depression is in its infancy. As discussed below, there is not even enough evidence to make a tentative statement of the efficacy of psychotherapy in manic depression.

This chapter is divided into pharmacotherapy and psychotherapy sections. The side effects and the evidence of treatment efficacy of commonly used drugs for manic depression will be reviewed first. This will be followed by a review of the efficacy of psychotherapy for manic depression.

PHARMACOTHERAPY

The most commonly used drugs specific to manic depression are lithium, carbamazepine and valproate. In addition, other major tranquillisers are often prescribed during an acute phase for the management of a very acute manic episode. Similarly, antidepressants are often prescribed for severe bipolar depression. However, the review of pharmacotherapy will concentrate on the drugs specific in the treatment of manic depression. Other chemical agents, including the newer drugs, will be reviewed briefly. In this section, the common side effects of lithium, carbamazepine and valproate will be described first. The evidence of the efficacy of pharmacotherapy in an acute phase will be reviewed next. This will be followed by a review of the evidence of pharmacotherapy as prophylaxis.

Side Effects of Common Drugs Specific for the Treatment of Manic Depression

The side effects of medication described in this section are summaries of the American Psychiatric Association's (1994b) Practice guidelines for the treatment of patients with bipolar disorder and the British National Formulary (1997).

Lithium is not protein bound or metabolised in the liver. It is distributed in total body water. Changes in hydration such as over-drinking, excessive sweating, diarrhoea and vomiting can affect the serum level. Diuretics will have to be prescribed with caution for patients on lithium medication. Up to 75% of patients on lithium report some side effects. These include polyuria (passing excessive amount of urine), polydypsia (thirst), weight gain, tremor, sedation, impaired coordination, nausea, vomiting, dyspepsia, diarrhoea, acne and oedema. Furthermore, it also has cognitive side effects, including dulling, impaired memory, poor concentration, confusion and mental slowness. It has also been reported that between 5% and 35% of patients on lithium developed hypothyroidism. This happens more in women and tends to appear after 6–18 months of lithium treatment. Lithium-induced hypothyroidism generally disappeared when lithium was discontinued. Lithium can also exacerbate any skin condition such as psoriasis. Concerns have also been expressed about irreversible kidney damage in 10–20% of patients receiving long-term lithium treatment (more than 10 years). The dose and frequency of the drug often have to be adjusted in order to eliminate or reduce these side effects.

Both carbamazepine and valproate are metabolised by the liver and are highly protein bound. Hence both may interact with other metabolised or protein-bound drugs. Carbamazepine decreases the metabolism of many drugs including neuroleptics, benzodiazepines, tricyclic antidepressants and thyroid hormones. Up to half of patients on carbamazepine experience side effects. The common ones include neurological symptoms such as diplopia (double vision), blurred vision, nausea and ataxia (unsteady gait). The common side effects for valproate include gastrointestinal upset, tremor, sedation, increased appetite and weight gain. However, these side effects of both drugs are normally reversible or alleviated by dosage reduction and, in cases of severe side effects, discontinuation of the drug.

Pharmacotherapy for the Acute Phase of Mania

Lithium has been the most commonly used and most evaluated drug for the treatment of mania. It has a latency period of one to two weeks before the drug takes effect. The response rate of acute mania to lithium is cited as between 70% and 80% (Prien & Potter, 1990). Carbamazepine is one of the most common alternatives to lithium in the treatment of manic-depressive disorders. In a review article, Small (1990) summarised 14 double-blind studies, totalling 175 manic patients, and concluded that 61% of subjects showed moderate to marked improvement in response to carbamazepine. Generally the evidence for carbamazepine as an effective treatment for acute mania is equivalent to lithium. Valproate, another anticonvulsant, is also commonly used as an alternative to lithium. Janicak et al. (1993) in a review of numerous studies (with a total of 297 patients) of the efficacy of valproate concluded that there was a moderate to marked response rate in 56% of patients. However, most of these studies had methodological flaws. In two recent randomised double-blind controlled studies comparing valproate with placebo (Pope et al., 1991) and valproate, lithium and placebo (Bowden et al., 1994) in the treatment of acute mania, the evidence pointed to valproate being more efficacious than placebo but equivalent to lithium. Furthermore, there was some tentative evidence from Bowden et al.'s (1994) study that lithium was more effective than valproate in 'classic mania' but that valproate was more effective in 'mixed mania' than lithium. As mentioned above, neuroleptics such as chlorpromazine or haloperidol are often used in the acute manic phase to tackle severe agitation and hyperactivity. Prien et al. (1972) reported that neuroleptics may have a quicker onset of action and are useful, at least initially, in the highly agitated or psychotic patient in a manic state. However, lithium may be superior to neuroleptics for the specific normalisation of mood. The American Psychiatric Association (1994b) also suggested that benzodiazepine should be considered in the treatment of the acute manic phase as it was considered equally effective when compared with neuroleptics and does not pose a risk of extra pyramidal symptoms or tardive dyskinesia.

Pharmacotherapy for the Acute Phase of Depression

The effect of drug treatment on bipolar depression is less clear. Lithium seems less robust in the treatment of bipolar depression. Fieve & Peselow (1983) reviewed 13 studies totalling 85 subjects and concluded that about 75% of subjects had achieved at least 'partial improvement'. Unfortunately, it is not clear from these studies whether subjects suffered from bipolar I or II disorders. The clinical significance of partial improvement is not clear either. The time frame for response to lithium in bipolar depression is even longer than in mania. It takes between six and eight weeks before the full response is evident. Prien & Potter (1990) made the criticism that there had been no placebo double-blind controlled studies of any drug other than lithium in bipolar I depression during the last two decades. Keck (1995) concluded that the evidence of efficacy of valproate and carbamazepine ranged from equivocal to weakly positive.

Because of the moderate effect of lithium and other anticonvulsants in the treatment of bipolar depression, the more traditional antidepressants such as tricyclics and mono-amine oxidase inhibitor (MAOI) and selective serotonin reuptake inhibitor (SSRI) are prescribed for patients suffering from bipolar depression. Zornberg & Pope (1993) reviewed seven controlled studies and concluded that the data indicated tricyclic antidepressants were superior to placebo in the treatment of bipolar depression. Sachs et al. (1994) reported in a double-blind trial of bupropion versus desipramine for bipolar depression that the two drugs were equally efficacious. However, significantly more patients on desipramine switched to hypomania or mania. But the sample was small ($n = 20$) and the findings need to be replicated. In another controlled study, Himmelhoch et al. (1991) showed that tranylcypromine, an MAOI, was significantly superior to imipramine in the treatment of the anergic subtype of bipolar depression.

More recent studies have been suggesting that the atypical antipsychotic drug, clozapine, may have a mood-stabilising effect as well as antipsychotic effects in manic-depressive patients with psychotic features (Suppes et al., 1992). Likewise, there is a suggestion that Lamotrigine, a relatively new antepileptic agent, is efficacious in treating both mania and bipolar depression, mainly as an add-on agent to standard drugs (Calabrese et al., 1996; Walden et al., 1996). However, again evidence comes from single cases (Walden et al., 1996). In clinical practice standard antidepressants tested primarily in unipolar patients or a mixed group of unipolar and bipolar depressives are prescribed for bipolar depression.

Summary of Pharmacotherapy for the Acute Phase

There is good evidence that lithium is efficacious in the treatment of the acute phase of mania. However, the relatively long latency period (of one to two weeks) for lithium to work has led the American Psychiatric Association (1994b) to recommend that major tranquillisers are used during an acute episode if patients become unmanageable with lithium medication alone. Both carbamazepine and valproate have been less stringently evaluated. However, the evidence of efficacy of both carbamazepine and valproate is at best equivalent to lithium. There is some tentative evidence that valproate may be more effective than lithium in mixed mania. Research on the drug treatment of bipolar depression is rare and often full of methodological flaws. Antidepressants tested on unipolar depressives are routinely prescribed to treat bipolar depression. There is an urgent need to evaluate the efficacy of antidepressants for bipolar depression.

Pharmacotherapy as Prophylaxis

Lithium has also been hailed as an effective form of prophylaxis. In the early 1970s a total of over 200 subjects in eight studies had been treated with lithium as prophylaxis in prospective, double-blind, placebo-controlled studies. The relapse rate for lithium ranged from 0% to 44%, while the rate for placebo ranged from 38% to 93%. However, Solomon et al. (1995) in their review article pointed out that the initial reports of efficacy of lithium seemed to be over-optimistic. More recent studies of lithium as a prophylactic drug reported that about 50% of manic-depressive patients relapse within two years compared with a relapse rate of about 35% in the studies reported in the 1960s. The authors speculated two reasons for the apparent drop in the efficacy of prophylactic lithium treatment. In the past there were tendencies for American psychiatrists to both under-diagnose mania and over-diagnose schizophrenia. Subsequently there has been a shift to classify schizo-affective or schizophrenic disorders as manic-depressive illness. Hence the samples in the more recent trials may have consisted of a more heterogeneous group of patients, some of whom responded less well to lithium prophylactic treatment. This may account for the reported decrease in efficacy for lithium as a prophylactic agent in more recent studies. The second speculation is that manic-depressive patients now referred to university-based clinics, where clinical trials are conducted, may be more complicated, suffering from comorbid psychopathology such as substance abuse or personality disorders. These complex cases may have responded less well to lithium as a prophylactic treatment.

The proportion of coexisting personality disorder and manic-depressive illness ranged from 4% (Baxter et al., 1984; Boyd et al., 1984) to 12% (Gaviria et al., 1982). The most common personality disorders among manic depressive patients are borderline and antisocial personality disorders. Generally patients with concurrent life-long difficulties such as a co-existing diagnosis of personality disorder or neuroticism are more difficult to treat. Neuroticism is known as an indicator of poor lithium prophylaxis response (Abou-Salch, 1983; Maj et al., 1984). Furthermore, the mere number of recent episodes may predict less favourable response to prophylactic treatment. Indeed Gelenberg et al. (1989) reported that little or no lithium prophylaxis effect was found in subjects with three or more episodes in the three years prior to randomisation.

Drug treatment by itself may not be adequate for all subtypes. The literature on lithium suggests that the rapid cycling subtype responds poorly to lithium prophylaxis (Dunner and Fieve, 1974). Calabrese et al. (1992) reported encouraging evidence of efficacy of valproate in 78 rapid-cycling manic-depressive patients in their non-randomised study. Likewise mixed mania, concurrent symptoms of mania and depression, is a predictor of a poor response to lithium prophylaxis (Tohen et al., 1990a). Hypothyroidism has been reported more frequently in rapid cyclers than non-rapid cyclers (Cowdry et al., 1983; Bauer et al., 1990; Oomen et al., 1996). Thyroid augmentation medications such as levothyroxine (Stancer and Persad, 1982; Bauer, Whybrow & Winokur, 1990) have been found beneficial in the treatment of the rapid cycling subtype. However, the samples were small and both studies used an open trial design. These findings on the efficacy of thyroid augmentation must be viewed as preliminary.

Two further issues relating to lithium as a form of prophylaxis for manic depression need to be discussed here. Firstly, there is a trade-off between a high serum level of lithium which causes more severe side effects that patients may find difficult to tolerate and a more favourable outcome. Gelenberg et al. (1989) found that standard serum level of lithium (0.8 to 1.0 mmol/l) produced better prophylaxis for manic-depressive patients than a lower serum level (0.4–0.6 mmol/l). However, some patients may stop lithium because of unacceptable side effects. This is particularly the case if a high serum level of between 0.8 and 1.0 mmol/l is aimed for. Most clinicians now aim for a range between 0.5 and 0.8 mmol/l (Peet & Pratt, 1993). Secondly, there is scant information about medically guided discontinuation of lithium treatment. One study by Faedda et al. (1993) reported a 5-year follow-up of 65 patients who had been determined clinically to discontinue lithium at different rates. Half of patients had a recurrence of mood episode within six months of lithium discontinuation. It is not clear whether the recurrences were due to a 'lithium withdrawal syndrome' or a recurrence of the disorder. Within five years, 75% had a recurrent episode and the overall risks of a new episode of both mania and depression were significantly greater after rapid discontinuation (less than 2 weeks) when compared with gradual discontinuation (2–4 weeks). The recurrence rate was found to be more elevated within the first 12 months of rapid discontinuation. From the second year onwards, the courses of survival over time were nearly parallel for both groups. The National Institute of Mental Health in the United States concluded in the 1989 Workshop on Treatment of Bipolar Disorders (Prien & Potter, 1990) that lithium as a prophylactic treatment was ineffective for at least 20–40% of classical manic-depressive patients, due to either inadequate responses or side effects.

The picture of carbamazepine used as a prophylactic agent for manic-depressive disorder is not so well researched compared to lithium as a prophylactic agent. Solomon et al. (1995) reported that four controlled trials examined carbamazepine as a prophylactic treatment for manic-depressive illness. Three studies (Coxhead et al., 1992; Lusznat et al., 1988; Small et al., 1991) reported no significant difference between lithium and carbamazepine. These studies also did not have a placebo group and hence the conclusion one can draw from them is limited. The other remaining study (Okuma et al., 1981) was published as a preliminary study and reported a non-significant trend for carbamazepine to out-perform placebo. Valproate is widely used as a promising prophylactic agent. However, again Solomon et al. (1995) criticised the evidence as retrospective (Fogelson et al., 1991; McElroy et al., 1988) and coming from uncontrolled open trials (Calabrese & Delucchi, 1990; Emrich et al., 1985; Lambert & Venaud, 1992). A literature search on Medline between 1991 and 1996 did not show any new studies that may alter Solomon et al.'s conclusions on lithium, carbamazepine and valproate as pharmacotherapy for manic-depressive disorders.

Since a significant proportion of manic-depressive patients do not respond well to the conventional prophylactic agents, other drugs are used as alternative or adjunctive maintenance agents. The most commonly used are neuroleptics. Unfortunately this widespread clinical practice has little empirical support from formal studies. Esparon et al. (1986) reported that flupenthixol decanote had no differential effect in the prevention of mania or depression and in fact some patients did worse on some clinical measures. Maintenance with adjunctive imipramine and lithium was reported to have no advantage over lithium on its own (Kane, 1988) and in another study it was reported to have run the risk of inducing manic episodes (Quitkin et al., 1981). However, virtually every antidepressant has been reported to be associated with the risk of mania, mixed episodes or rapid cycling. More systematic studies are warranted to examine whether different agents are more or less likely to induce the 'switch process'.

Summary

A significant proportion of patients, ranging from 20% to 40% of classic manic depressive patients, are not protected by lithium alone. Characteristics of 'difficult to treat' patients such as a coexisting diagnosis of personality disorder, long-term personality traits such as neuroticism and frequent previous episodes such as rapid cycling or simply more than three episodes in the past 5 years are all reported to be associated with poor outcome for lithium as a prophylactic agent in manic depression. The evidence of other pharmacotherapeutic agents such as carbamazepine and valproate as prophylaxis is only tentative and most studies reported equivalent efficacy to lithium.

PSYCHOTHERAPY

Psychotherapy for manic depression has been under-developed and the evidence of treatment efficacy is scanty. There are possibly two reasons for this. Firstly, there is the erroneous assumption that because there is a strong hereditary element in manic depression, physical treatment is more appropriate. Mood stabilisers such as lithium and carbamazepine had been hailed as a very effective prophylaxis for manic depression. This rather reinforces the notion that physical treatment is appropriate. Secondly, manic depression is traditionally seen as an episodic illness with a good prognosis. Kraepelin (1913) described dementia praecox (schizophrenia) and manic depression as the two major psychiatric illnesses. Dementia praecox was said to be chronic and to follow a deteriorating course. Manic depression was described as episodic and having a good prognostic prospect. Patients suffering from manic depression were said to make a good recovery with very little deterioration. Kraepelin's initial view was later modified (Jablensky, 1981). He acknowledged that some dementia praecox patients appeared to recover, whereas some manic-depressive illness followed a progressive chronic course. However, his initial views seem to have had a great impact on the treatment of the two types of psychosis. Manic-depressive patients traditionally receive very little care between episodes. Given that psychotherapy seems only feasible during the non-acute phase, not much attention has been given to this aspect of treatment of manic-depression patients.

Psychotherapy is perceived to be minimally effective during an acute phase. Generally patients are hard to engage during an acute manic phase or during a deeply suicidal or psychotic depressive episode. Hence most of the evidence of efficacy of psychotherapy is about therapy when patients were not in an acute phase. In this section, evidence of treatment efficacy of individual therapies, family therapy and group therapy will be reviewed. Individual therapies include psychoanalysis, cognitive therapy and interpersonal therapy. Traditionally manic-depressive patients were seen as unsuitable for psychotherapy by psychoanalysts. For example, Fromm-Reichmann (1949) compared manic-depressive patients unfavourably with schizophrenic patients. He wrote about manic-depressive patients' dependency, unyielding grandiosity, lack of introspection and lack of any close interpersonal relatedness. Abraham (1953) also focused on the inattentiveness of the manic patient and the danger of mistaking spontaneous remission from depression for cure. However, these are early writings. As discussed below, in more recent days, psychoanalytically orientated therapists acknowledged the need to work with manic-depressive patients and attempts have been made to do so.

One of the characteristics of psychotherapy for manic-depressive patients is the promotion of medication compliance. This is based on the clinical observation that a significant proportion of patients find taking long-term prophylactic medication hard to come to terms with. Often patients' response to being told that they are suffering from a chronic, recurrent and serious psychiatric illness and that they will have to take long-term medication is a mix of denial, anger and anxiety. Psychotherapy is increasingly seen as necessary to help patients to adjust to their illness, including their emotional response to it. Both individual cognitive therapy and interpersonal therapy address this point. In a cognitive therapy study, Cochran (1984) dealt with medication compliance within the cognitive model (Beck et al., 1979). Interpersonal therapists use the model of loss to deal with the loss of sense of healthy self and having to take long-term medication.

The rationale for intervening with the family is that the patient's family environment has been found to be an important intervening variable in deciding how patients fare with their illness. Miklowitz et al. (1988) reported that two indexes of family attitudes, expressed emotion (EE) and affective style (AS), predicted relapses in a mix of pure manic and schizoaffective manic patients in a 9-month follow-up study. The predictive relationships were significant when patients' medication compliance, treatment regimen, baseline symptoms and illness history were controlled for. The finding that family atmosphere predicted relapses in manic depression has since been replicated by O'Connell et al. (1991) and Priebe et al. (1989). In family therapy for manic depression, a psycho-educational approach is often adopted with families seen as having valuable potential to help patients. Family therapy has the advantage of recruiting the family members to help deal with the illness. This may be an option for treatment when the patient is living with a family or has family members who are closely involved. However, sensitivity is needed so that the family do not feel over-burdened and the patient does not resent that their sense of autonomy is being curbed unnecessarily.

Several advantages of working with manic depressive patients in groups have been raised. For example, Davenport et al. (1997) highlighted the following advantages: to reduce anxiety over issues of one-to-one intimacy through diffusion in the group; mutual support for the fear of the genetic aspects of the illness; to support and reinforce socially acceptable behaviour through group cohesiveness; and to promote sensitivity to early warning signs so that prompt drug or psychotherapeutic intervention can ensue. Pollack (1990) discussed the possible value of the group process for allowing information-sharing about the illness, learning strategies to cope with the illness and to improve interpersonal relationships. Other advantages of treating manic-depressive patients in groups include facilitating problem solving and focusing on reality issues by evoking group processes rather than dwelling on the past (Volkmar et al., 1981) and allowing group members to discuss the worth of the group (Wulsin et al., 1988). Several group therapists have discussed the curative factors in group therapy for manic-depressive patients. Three curative factors have been considered as important by Shakir et al. (1979). These included interpersonal learning, instillation of hope and imparting of information. In addition to these three curative factors, Kripke & Robinson (1985) included on their list universality, altruism, imitative behaviour, and group cohesiveness. Pollack (1990) wrote about similar issues and thought group cohesiveness, universality and instillation of hope can facilitate patients' learning to cope with the illness and the goal of improving interpersonal relationships can be facilitated by interpersonal learning and the development of socialisation techniques.

Individual Psychoanalysis

Like other schools of psychotherapy reviewed here, data on the efficacy of psychoanalytically orientated psychotherapy for manic-depressive patients is scarce. Cohen et al. (1954) applied the developmental theories of Melanie Klein when working intensively with 12 manic-depressive patients and claimed some long-term success. In their formulations, the problem was traced back to late oral stage when the ability to relate to others as individuals distinct from oneself developed. This led to a dependent state and the inability to integrate the concepts of 'good or bad mother' into a single person. It was said that these families were frequently set apart from others due to some factors such as economic or racial ones. This led to pressure of achievement or upwardly mobile pressure while dependency needs and insecurities were denied. Depressive episodes were seen as intensifications of the emptiness felt inside. Manic episodes were seen as a defence against this painful emotional state. Benson (1975), in a 41-month open trial, treated 31 patients with psychotherapy in addition to lithium maintenance and reported 68% of patients had a good outcome. Leob and Leob (1987) reported their use of transference in their work with three manic-depressive patients. During early stages of hypomania, the increased sexual drive was manifested in transference material. Patients were helped to be made aware of the hypomanic cycle early, allowing for early intervention. However, none of these studies used a randomised controlled design and the results must be interpreted cautiously.

Individual Cognitive Therapy

Cognitive therapy (Beck et al., 1979) has been demonstrated to be an efficacious form of psychotherapy for unipolar depression (Dobson, 1989; Hollon et al., 1991) and a viable alternative to pharmacotherapy (Jacobson & Hollon, 1996). However, there is no good evidence of the efficacy of individual cognitive therapy for manic-depressive patients. The study by Cochran (1984) was a rare study in the field of psychotherapy for manic-depressive patients, using a randomised controlled design and a relatively large sample. Therapists used Beck et al.'s (1979) cognitive behavioural principles to enhance manic depressive patients' drug compliance. Treatment consisted of six 1-hour weekly sessions. Results were mixed. There was no difference between the treatment group and the control group at post-treatment, 3-month or 6-month follow-ups in terms of self-reports or informant-reports. Nor was there a significant difference between the two groups in terms of serum lithium levels at post-intervention. Moreover, serum lithium levels were unavailable in a significant proportion of subjects at 3 months (54%) and at 6 months (64%). However, there was better compliance according to the physician's rating and the compliance index at post-intervention and at 6 months, favouring the therapy group. Unfortunately the physician was not blind to the patient's group status and this knowledge might have biased his rating. The difference in the compliance index was not significant at 3-months follow-up. It was also reported that patients in the control group 'had affective episodes more likely precipitated by lithium non-compliance (p. 875)' at the 6-month follow-up. It was not clear from the study how episodes precipitated by lithium non-compliance was defined or rated. Clinically, it is not easy to decide retrospectively whether patients stopped taking medication because they were in the early stages of another episode, or whether their non-compliance with the medication caused their relapses. Since the serum level was generally unavailable at the 6-month follow-up and the physician was not blind to patients' group status, the beneficial effect of the treatment group could easily have been due to the cognitive behavioural skills patients learned, leading to a general beneficial effect.

Individual Interpersonal Therapy

Like cognitive therapy, interpersonal therapy has been found to be efficacious in the treatment of the acute phase of unipolar depression (Elkin et al., 1989) and in maintenance therapy for unipolar depression (Frank et al., 1990; Kupfer et al., 1992). Recently a form of modified interpersonal therapy called interpersonal and social rhythm therapy (Frank et al., 1994) has been developed for manic-depressive patients. It is based on the hypothesis that stressful life events affect the course of the illness in part by disrupting daily routine and social rhythms (sleep–wake habits). Disruption in social rhythms in turn disrupts the sleep–wake cycles and other circadian rhythms. Therapy aims are: to help manic-depressive patients to stabilise their social and possibly their circadian rhythms in the face of provocative life events; to intervene in the interpersonal functionings that lead to mood disorder symptoms; and to evaluate and renegotiate the patients' lifestyle of coping with their social environment. A new component is to track patients' social rhythms by means of the social rhythm metric (Monk et al., 1990) and to identify environmental factors that disrupt these social rhythms. In addition to the social rhythms component, the four foci used for interpersonal therapy in unipolar depression are employed when working with manic-depressive patients. These include interpersonal disputes, unresolved grief, role transition and interpersonal deficit. Interestingly with manic-depressive patients, the concept of grief includes grief over loss of the sense of a healthy self. Patients are recruited during an acute phase of the illness. However, the emphasis of the work is preventative during the non-acute phase of the illness. Recruitment of patients is still being carried out and no results have been published.

Family Therapy

The evidence for family therapy for manic-depressive patients is also tentative. Miller, et al. (1991) reported a small pilot study of 14 families with one member suffering from manic-depressive illness. The families were randomised to 'standard clinical treatment' (pharmacotherapy and clinical management) or 'standard treatment' and family therapy. Patients in the combined treatment had a higher full recovery rate and fewer hospitalisations over two years. Miklowitz et al. (1988) reported that in an open, non-randomised trial, the patients in the nine families had fewer hospitalisations at nine months when compared with the author's previous similar sample managed by medication alone. The group used the behavioural family management approach developed by Falloon for schizophrenic patients. Clarkin et al. (1990) reported a randomised controlled study of 21 manic-depressive inpatients involving six sessions of psycho-educational family intervention in addition to the usual standard hospital treatment. The goals of family interventions were: acceptance of the illness and development of an understanding of the current episode; identifying possible precipitating stresses in the current episode; identifying likely future stresses within and outside the family; elucidating family interactions that produce stresses on the patient; planning strategies for managing and/or minimising future stresses; and acceptance by patients and families of the patients' need for continued treatment after discharge. Patients in the psycho-educational group did better on global symptoms and role functioning at both 6 and 18 months. However, the treatment effect was exclusive to the female patients and was attenuated over time. There was also a trend that patients in the family intervention group created less family burden at the 6-month follow-up. Interestingly the authors also reported that family intervention had the opposite effect in a group of 29 patients suffering from unipolar depression. Unipolar depressed patients did better when they only received the standard medication regimen and outpatient follow-up. Honig et al. (1997) also reported a psycho-education model of intervention in bipolar disorders. Key relatives were educated about the illness for three sessions. Adaptive coping with the illness was discussed in a further three sessions. There were significant changes at post-treatment from high to low expressed emotion for the key relatives in the psycho-education group. There was no change from high to low expressed emotion in the waiting list control group. Davenport et al. (1977) reported that couple therapy plus lithium showed a lower relapse rate and better marital adjustment and social functioning than the lithium group alone. However, the study did not employ a randomised controlled trial and there were marked initial differences in patient characteristics. Hence it is difficult to draw any firm conclusions.

Group Therapy

The data for the efficacy of group therapy are also preliminary and evidence comes from small open trials. Davenport et al. (1977) reported a follow-up study of between 2 and 10 years of the 65 manic-depressive patients admitted to the National Institute of Mental Health research ward for the treatment of acute mania. The study consisted of three groups: 12 patients who received both medication and weekly couple group therapy; 11 patients who received medication alone and 42 patients who were referred back to their community for medication management. Patients who received weekly couple group therapy plus medication did better than the other two groups in terms of rehospitalisation, marital failures, global functioning and family interaction. The therapists in this study apparently adopted a relatively non-directive and accepting stance. However, patients in the therapy group were significantly older and had been married longer. Wulsin et al. (1988) reported substantial hospitalisation rates in a long-term group carried out over 4 years in the community. However, the attrition rate was high and 12 of the 22 patients left group treatment in an unplanned manner. Kripke and Robinson (1985) reported decreased rates of hospitalisation and better socio-economic functioning in the 17 patients treated in a group-therapy programme over 11 years. Initially the goal of the group was to provide a forum for lithium administration and compliance monitoring. However, gradually the patients bonded to form a bi-weekly psychotherapy group that met for an hour and a half. The group was run on the basis of a psychodynamic analysis of group interactions, self-revelation and later problem-solving of current difficulties. At the beginning of each session, patients' medication and blood levels were reviewed. Shakir et al. (1979) reported that the 15 patients receiving group therapy had a higher mean level of lithium and less time in hospital during the 2 years of group therapy when compared with the 2-year period prior to group therapy. Palmer et al. (1995) reported a small cognitive behavioural therapy group of six subjects. The results were encouraging but the dropout rate was high (2/6) and it was not clear what the inclusion criteria were. The referral criterion consisted of a psychiatrist's judgement of these patients being suitable for group treatment.

Summary

Psychotherapy for manic depression is often carried out during the non-acute phase of the illness. It is seen as a helpful addition to pharmacotherapy. Evidence for the efficacy of psychotherapy for manic-depressive affective disorders is extremely tentative. There are only a few psychotherapy studies for manic-depressive affective disorders, most of which are small, open trials. Some of these studies amount to not much more than a description of clinical practice. Only a couple of small pilots using a randomised control design have been reported. There has been one cognitive therapy study (Cochran, 1984) using a randomised control design to promote lithium compliance. Unfortunately no report of its treatment efficacy beyond 6 months was published. Prien & Potter (1990) concluded that the situation of psycho-social intervention in 1989 was akin to that in 1979 for schizophrenia. Since then no major psycho-social interventions for manic-depressive disorders have been reported. Thus there is a need for randomised controlled trials of psychotherapies specifically designed for this disorder.

CONCLUSION

A review of the current available treatment for manic depression suggest that both pharmacotherapy and psychotherapy need further research and improvement. However, clinically manic-depressive patients routinely are prescribed mood stabilisers. They are seldom referred for psychotherapy. Manic-depressive patients need both and pharmacotherapy and psychotherapy which should work hand in hand. As a patient put it:

> Lithium may prevent my seductive but disastrous high, diminishes my depressions, clears out the wool and webbing from my disordered thinking, slows me down, gentles me out, keeps me from ruining my career and relationship, keeps me out of hospitals, alive and makes psychotherapy possible. But ineffably, psychotherapy heals. It makes some sense of the confusion, reins in the terrifying thoughts and feelings, returns some control and opens the possibility of learning from it all.... No pills can help me deal with the problem of not wanting to take pills; likewise, no amount of analysis alone can prevent my manias and depressions. I need both. (Goodwin & Jamison, 1990)

Most bipolar patients will struggle with some of the following issues between episodes: the meaning of being diagnosed as suffering from a major psychiatric illness; being told to take prophylactic medication for the foreseeable future if not forever; problems of stigmatisation; losses including the loss of self-esteem and loss of sense of healthy self; fear of recurrence and any mood swings; interpersonal difficulties associated with previous episodes; financial, occupational or educational loss because of previous episodes; issues of independence and separation from parental homes for those whose onset of the illness is early; issues relating to becoming a parent due to the fear that the illness may be passed on; issues relating to pregnancy due to the side effects of long-term medication on the offspring. When patients become less symptomatic or between episodes, they must deal with the psychological consequence of past episodes, the ongoing vulnerability and for some patients the emotional subsyndromal lability between episodes. Individual cognitive therapy can address these issues by providing psycho-education about the illness, behavioural cognitive skills to cope with the illness, goal-setting and problem-solving. Cognitive skills can help patients to look at evidence, advantages and disadvantages, and to address irrational fears. Patients are in a better position to gain control of their illness and to work with their psychiatrists and genetic counsellors in a more informed and collaborative way.

Chapter 3

PSYCHO-SOCIAL MODELS IN BIPOLAR DISORDER

As the preceding discussion has indicated there is now a substantial body of evidence supporting the need for additional approaches in the treatment of bipolar disorder. There are important limitations to lithium therapy alone, leaving up to 40% of patients unprotected against relapse. In addition to efficacy issues there are also difficulties in terms of compliance with medical regimes for which there are significant side effects to be endured by many patients.

A number of small-scale research projects have investigated psychotherapeutic approaches to bipolar illness, and results appear promising. However, none of these reports have addressed the application of a cognitive behavioural approach designed specifically for people with this type of diagnosis. In this chapter information will first be presented on the role played by psycho-social factors in the onset and maintenance of bipolar disorder. The findings that life events play a significant role in bipolar illness and that there is a significant delay between event and illness onset suggests that there may be scope for psychological intervention in this period. As indicated previously in Chapter 1 many people with bipolar illness can successfully identify when they are experiencing prodromal manic and (to a lesser extent) depressive symptoms. If this awareness of prodromes can be associated with a use of appropriate coping strategies then it may be possible to avert potential relapse of the disorder.

Three diathesis–stress models are discussed which have been influential in psychiatric conceptualisations of bipolar disorder: (1) biological dysregulations and behavioural engagement system model (Depue et al., 1987); (2) behavioural sensitisation and kindling model (Post et al., 1986b); (3) circadian rhythm and life events. All three models indicate possible roles for psychological interventions in bipolar disorder in terms of education, development of structure and routine and the use of specific cognitive behavioural techniques.

This background information leads into a discussion of our specific approach in the next chapter, which assumes that clinical episodes derive from an interaction between stressors (e.g. life events, disruption of social routine, sleep deprivation) and biological vulnerabilities (e.g. sensitisation effects, weak regulatory systems or circadian changes). These initially lead to prodromes which can be moderated by the applications of appropriate coping skills. The form of intervention described highlights the use of psycho-education, training in cognitive behavioural skills, importance of sleep and routine and dealing with long-term vulnerabilities.

This chapter will set out the background to the approach described in detail in the rest of the volume. It derives from several years of research employing a randomised controlled trial of CBT versus waiting list control in patients with this disorder.

PSYCHO-SOCIAL RESEARCH: LIFE EVENTS AND RELAPSE

Although there is much research to indicate a significant biological basis for bipolar disorder there is increasing evidence for important effects of psycho-social phenomena, such as life events, in onset and relapse of both depressive and manic episodes. Bebbington et al. (1993) investigated whether there was any evidence for increased numbers of life events in individuals prior to the onset of psychosis. They studied 97 patients who had developed psychosis of which 31 were manic and 14 depressive psychoses (the remainder being schizophrenic). Life event histories for these patients were compared with those from a control group drawn from the same geographical area (Camberwell). In all groups there was a significant excess of life events compared to controls, a pattern that was particularly strong in the 3 months prior to onset of illness. This pattern was sustained even when events were excluded which might have been non-independent (i.e. caused by the developing illness itself). Mathew et al. (1994) reported from a study of 46 manic patients that life events were present in the 6 months prior to onset of the first manic episode and that stress reported in response to these events was also elevated prior to onset. This pattern was particularly clear in young males. Kennedy et al. (1983) studied 20 manic patients and reported, in comparison to matched controls, that there was a doubling of life events in general in the 4 months prior to hospital admission and that independent life events were also significantly more common.

Hammen & Gitlin (1997) found that bipolar I patients ($n = 52$) who were followed up over a 2-year period were more likely to have an episode of illness if they had experienced severe stress in the preceding 6 months and increased stress in the preceding 3 months in comparison to those who did not have such an episode. Furthermore this association with stress was strongest for those who had more previous episodes, indicating that if anything stress sensitivity increases over the course of the bipolar illness. Ellicott et al. (1990) also followed up a similar sized group of bipolar patients ($n = 61$) over a 2-year period. They reported a significant association between life events and relapse which it was noted was not mediated by medication level or compliance factors. Ambelas (1987) compared patients having their first admission for a manic episode with patients experiencing a manic relapse of an ongoing condition and controls with acute medical conditions. Life events were reported as a significant factor in the first onset of mania in 66% of cases. This was three times the rate in manic relapse and almost ten times higher than that observed in the medical cases. Ambelas argued on the basis of this data for a strong link between life events and mania with an apparently lower threshold for precipitation of mania in subsequent episodes. Glassner & Halpidur (1983) reported that life events were particularly associated with illness in patients with late (>20 years) as opposed to early onset bipolar disorder. Hunt et al. (1992) investigated 62 bipolar patients over a 2 year period. Increased life events were reported in the month prior to relapse. 19% of relapses were preceded by a severe event as compared to a baseline rate of 5% for such events in 'normal' months. In addition, Isometsa et al. (1995) studied the association between life events and suicide in patients with unipolar or bipolar depression. They reported that in two thirds of the cohort studied ($N = 81$) a life event occurred in the preceding 3 months and in 42% in the final week. In the case of bipolar patients it was less clear whether these events were independent of mood factors or associated with them.

Johnson & Roberts (1995) reviewed a number of studies of life events suggesting that the better controlled studies do support a role for life events in influencing the course of bipolar disorder, although there is still inadequate information on what particular type of event or life stress is particularly important. Johnson & Miller (1997) identified that life events are not only important in the triggering of bipolar episodes but also in duration of episodes once started. Thus they reported that individuals with severe negative life events took three times as long as those not having experienced such events to achieve recovery and further that this effect was independent of medication compliance. These reports clearly indicate that life events have an important impact on patients with a bipolar diagnosis. Beck (1983) has argued that particularly for unipolar depression performance in interpersonal and achievement relevant areas can have different effects on different individuals depending on how they evaluate themselves. Beck et al. (1983) have devised the sociotropy–autonomy scale

(SAS) in an attempt to distinguish individuals' personally relevant schemas for interpreting the events which occur to them. Subjects with high sociotrophy scores have tended to be associated with a propensity for reactive depression, and subjects with high autonomy scores have tended to be associated with endogenous depression. Hammen et al. (1989) have investigated how sociotropy and autonomy relate to individuals' reactions to specific life events. They studied 25 unipolar and 25 bipolar patients over a period of six months. They found that when life events were congruent with patients' grouping on the basis of SAS score, there was significantly greater likelihood of symptom exacerbation in the unipolar patients. In bipolar patients who exhibited an exacerbation of symptoms four out of six showed the same pattern of congruence, although this did not reach statistical significance. They have argued that one possible explanation for the discrepancy observed between the two patients groups might be that the pattern in bipolar patients (given the small number of exacerbations observed) might be observable over a longer time course. All symptom exacerbations in both groups were associated with preceding life events even when congruence was not observed.

Research does not as yet indicate therefore which particular events might be most important in onset or relapse, although there are suggestions (as yet unproven) that the clinician should be aware of the issue of individual relevance of particular events to the individual's particular schema. It is clear that there tends to be a significant lag in many cases between life event and illness onset, it is therefore possible that this period may represent a therapeutic opportunity in which appropriate clinical intervention post event might prove important in protecting patients from further relapse. As discussed later in this chapter one of the roles for a cognitive therapy approach is to provide tools for the patient to use in these situations. Although life events are clearly important it is also the case that relapse or onset can occur in the absence of obvious stressors. However, even when this is so it is usually possible for the patient to identify a prodromal period which precedes onset of the full illness episode.

Conclusion

Although there is clear evidence of biological or genetic factors in the development of bipolar disorder this forms only part of the picture. In terms of depression generally life events appear to be important in development of psychiatric episodes. The work of Brown and Harris (1989) demonstrates that life events are substantially more frequent in periods prior to illness than in euthymic periods. Similarly research on mania indicates that events which disrupt routine are associated with elevated rates of relapse. As discussed in Chapter 1, both low and high mood people appear to be able to identify subclinical changes or prodromes which identify that 'all is not right'. Research indicates that some people are able to use this information to trigger coping strategies which may avert exacerbation of mood problems at this time. This raises the possibility of formalising the identification of prodromes as a therapeutic strategy for people with this type of disorder.

THREE DIATHESIS STRESS MODELS AND THEIR IMPLICATIONS FOR THERAPY

Biological Dysregulations and Behavioural Engagement System

Depue et al. (1987) proposed that weak regulation of a hypothesised integrative system which influences mood and mood-related behaviour leaves the individual vulnerable to extreme variations in mood. When regulatory control is lost (dysregulation) a clinical episode of depression or mania or hypomania is observed. It is proposed that dysregulations can be associated with internal biologic factors and external socio-environmental factors. From the model it is predicted that if dysregulation is an important influence on mood then high intra-individual variability in mood and mood-related behaviour should be apparent in bipolar disorder. It would also be predicted that effective treatment should improve both clinical symptoms and variability. Depue et al. (1987) argued that positive affect is underpinned by a behavioural engagement (BE) which tends towards extreme values in bipolar illness and low values in depression. Krauss et al. (1992) tested this prediction by comparing the variability in BE in bipolar seasonal affective disorder (SAD) sufferers before and after phototherapy. SAD patients showed lower overall BE ratings, were more likely to show diurnal variation in BE, were more variable between days in diurnal rhythm and varied more in BE over short (3 hour) periods. These group differences did not persist after bright-light treatment. These findings were interpreted as consistent with Depue's model. It was also, however, acknowledged that patterns of dysregulations may be interacting with circadian rhythms in the recovery process through phototherapy. There is however little further empirical evidence with respect to this interesting model except for a more recent study of Lovejoy & Steuerwald (1995) which indicated high levels of between-day mood variability in young adults with cyclothymia and intermittent depression compared to non-clinical controls—cyclothymics alone showed particular variability in terms of negative affect.

Behavioural Sensitisation and Kindling

Post et al. (1986a) report on a model of affective illness which they suggest might accommodate several important aspects which previous models had not accounted for, in particular the recurrent nature of affective illness, the increased frequency of relapse with increasing age and number of previous occurrences and the finding that symptoms tend to repeat across episodes, with additional symptoms being overlaid onto these. Although presented as a biological model it explicitly accommodates the evidence that psycho-social stress has an important role in the onset of episodes particularly in the early stages of the illness. They describe two phenomena first observed within animal research, namely kindling and behavioural sensitisation. Kindling is described as a 'long lasting, possibly permanent change in neural excitability'. Electrical kindling (Goddard et al., 1969) describes the production of major motor seizures in animals using an electrical stimulus which is usually sub-threshold in its effects, but triggers seizure following repeated intermittent application. Similar findings have also been reported for pharmacological agents (Post et al., 1982). In higher mammals although full seizures are difficult to kindle, threshold and behavioural changes are observable (Post et al., 1984). It is suggested that the intermittent presentation of stressors to humans may also exert a kindling effect with initial episodes being triggered only by substantial stress, but later episodes (having been kindled) being triggered by much lower levels of stress or in some cases becoming self-generated.

Behavioural sensitisation is the observation of increasingly rapid and substantial behavioural changes in response to repeated intermittent doses of psychomotor stimulants (Kilbey & Ellinwood, 1977). Although similar to kindling in many respects it is thought that different neurotransmitter pathways underlie the two phenomena and that conditioning forms an important component in behavioural sensitisation (Post et al., 1985b). Post et al. (1986) also suggest that drug or environmentally induced changes in brain biochemistry can be conditioned in animals.

These models led to the suggestion that symbolic aspects of previous triggers of affective episodes might over time become conditioned to the point that they themselves can trigger later episodes in the absence of the substantive trigger itself. Thus anticipated loss or stress might impact to cause an episode rather than actual loss or stress. It is suggested that biological and psycho-social mechanisms might interact progressively—with patterns of both reactive and endogenous reaction possible in the same individual, consistent with Paykel's report (1979). As noted in the earlier section on psycho-social losses there is some evidence that affective episodes are particularly associated with significant stress in the early course of the illness (Ambelas, 1979). If indeed sensitisation occurs through the course of illness it would be expected that this pattern should weaken over time as the ability of 'symbolic' triggers to generate episodes becomes conditioned. Also within mania more rapid onset of mania is observed in later episodes, which would be consistent with earlier presentation of conditioned responses over time and progressively quicker generation of motor hyper-activity in behavioural sensitisation experiments. In terms of the observed time lag between lithium treatment and clinical response, Post argues that this may be explained by the time taken for patients to unlearn the conditioned psychological responses developed during their symptom history against a new background of lithium-controlled biochemical function.

As different drugs are differentially effective in modifying seizure responses at different points in the development of kindling, a suggestion is made that different pharmacological interventions might themselves be differentially effective during the development of recurrent episodes (Post & Weiss, 1989). In particular lithium and carbamazepine together are suggested as potentially potent interventions when mood episodes have become relatively autonomous.

An important role for psychological intervention is implied by the conditioning and sensitisation model. Post et al. (1986b) highlight the importance of cognitive restructuring techniques (Beck 1976), desensitisation (Wolpe, 1973) and social support (Weissman, 1979), but also suggest psychological interventions specifically targeted at bipolar or recurrent illness. This includes a role for systematic symptom history and life event information to be collected to obtain critical incident or sensitivity information for individual patients, to form the basis of psychological treatment including desensitisation. Furthermore this model provides a possible basis for psycho-educational information which brings together the biochemical and psychological aspects of bipolar disorder. Commonly people are presented with polarised views with respect to these aspects and accommodation of often conflicting information is left to the patients. Within this type of diathesis–stress model, however, integration of both is explicit which is likely to be beneficial in enhancing patients' understanding of their own illness process and the importance of combined psychological and medical treatment in effective therapy.

Circadian Rhythm and Life Events

Circadian system functioning has been widely studied in basic science as well as clinical research. Klein et al. (1991) indicate that the timing for this is importantly associated with the suprachiasmatic nucleus in the hypothalamus which regulates pineal secretion of melatonin. Circadian rhythms have been studied for some time in relation to depression. More recently Healy & Williams (1989) have proposed a model for interaction between life events and disruption of circadian rhythms in depression and mania. Wehr et al. (1983) reviewed studies of apparent circadian rhythm disruption in manic-depressive illness. They noted that a number of clinical features of this disorder including diurnal mood variation, early morning wakening and the cyclical or seasonal pattern of relapse might be associated with circadian disruption. Although a number of possibilities are considered in terms of the form this disruption might take, the main focus of Wehr et al. (1983) is to call for further more detailed assessment of circadian functioning in these patients. In a later paper Wehr et al. (1987) suggested that the effects of interpersonal, environmental and pharmacological events which impact on mania may act through their ability to cause sleep deprivation. Previous evidence is cited that sleep deprivation is associated with mania onset and that mania itself can then cause further sleeplessness, exacerbating the manic state.

Souetre et al. (1986) reported on the circadian rhythm of plasma thyrotropin in depressed and normal control. Particular abnormalities were observed in bipolar patients, these being in terms of reduced amplitude and peak night time values for secretion. Tsujimoto et al. (1990) looked at circadian rhythms in body temperature 2 hourly over a 48-hour period. They found that disturbances in temperature amplitudes and phase variability (but not advance) were apparent in depression and mania. In both cases instability of rhythm appeared to be critical. Feldman-Naim et al. (1997) investigated diurnal variation in mood switching in rapid cycling bipolar disorder. They reasoned that since melatonin is important in circadian function and the secretion of melatonin is promoted by daylight hours, a change from depression to mania or hypomania should occur during the day and reverse at night in these patients. Their data supported this pattern, leading them to argue for the importance of increased sleep, reduced activity and darkness in triggering depression and for the reverse pattern being important in triggering mania. Linkowski et al. (1994) took plasma samples over 24 hours from manic and healthy subjects. They reported that circadian rhythms in variations of cortisol levels were disrupted in mania, in a manner similar to, but less severe than, that observed previously in depressed subjects.

If circadian rhythms are important in bipolar illness then it might be expected that effective therapeutic agents would be shown to have actions on this system. Seggie et al. (1987), on the basis of study of the effects of chronic lithium administration in the rat, suggested that lithium works by affecting melatonin levels along the retinal–hypothalamic–pineal pathway, which provides a 'healthier' trigger for synchronisation of circadian rhythms. These effects of lithium were most significant during the dark phases of a split 24 hours dark light cycle. Welsh & Moore-Ede (1990) found that circadian periods were lengthened by chronic lithium treatment in primates assessed in behavioural terms (perch hopping), a finding also observed in lower animals, which again indicates a circadian role for the mechanism of action of this anti-mania drug.

Healy & Williams (1989) argued that behavioural stressors of the type observed in learned helplessness are also associated with circadian disruption and that such disruption would itself be likely to be associated with the kinds of cognitive distortions associated with negative affect. Also that desynchronisation of rhythms caused by substantial changes to external environment might be associated with mania. In animals it is noted that sustained bright light over extended periods led to loss of normal rest-activity cycles in chaffinches (Wever, 1980) to be replaced by restless hyperactivity. In humans jet travel eastwards, associated with greater jet lag and by implication more profound circadian disruption, is associated with higher rates of mania than travel in the opposite direction (Young, 1995). In general they suggest that conjunctions of disrupted social routines along with disruption of physiological functioning, such as sleep disruption, might together have equivalent effects in humans to those observed in chaffinches by Wever (1980).

It is argued that disruption of circadian rhythms tends to lead naturally to dysphoria, which whilst most obvious in depression is also observable in many manic patients. Indeed, as Healy & Williams note, the parallel presence of dysphoria and elation during mania has often been an unexplained paradox. They argue, however, that elation is a secondary effect deriving from the patients' normal reaction of 'explaining' their increased levels of psychomotor activity and associated increases in cognitive activity. They cite the fundamental attribution error commonly found in assessments of human judgements in which there is a basic tendency to attribute outcomes to internal causes. Hence elation may therefore be a side effect of internal attribution of changes in energy levels and cognitive functioning (i.e. I am stronger or more unstoppable than a thought). It is suggested that these attributions feed on the original and possibly quite mild dysphoric changes to generate further disruption of functioning. Since the attributions employed are therefore not in themselves 'illogical' in the sense that they are normative, there is an implication that such a process should be amenable to cognitive techniques in much the same way as those of depression are. Circadian disruptions normally resolve over time, as in the case of jet lag. However, in mania it is suggested that the behavioural responses of individuals to the cognitive distortions associated with increased activity levels tends to disrupt the very social routines which would normally provide the stable context within which normalisation would occur.

As noted previously there is considerable evidence of associations between manic episodes and life events which would be consistent with the circadian disruption hypothesis. Furthermore the observation that particular life events can at different times trigger either mania or depression would be more consistent with the affective state being secondary to interpretation of changes in motor activity levels. Healy & Williams (1989) also argue that the evidence which exists for neurochemical abnormalities in mania is most consist with generalised dysregulations associated with circadian rhythm disturbance rather than with specific disruption in particular neurotransmitter pathways. Thus the most specific evidence is for increases in melatonin levels in mania, which is secreted by the pineal gland which is important in co-ordinating rhythmic functioning. In pharmacotherapy of both mania and depression it is suggested that drugs act to harmonise circadian functioning and also that there is overlap in therapeutic effectiveness between drugs which are traditionally regarded as anti-manic and those which are regarded as anti-depressant. It is usually argued however that tricyclic antidepressants can cause mania, which would not fit with this model. The argument of Healy and Williams is that better controlled studies do not in fact support this and that the apparent findings of mania induction with this medication may in fact be an artefact of the popularity of this medication in association with the cyclic course of affective disturbance. They cite evidence that a wide range of other medications have also been reported as mania-inducing, including even lithium. It is also argued that whilst neuroleptics are useful in the acute stages of mania this is more in terms of behavioural containment rather than specifically anti-manic actions, which leads them to argue that it is likely that dopaminergic function in mania is probably normal.

Since this model argues for the presence of cognitive distortions in mania it raises the possibility of psychological intervention in a disorder which is traditionally regarded as only biologically treatable. Treatment might include psycho-education with respect to the interaction between biological changes and cognitive attributions for these changes as well as techniques for addressing such attributions. Furthermore it is suggested that medication compliance might be enhanced by patients appreciating the role that medication has in addressing the medical complaint responsible for their psychological distress rather than feeling that such treatment merely serves to mask their real feelings. As the authors indicate, however, there is still much research to be done in mania to progress understanding of the cognitive processes to the extent that they are understood for depression.

Chapter 4

A MODEL OF COGNITIVE BEHAVIOURAL INTERVENTION FOR BIPOLAR DISORDER

Our model, which forms the basis for our current approach to cognitive therapy, does not attempt to resolve all of the conflicting issues raised within the diathesis–stress models presented above. There is evidence which supports kindling, biological dysregulation and circadian rhythm effects as being linked to bipolar disorder. Evidence is not, however, sufficiently advanced to clarify whether these are competing models or in fact complementary descriptions, explaining the process of the developing bipolar illness at different physiological and psychological levels. However, all three models share a diathesis–stress approach in which physiological and psychological factors interact and suggest that the ways in which the individual copes with early onset of changes predicts likely clinical outcomes. A complex picture of biological, psychological and social elements surrounding manic depression is discussed, pointing to a holistic approach to the illness. Any model that does not incorporate these elements of the illness can miss out on important implications for intervention. Figure 4.1 depicts the holistic model of bipolar illness for psycho-social intervention. The model is largely pragmatic and incorporates research findings, clinical observations and speculations that need testing.

Consistent with Healy & Williams' (1989) proposition, we also propose that the inherent biological vulnerability in bipolar illness in the holistic model is the instability of circadian rhythms. Circadian rhythms are said to be entrained to social events and routine (Minors & Waterhouse, 1986). Disruption of routine and sleep can lead to a bipolar episode through the disruption in circadian rhythms. This aspect of interaction between the trigger (stress) and vulnerability (circadian rhythm unstableness) has important implications for intervention. Patients should be educated about the regularity of social routine in order to minimise disruption of their circadian rhythm. Prediction, anticipation and prevention of such disruption in routine and sleep by stressors such as life events can be an important

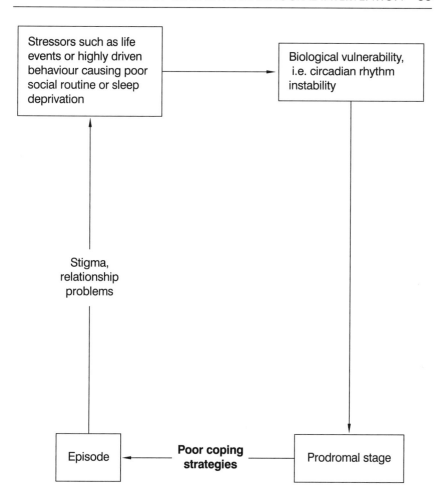

Figure 4.1   Diathesis–stress model for psycho-social intervention in bipolar affective disorders

aspects in the psycho-social management of bipolar affective disorders. However, in addition to acute stress proposed in Healy and Williams' model, it is further proposed in this model that an irregular life style that lacks in routine can also act as a stressor for individuals vulnerable to manic depression. Clinically it has been observed that chaos can lead to more episodes and hence having regular routine seems very important for bipolar patients. Beck (1983) proposed that individuals in a manic phase can exhibit an autonomous trait. If indeed autonomy is a personality trait in some bipolar patients, the drive to succeed can lead periodically to working excessively long hours, neglect of other important social routines such as regular meal times and lack of exercise. In extreme cases, this can involve sleep deprivation and total disruption to social routines, which can lead to a disruption of circadian rhythms. Hence, in this model, the disruption of circadian rhythms can be due either to acute stress or to a chronic unhealthy life style leading to progressive development of an episode.

It is proposed in our model that disruption of circadian rhythms does not necessarily lead to acute episodes. Patients go through prodromal stages of mania or depression of various lengths. Bipolar patients have idiosyncratic patterns of prodromes. Research in prodromes in bipolar patients suggests that most patients can report prodromes (Molnar et al., 1988; Smith & Tarrier, 1992; Altman et al., 1992; Lam & Wong, 1997). Furthermore, they are reported to have a fairly consistent pattern of prodromes over time (Molnar et al., 1988). Good coping was associated with higher social functioning (Lam & Wong, 1997), which in turn predicted longer intervals between episodes (Gitlin et al., 1995). These findings suggest that intervention at the prodromal stages can be important for the management of bipolar illness.

It is further proposed here that intervention at the prodromal stage can affect whether the patient proceeds to an acute episode. The prodromal stage can develop into a full-blown episode or can revert to a relatively stable mood, depending on the individual's coping strategies. Bipolar patients are thought to show more disregulation in the behavioural engagement system which regulates mood, incentive–reward motivation, sociability–social potency, desire for excitement, motor-activity arousal as well as positive mood state (Depue, Krauss & Spoont, 1987). Gray (1982) proposed that the behavioural engagement system is sensitive to environmental experiences and is turned on by signals of rewarding goal objects and turned off by signals of frustrative non-rewards. It is proposed here that bipolar patients are more sensitive both to environmental signals of rewards leading to goal-directed activity during the early stages of hypomania and to signals of frustrative non-reward leading to disengagement during the early stages of depression. Healy and Williams (1988, 1989) proposed that cognitive elements have a role in the genesis of full-blown episodes. They posited that misattribution of bodily symptoms to personal weakness or self-potency can further the course of developing from the prodromal stage into an acute episode. The mood state can further lead to selectively abstracting mood-congruent information in the environment to feed into the vicious circle. If the behavioural engagement system is turned on and off by environmental stimuli, it implies that manipulation of the environment can be helpful. It can help patients to maintain mood stability and during the prodromal stage may affect the development of an episode. Consistent with the cognitive model for affective disorders (Beck et al., 1979) that thoughts, mood and behaviour affect each other, bipolar patients' behaviour during the prodromal stages can also affect the course of an episode. Patients can be taught to resist the temptation of seeking more rewarding goal-directed behaviour in the prodromal phase of mania and to resist staying immobile during the prodrome of a depression to prevent a full-blown episode. Clinically, it has been observed that mania can fuel itself and depression can spiral down. Hence patients' coping during the prodromal stage can have important implications for the development from prodromal stages to full-blown episodes. For example, avoiding the temptation to seek further stimulation and engage in calming activities in the prodromal phase of mania may prevent a full-blown manic episode. Likewise, engaging systematically in pleasure or mastery activities, seeking support and reality testing one's negative cognition during the prodrome of a depression can prevent a full-blown depressive episode.

The model also proposes that an episode can beget further episodes by generating factors which can lead to further potential stress. For example, manic phases are more public and the expansive mood, increased goal-directed activities, increased pursuit of pleasurable activities, irritability and grandiose ideas are more noticeable and may have immediate or long-term consequences associated with occupational or financial loss and social embarrassment. During the manic phase, patients can be insensitive to their partners' needs or become flirtatious or even sexually promiscuous due to sexual over-arousal. Partners or spouses may resent this. Recurrent severe depression may also hinder the sufferer's social functioning. During the depressed phase, patient can be withdrawn, hopeless and suicidal, which could be construed differently by the spouse or family. The long-term burden associated with financial difficulties, child neglect, marital problems, infidelity, loss of status and prestige and fear of recurrence of the illness can all contribute to stress which can lead to another episode. Stigma is another important issue that may contribute to further vulnerability. Link et al. (1989) suggest that stigma can decrease self-esteem and social interaction. This in turn can contribute to decreased social support and result in a maladaptive style of coping. This implies that it is important to intervene at an early stage of the illness to prevent a course of frequent relapses, each leading to increased vulnerability to further episodes.

ARGUMENT FOR COGNITIVE–BEHAVIOURAL THERAPY

It is argued that individual cognitive–behavioural therapy can be a useful framework under which the following elements of psycho-social intervention for bipolar affective disorders are carried out. The model suggests four important aspects for psycho-social intervention:

1. *Psycho-educational.* Patients are educated about bipolar illness as a diathesis–stress illness. It is explained that there is a prominent genetic component in manic depression but that stress can lead to an episode. Therapy is introduced as being able to help patients to learn skills to problem-solve, to limit mood swings and to establish a routine in daily living in order to avoid excessive stress.

2. *Cognitive behavioural skills to cope with prodromes.* Clinically, we have observed that some patients who have a chronic course of frequent relapses find it hard to discriminate normal range of mood swings from an episode. The techniques of monitoring and rating mood and relating mood fluctuations to events in their activity schedules can be a very useful way of teaching these patients what their normal mood fluctuations are and how events can affect these. This approach also aims at promoting patients' ability to recognise prodromes and effective coping strategies for prodromes as important aspects of treatment. Patients are taught to resist the temptation of seeking more goal-directed behaviour in the prodromal phase of mania and to resist staying immobile during the prodrome of a depression to prevent a full-blown episode. The model of how thoughts, behaviour and mood can affect each other is a convenient way for patients to grasp the basis of cognitive–behavioural techniques.

3. *Importance of routine and sleep.* It has been observed that chaos can lead to more episodes. Sleep and routine appear to be very important for bipolar patients (Wehr et al., 1987). This is consistent with the vulnerability of the circadian rhythms of bipolar patients proposed by Healy & Williams (1989). As the circadian rhythms in humans are attuned to social events and routine, this model suggests the importance of educating patients to have a good social routine in order to minimise the disruption of their circadian rhythms. Patients are taught behavioural skills such as activity scheduling as a useful means of establish systematic routines.

4. *Dealing with long-term vulnerabilities.* A careful assessment of triggers for past episodes can reveal the individual's vulnerability to specific themes, such as extreme achievement-driven behaviour leading to stress and relapse periodically. Our experience suggests that therapists and patients can work towards modifying these vulnerabilities.

FURTHER DESCRIPTION OF THE APPROACH

Collaboration

An essential ingredient of the approach outlined below is that, as with most cognitive approaches, it is based on collaborative working between client and therapists. There is a focus of guided discovery throughout treatment such that the information collected with the client is used to allow clients themselves to identify useful changes in their approach to their illness. Whilst in certain phases of treatment alternatives will be suggested to clients, this is best done in the spirit of an experiment to test out a particular view rather than a didactic instruction. Thus, even when changes required for a particular client would seem extremely obvious, it is critical that the therapist does not try to impose these. Often the 'unhealthy' routines and behaviour of clients can serve important psychological functions which need to be grasped before steps towards change can be effected. If such steps are omitted then the collaborative relationship can be damaged, which can hinder progress and increase the likelihood of later withdrawal from treatment.

Adjunctive to Medication

Historically there has been a contrast between psychiatric and psychological approaches in the literature. In the former the focus is predominantly on finding the right medication for the condition under consideration, whilst in the latter it is supposed that medication may merely serve to 'cloud the issue'. Happily this dichotomy is less apparent currently and both psychological and psychiatric clinicians are more appreciative of the important interactions between pharmacology and psychotherapy in enhancing clinical outcomes.

The approach described in this book accepts that there is a significant biological component to bipolar illness and further that medication is likely to be a crucial component in the effective treatment of this illness. Cognitive therapy is presented as adjunctive to medication. It provides educational information to help clarify what role such medication might have and encourages an active debate between client and prescribing clinician with respect to medication regimen. It is believed that if the client has a good understanding of the rationale for each of the pharmacological treatments offered and is able to collaborate with their doctor to titrate medication required against current mental state the likelihood of regular compliance with maintenance medication is substantially increased.

Skill Acquisition and Relapse Prevention

The skills to be acquired during the course of treatment are diverse. Basic skills in monitoring and developing balanced social and work routines will be important. In addition self-management in terms of sleep, diet, sensation-seeking behaviour and substance abuse will need to be covered in therapy. Many clients will not readily alter work and social patterns which may have been familiar to them over many years. It is therefore incumbent upon the clinician to work with the client to identify why and how such changes may be of benefit and where necessary to reach appropriate compromise when clinically optimal changes are not possible for other psychological or practical reasons.

Traditional cognitive therapy elements of planning in rewarding activity in depression and rest periods in manic phases are included. Monitoring of cognitions and development of techniques for challenging dysfunctional cognitions and assumptions are employed during therapy. This approach is used in both depressive periods to reduce the impact of negative thinking and in manic prodromes to moderate over-optimistic thinking.

The issue of lithium compliance and its likely role in relapse prevention is tackled in therapy. Detailed symptom history information and cost–benefit analyses are used with the individual client to test out the extent to which lithium has been of benefit to them in maintaining mental health.

To enhance detection of prodromes ongoing symptom reports and symptom history are used with the client to describe early warning signs profiles. These signs are discussed in relation to likely interventions which might be of benefit in the early prodromal stages of illness.

Therapy will also cover issues in relation to the consequences of mental health history. This may include issues of stigma with respect to diagnosis and issues of guilt and grief. These may be in relation to their own behaviour during previous periods of mental illness or the consequences of labelling. This might also include discussion of marital and family relationships and child care issues.

Timing of Therapy in Relation to Illness

It is unlikely that patients would benefit from the approach described in this book if they were in a frankly manic or deeply depressed phase of illness. Although it is not necessary for the client be in full agreement with the therapist, some degree of insight and ability to cooperate is important. In the studies conducted to date patients who scored at extreme values of the Beck Depression Inventory of the Mania Assessment scale were excluded. However, this did allow many patients who continued to have significant levels of depressive or manic symptomatology to enter therapy.

Once in therapy efforts are made to continue work during exacerbations of symptomatology and indeed once skills have been developed *in vivo*, demonstrations of the efficacy of these coping skills in prodromal phases can form an extremely useful aspect of treatment.

OUTLINE OF TREATMENT

Typically cognitive therapy, as described in this volume, consists of about 20 therapy sessions in three stages. Session content provided below is intended as a guide. Individual patients vary in the speed with which particular approaches can be applied and in the degree to which support is required in implementing changes to structure and routine.

Stage 1. Initial sessions focus on education with respect to manic depression and both psychological and pharmacological treatments. This will usually be followed by the development of a detailed symptom or life event history and individual goal setting.

Stage 2. Subsequent sessions will cover a range of cognitive approaches, detailed below. It is intended that each subject will complete therapy with an understanding of their own particular warning signs for early onset of depression and mania or hypomania along with a 'fire drill' of actions to take to address these warning signs, with a view to avoiding relapse.

Stage 3. Sessions following active treatment will focus on continuing practice of techniques learnt previously and on behaviour changes where required if potential problems are identified.

Sessions contain the following elements:

Stage 1 (Sessions 1–5)

Treatment Structure

Patients will usually be offered 20 appointments, beginning twice weekly and becoming less frequent as treatment progresses, the final eight sessions being fortnightly. Information is provided on session length and, if relevant, on method of session recording. The importance of shared responsibility in the effective use of therapeutic time is emphasised.

Education or Development of Therapeutic Alliance

Introduction to the diathesis–stress model in which manic depressive illness is viewed as the outcome of a combination of genetic predisposition and environmental effects and to the cognitive model highlighting the role of thoughts and behaviour in relation to mental health problems.

Patient is informed of the structured approach used within cognitive therapy and in particular the use of an agenda is introduced. It is explained that an agenda will be set at the start of each therapy session to ensure that important aspects of the intervention are addressed. There will be opportunity for the patient to prioritise particular issues during this process. This process is begun in the first session and will be expected to continue during the first stage of treatment. For manic depression specifically there is evidence that routine is important, particularly in relation to work, sleep and diet; these issues are highlighted.

Symptom History

A detailed symptom history is begun at the first session and again will be expected to continue through stage 1. In combination with this the therapist and patients work to develop a detailed list of early warning signs associated with the symptom history which has been collected. A normalisation approach is taken towards the onset of symptoms, using the symptom history to introduce the idea of the patient reacting 'normally' at times to an abnormal environment (including the experience of manic or hypomanic symptoms). This information is discussed in detail in session, and patients are also provided with written educational sheets to promote generalisation of information learnt within session. A symptom history record is generated which patient and therapist can refer to during the remainder of therapy.

Self-monitoring

It is explained during the first session that self-monitoring will be an important part of treatment. Patients will be expected to complete a measure of mood, general mental state and to answer a few questions on medication at each session. They are also informed that more detailed monitoring of activities, mood and thoughts will be important aspects of therapy in later stages. The role of homework is discussed in relation to this and the importance of the patient's active participation with this process to optimise treatment outcome is emphasised. The following questionnaires are usually administered before each session: Beck Depression Inventory, Internal States Scale and Beck Hopelessness Scale (see Chapter 4 for more details on assessment issues).

Goal Setting

The focus here is on eliciting the patient's own functional goals, which may or may not be symptom related. This is introduced at session 2 but will usually be returned to and expanded upon during stage 1. Information from goal setting will usually inform the treatment process within stage 2.

A problem-solving approach is used to analyse steps towards these goals, which will include use of the cognitive techniques described below. An important issue here is an analysis of how to continue achieving important goals in spite of the presence of particular symptoms, rather than always having a strategy of withdrawal or avoidance.

An initial list of goals is generated. Problems associated with goals achieved and likely steps to overcome such problems are identified and discussed.

Stage 2 Intermediate (Sessions 5–16)

Cognitive Behavioural Techniques

Activity schedules. Introduction of activity scheduling, including daily mood ratings. Sheets provides for the monitoring of activity and routine through each 24-hour period. Rationales in terms of identifying natural variations in mood, checking for changes in sleep patterns, noting type and range of tasks undertaken. This monitoring is to be continued through this stage in particular. Information from activity sheets will often be inspected and discussed in relation to changes in mood or internal states scores and suggestions for behavioural change developed. If BDI or ISS indicate the presence of prodromal symptoms, then therapist investigates whether behavioural factors are associated with this. Balance between task and non-task activity, amount and regularity of sleep, pattern of routine or chaos is identified.

Use activity records as a basis for planning of appropriate activities: if there is evidence of excessive task-centred behaviour, then targets for relaxation or recreation are set. If lack of activity is associated with low mood, manageable task-oriented targets are set. Variability in sleep patterns if noted indicates a possible role for relaxation training which could then be set as an agenda item for next session. Also suggests a need to set regularity targets with patient in relation to sleep times etc.

Thought monitoring. Thought monitoring is introduced in the context of the CBT model. Therapist describes the way in which negative thoughts are associated with depression and overly positive automatic thinking can be associated with mania. Targets are to take a more objective approach to evaluation of circumstances which can begin with developing data on patients' own current patterns of negative or positive thinking. Records sheets and explanatory handouts are provided. Thought monitor records are reviewed, and any difficulties noted in capturing thoughts are discussed. The process of looking for patterns or themes in terms of thinking reported is begun here.

Thought challenging. Introduction of thought challenging. Written information with examples of challenges along with thought-challenge record sheets is provided. The process of challenging with respect to thoughts recorded on thoughts monitor is modelled. Thought challenge records are reviewed, and any problems encountered with challenging techniques are discussed.

Behavioural experiments. Introduction of role of behavioural experiments, which are explained in terms of concrete examples. If appropriate therapist identifies behavioural experiment to undertake during next week. At the next session therapist reviews behavioural experiment if attempted, if not then tries to identify a suitable behavioural experiment for the coming week, and discusses the importance of these in relation to effective challenging. The outcomes of behavioural experiments in terms of previous challenges of automatic thoughts are reviewed.

Dysfunctional assumptions. Therapist relates observed patterns of thinking to probable dysfunctional assumptions being made by the patient. He discusses the importance of addressing assumptions of this type for the purpose of capitalising on gains made in previous sessions and with a view to relapse prevention. He discusses within sessions possible alternative assumptions. Thought challenge records are used to further model approach to dysfunctional assumptions. Patient learns to demonstrate his or her own ability to challenge these. Methods for putting challenges discussed into practice behaviourally are planned.

Early Warning Signs

Focus here is on bringing together the information on early warning sessions collected during treatment. This will include information from symptom history, activity schedules, mood ratings and thought monitors which might be indicative of possible manic or depressive prodromes for the particular patient. Early warning signs identified in previous sessions are drawn together with idiosyncratic signs identified as homework. These are used to construct an early warning signs profile. The profile is then discussed with reference to which of the treatment approaches discussed above are most likely to be of benefit in alleviating the early warning signs identified when they occur.

Medication (Lithium) Compliance

Therapist introduces discussion of medication. Again this will be an issue returned to over several sessions. Verbal and written information is provided on available medications, their advantages and limitations. The patient is encouraged to report his or her own views and experiences. On the basis of information provided symptom history is used to review the patient's own experiences of symptoms with and without appropriate medication. Costs and benefits of compliance or non-compliance are identified. Importance of the patient having an active role in organising medication with the psychiatrist is addressed.

Stage 3 (Sessions 16–20)

Review

Review of cognitive-behavioural approaches introduced during the previous section. Discussion focuses on how these approaches have been applied in the individual patient and how the continuing use of such approaches after the formal treatment period is over is likely to be beneficial in terms of relapse prevention. This will include assessment of the degree to which the approaches associated with this part of the cognitive model have been internalised by the patient (e.g. the extent to which thought challenges have become 'automatic').

Self-management

Reviews self-management issues raised through the course of treatment, again with reference to historical information as well as information collected during treatment sessions. This includes the importance of sleep, diet and routine. Also the risks of sensation-seeking behaviour and substance use or abuse.

Consequences of Mental Health History

This covers issues of stigma, guilt and grief in relation to their history of mental health problems and their consequences. These may be in terms of patients' own behaviour (e.g. gambling, promiscuity, fraud) or in terms of the consequences of labelling. This will involve discussion of the effects of family relationships and child care issues.

CONCLUSIONS

This chapter has shown that whilst bipolar disorder is clearly an illness with significant biological and genetic components there remains a substantial contribution for social and psychological events in the development of illness episodes and in their remediation. Life events are disproportionately frequent preceding illness onset, particularly earlier in the course of the illness, and response to such events can determine whether an illness episode develops. A brief discussion of three diathesis–stress models of bipolar illness in the previous chapter served to show that all lead to a role for psychological intervention. Although these models are of interest there is not currently sufficient evidence to choose between them in terms of clinical relevance and it may indeed prove that the effects described are complementary. The psycho-social approach described in this chapter therefore views relevant stressors as including life events, disruptions of routine and biological functions (e.g. sleeps) as well as cognitive interpretations put on to 'normal' events as a functioning of distorted cognition's (positive or negative) and/or dysfunctional assumptions. The intervention which is summarised introduces the client to a psycho-social model of their illness which is combined with detailed history of the client's own illness experience and how this relates to psycho-social factors. Specific cognitive and behavioural approaches are described in relation to management of prodromal stages and long-term management issues are discussed in particular in relation to long-term self-management. The remaining sections of the book will provide detailed descriptions of each stage of the psychological intervention described above, which are illustrated through use of anonymous clinical examples.

Chapter 5

PRE-THERAPY ASSESSMENT

A systematic assessment is necessary prior to any formal therapy session. In addition to assessing the patient's current level of mood and suicide risks, therapists need background information about the patient's upbringing, the history of the illness and the patient's perception of current and past treatment in order to put the illness in the patient's context. Enquiries should also be made into how the patient has coped with the illness and how the patient is functioning in a wider social setting. Therapists should also find out the social support available to the patient.

It is important to point out that assessment and therapy are often intertwined. Some assessment procedures can be inherently therapeutic and often a therapeutic intervention may yield further information. Examples of the former include the life chart which enables the patient to put the illness in a personal context; to link it up with stresses and to examine whether there is a pattern of particular stresses to which the patient is vulnerable; and to examine the responses to treatment over a longer time perspective. An example of the latter is that sometimes tasks which involve spouses can reveal the quality of support from significant others that hitherto has not come to light. More detailed enquiries about it are often warranted. Hence assessment should be a continual process all through therapy. However, a formal assessment precedes formal therapy sessions. This chapter is concerned with the systematic assessment before the formal therapy session is started. It often takes a couple of sessions. The areas to be covered in the pre-treatment assessment can be divided as follows: (A) personal history, including the onset of the illness, stresses related to the onset of the illness and subsequent episodes; (B) the patient's perception of the illness and medication compliance; (C) the sense of self as well as other vulnerability issues including dysfunctional beliefs and sense of stigma; (D) how the patient is coping with the illness including mood swings and prodromes; (E) the patient's current mood state; (F) hopelessness and suicidality; (G) social functioning; and (H) the patient's formal and informal social support. These areas will be discussed below.

PERSONAL AND FAMILY HISTORY

The patient's own personal history is important. It helps the therapist to understand what the patient's background is, particularly early experiences. An important concept in cognitive therapy is beliefs about ourselves (core beliefs), other people and events, as introduced by Beck (1983). These important beliefs are thought to have developed in relation to early experiences. They guide our construction of, and interaction with, the outside world. Hence to gain an insight into the patient's internal world, therapists must enquire into any salient childhood events. During the assessment stage, patients should be asked to give an account of their upbringing and schooling experience. Any history of early losses due to separation or death and any physical or psychological traumas should be noted. Furthermore, the patient's own perceptions of his or her parental attitudes, relationships with peer groups and authority figures are also important. In the context of manic depression, there is often a family history of mental illness. Many manic-depressive patients have first-degree relatives who suffered from unipolar depression or manic depression. The impact of having a parent whose life has been disrupted by repeated episodes of mania and depression should not be taken lightly. Some patients may feel that their family environment was very unstable and may resent it. When the ill parent was depressed, the patient was often neglected or criticised. When manic, the ill parent became demanding, loud and embarrassing. Some patients also mourn not having the opportunity to know their ill parents because of frequent absences due to hospitalisation.

In terms of the history of the illness, a life chart can summarise it well and patients and therapists often find it useful to look at patterns of illness, stresses, academic or occupational achievement and relate them to medication. Bipolar episodes and their severity (mild, moderate and severe); treatment; any triggers that might have precipitated each; and occupational and educational stages over the course of the illness are marked on the vertical axis. These can then be charted over time on the horizontal axis. Figure 5.1 is an example of a life chart of a patient. By drawing together the information about the illness, therapists and patients can examine the pattern of the illness, whether the episodes were precipitated by any stress and the effectiveness of different prophylactic medications. Furthermore, the therapist and the patient can explore whether the patient is vulnerable to a particular type of stress, e.g. frustration about achievement or interpersonal events. The effect of medication, not only in relation to the frequency of bipolar episodes, but also in relation to how well the patient is performing at work or studies due to stability of mood can also be pointed out.

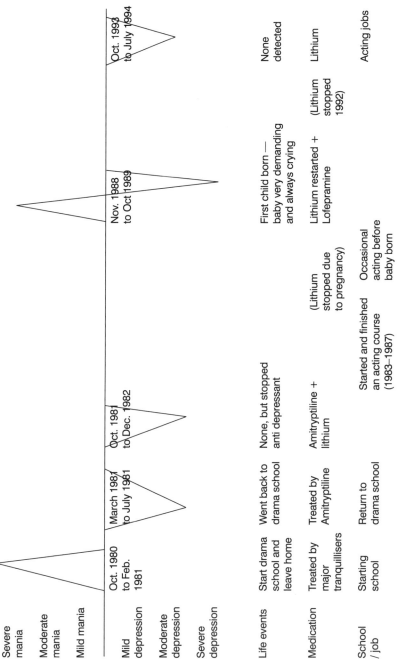

Figure 5.1 Life chart of Jane

Case example

Jane is a 37-year old actress. She has been suffering from manic depression for almost twenty years. There is a family history of depression in her mother's family. In fact her mother suffered from severe depression from time to time. Jane's life chart depicting the history of her illness, triggers, medication and academic/career attainment was reproduced in Fig. 5.1.

Jane had a very protected childhood. Her parents were indulgent in many respects and she was allowed to make a lot of choices and demands within the home. However, her parents were very strict about her going out with friends, particularly with boyfriends. Jane said that she had never spent even one night away from her parents before she went to drama school at the age of 17. As her life chart reveals, Jane's first episodes started when she left home to study drama. She described how excited she was about the prospect of going away from home and being totally free of any parental restriction. She had her first episode of mania two weeks after she started her drama course. Looking back, Jane said that she had so much freedom that she did not know how to handle it. She talked to a lot of people of her age and had a lot of late nights and partying. She went into a manic episode very quickly and had to be brought home. Initially her family tried to deal with the illness without any medical input. However, Jane was very disturbed and her parents very quickly realised that they could not cope with her illness on their own. A psychiatrist paid a home visit and prescribed major tranquillisers. Jane's first manic episode was followed by an episode of moderate depression. Then her mood was fairly stable for about five weeks before Jane made a second attempt at going back to drama school in the spring. However, she quickly developed into a severe depression. Jane described how she found it hard to fit in with her peers. She also said she felt totally humiliated and shameful about her breakdown. Jane had to return home a second time and gave up her place in the drama school. She was treated this time with Amitryptiline, an antidepressant. Jane's depression remitted in July 1981. However, Jane stopped her antidepressants and had an episode of moderate depression a few months later. This time lithium was added as a prophylactic medication. Jane continued with lithium prophylaxis and for five years she did not have any bipolar episodes. During this time she also managed to finish an acting course and was able to pursue a fairly successful acting career, appearing on London stages and some advertisement films. Then in 1988 Jane became pregnant unexpectedly. Both she and her boyfriend decided to continue with the pregnancy. She followed medical advice to stop taking lithium which can have harmful effect on a foetus. After the baby was born, Jane had a severe episode of mania, followed immediately by a severe depressive episode. Lithium was restarted and she was also treated with an antidepressant. She recovered in June 1989. In 1992, three years later,

Jane wanted to try without lithium as she was hoping to have a second child. Unfortunately she had another episode of moderate depression.

Constructing the life chart has been a very useful exercise for Jane. She said she never saw the history of her illness so clearly. She managed to identify with the idea that her manic episodes are triggered by disruption in her sleep and wake cycle. The first time, she was thrilled about starting college, being totally independent and mixing with people of her age. She slept very little several nights prior to the manic episode. The second manic episode was preceded by lack of sleep because the baby was very demanding and crying frequently at night. Jane also had to feed the baby every two to three hours. Most of her depression seemed to follow a manic episode. Jane thought that the first two depressive episodes were due to a sense of being a failure and being humiliated. She also described a tremendous sense of stigma. Similarly, Jane thought the depressive episode following child birth was due to feelings of guilt and shame at not being able to be a good mother and to give her baby a good start. Lithium seemed to have a protective effect against bipolar episodes. Jane did not have any bipolar episodes whilst she was taking lithium. She was able to finish an acting course and to pursue an acting career when she was taking lithium. Jane made a 'discovery' that lithium not only prevented acute bipolar episodes but also allowed her to pursue her life goals such as education and career. Furthermore, whenever lithium was stopped, Jane seemed to be vulnerable to a further episode.

For some patients who are not happy with taking prophylactic medication, the life chart can provide very useful evidence to weigh up the pros and cons of taking it. Jane was willing to continue taking lithium for the foreseeable future. However, she thought the life chart would also be useful in helping her to make future decisions about whether to continue with it. She could show her psychiatrist the chart and discuss it sensibly with him. Of course, it can be true that prophylactic medications have not shown any protective effect and have not reduced the frequency and severity of bipolar episodes. In these cases, a careful charting of the illness can demonstrate the differential effectiveness of different types of prophylactic medication, either singly or in combination. This information can be very useful for the patient to make an informed decision with his or her psychiatrist about prophylactic medication.

PATIENT'S PERCEPTION OF THE ILLNESS AND MEDICATION COMPLIANCE

As the model of cognitive therapy is one of collaboration, it is important that therapists understand the patient's view about manic depression. The importance of educating the patient, having a shared model and agreeing on shared goals and shared tasks are discussed in Chapter 6. Suffice it to emphasise here that therapists should have a clear view of the patient's understanding of the illness. Their views and understanding of having an illness which is relapsing in nature and the possibility of life-long pharmacological prophylaxis are particularly important. Patients may have varying degrees of acceptance of the diathesis–stress model. Some patients come to therapy with a view that their illness is caused by 'stress' or 'intrapsychic conflicts' and want to substitute medication with therapy. There is no evidence that psychotherapy alone is efficacious in treating manic depression. Our approach of carrying out psychotherapy in conjunction with medication should be made clear to patients. Often patients can be persuaded to give the approach of combining cognitive therapy and medication a try. When they have had a long period to put the skills learnt from therapy to use and a period of mood stability, they can then often be in a better position to discuss the pros and cons of discontinuing prophylactic medication with their prescribing doctors.

We have used the Insight Interview by David et al. (1992) to assess patients' attitude to their illness and medication-taking as well as to their model of their illness. We have found it appropriate to manic-depressive patients. The Insight Interview is a semi-structured interview and can be a systematic way of exploring patients' views. It has three components: treatment compliance (two questions), recognition of mental illness (three questions) and relabelling of psychotic phenomena (two questions). Each question is scored as: 0 = full insight; 1 = as much insight as social background and intelligence allow; 2 = agrees with nervous condition but does not really accept explanation in terms of nervous illness; 3 = denial. The section on relabelling psychotic phenomena is often not applicable when assessing manic-depressive patients who are not in an acute episode since they are no longer psychotic and tend to realise that previous psychotic experiences were part of their illness. The authors also reported good construct validity of the Insight Interview in the validation paper. See Appendix 5.1 for the Insight Interview.

THE PATIENT'S SENSE OF SELF, DYSFUNCTIONAL BELIEFS AND SENSE OF STIGMA

Sense of self in manic depression is an interesting issue which has not been investigated. Beck (1983) hypothesised that the relevant core beliefs in therapy were related to the themes of sociotropy or autonomy. He described the sociotropic individual as 'dependent on these social inputs for gratification, motivation, direction and modification of ideas and behaviour. The motif of this cluster is receiving' (p. 272). And the autonomous individual's investment was described as 'in preserving and increasing his independence, mobility, and personal rights; freedom of choice, action and expression; protection of his domain; and defining his boundary' (p. 272). In the case of manic depression, Beck hypothesised that when bipolar patients are depressed, issues of lovability are important whereas when they are in a manic phase, the issues of autonomy become more pertinent. However, the hypothesis of autonomy and sociotropy being related to mood state in manic depression has not been empirically tested. Clinically some highly sociotropic manic-depressive patients see the state of being slightly 'high' as their normal self and find it an attractive state to be in: they consider themselves more creative, energetic and confident. They find lithium intolerable as it takes away the 'rough edges' of the highs as well as the lows. Empirically the Sociotropy–Autonomy Scale (Beck et al., 1983) has been found not to measure the autonomy arm well (Robin et al., 1985). Instead the Dysfunctional Attitudes Scale (Beck et al., 1991; Power et al., 1994) has been found to be a better measure of the two concepts. In therapy, patients and therapists often work together to unearth patients' dysfunctional assumptions by examining the themes in automatic thoughts in therapy and by examining longitudinally the themes in stressful events that may lead to previous episodes. However, during the assessment stage prior to therapy, the Dysfunctional Attitude Scale can be useful in examining the extent of extreme scores of the dysfunctional beliefs so that therapists have an idea of the patient's belief system. See Appendix 5.2 for the 24-item Dysfunctional Attitudes Scale by Power et al. (1994).

A related issue with sense of self is the sense of being stigmatised as a sufferer of manic depression. The negative impact of stigma on the individual is discussed in Chapter 11. To assess the sense of being stigmatised as a sufferer of manic depression, the Views on Manic Depression Scale by Hayward et al. (paper in preparation) can be a useful instrument to assess the extent the patient feels stigmatised. However, it is important to realise that some patients do not say that they feel stigmatised. And yet they behave as if they feel very stigmatised. For example, they avoid social contact or cut out contacts with previous friends and relations even though they deny feeling prejudiced against them when asked. Therapists should be alert to this. See Appendix 5.3 for the Views on Manic Depression Questionnaire.

PATIENT'S GENERAL COPING WITH THE ILLNESS, MOOD SWINGS AND COPING WITH MANIC-DEPRESSION PRODROMES

Assessing how patients cope with their illness is an important aspect of the pre-therapy assessment. A thorough assessment of how patients are coping with their illness can be difficult to achieve during the first couple of sessions. However, one way of asking how patients cope with their illness is to be problem-focused. Patients can be asked what sort of problems come about as a result of their manic depression. Then the therapist can enquire how the patient copes with each problem specifically. The Self-Control Behaviour Schedule by Rosenbaum (1980) is a useful self-report questionnaire mapping into patients' use of cognitions to control physiological and emotional responses, patients' problem-solving skills, any harmful behaviour as a means of coping, their ability to delay immediate gratification and their belief in self-control in the face of behavioural problems. It consist of 36 items and each item is scored from +3 to –3. Good reliability and validity were reported by the author. The questionnaire can be used to obtain some idea of the patient's coping in the face of problems. The instrument is useful in getting a sense of how patients cope with behavioural problems. See Appendix 5.4 for the Self-Control Behaviour Schedule.

Patients' coping with prodromes will be discussed more fully in Chapter 10. However, during the pre-treatment assessment stage, it can be assessed by using open-ended questions (Lam & Wong, 1997). Patients are asked from their experiences what makes them think they are going either high or low and how these prodromes are different from a full-blown depression or mania. Then they are asked what they do when they have these prodromes. We recommend the open-ended questioning approach which has the advantage of being able to access subjects' more idiosyncratic prodromes and anchoring the prodromes in their individual contexts. This is important, as later in therapy the purpose is to teach and further develop the patient's ability to detect and cope with prodromes.

PATIENT'S CURRENT MOOD STATE

The evaluation of the patient's current mood state can be assisted by self-report or observer-rated mood instruments. It is advisable not to rely on just self-report or observer-rated instruments. Self report and observer rating do not always agree with each other. For patients who have been chronically depressed, there is often a time lag before self reports catch up with observer ratings in improvements of depressive mood state. Furthermore, when patients are manic, it is unlikely they will collaborate in filling out a questionnaire and it is dubious if their self-report will be accurate. The following is a collection of assessment instruments suitable for assessing manic-depressive patients. All these scales are designed to measure the severity of symptoms, not for making a diagnosis.

1. *Hamilton Rating Scale for Depression* (Hamilton, 1960) is an observer-rated instrument. All clinical information should be taken into consideration when completing the ratings. The scale maps into the cognitive, behavioural and somatic aspects of depression. It is particularly thorough in enquiring into the somatic aspects of depression. There are various versions of the scale, including a 21-item and a 17-item version. On balance the 17-item is more commonly used. Each item is rated either on a 0–4 or 0–2 scale. Good validity and interrater reliability have been reported. Grading guidelines are published. The score interpretation guide is:

0–7	None/minimal depression
8–17	Mild
18–25	Moderate
26+	Severe

    See Appendix 5.5 for the Hamilton Rating Scale for Depression.

2. *Beck Depression Inventory* (Beck et al., 1961) is a 21-item inventory designed to measure the severity of depression in adults and adolescents. The inventory enquires into the somatic, cognitive and behavioural aspects of depression. The factorial composition of the scale varies, to some extent, according to the extraction procedure. However, it seems to reflect Negative Attitudes Towards Self, Performance Impairment and Somatic Disturbance. *The time frame is 'the last week including today'.* Good validity is reported. The best review of the psychometric properties of the BDI is Beck et al. (1988). The instrument can be administered orally if necessary (instruction in the manual). Item 2 measures pessimism and Item 9 measures suicidality. Each item of the BDI is scored on a four-point scale (0–3). The Center for Cognitive Therapy in Philadelphia uses the following guidelines with depressed patients:

0–9	asymptomatic
10–18	mild-moderate depression
19–29	moderate-severe depression
>29	extremely severe depression

    In 1996 BDI-II, a new version, was published. Four items (Weight Loss, Body Image Change, Somatic Preoccupation and Work Difficulties) were replaced by new items (Agitation, Worthlessness, Concentration Difficulty and Loss of Energy) in order to index symptoms typical of severe depression or depression warranting hospital admission. Furthermore, the items on appetite and sleep were changed to allow for increases as well as decreases. The new version was influenced by DSM III-R on Major Depression. *The time frame has also been changed to two weeks* in order to be consistent with the criteria of Major Depression according to DSM-IV. So far, BDI-II has less data on the psychometric properties. The following guidelines for cut-offs have been suggested for BDI-II.

0–13	minimal
14–19	mild depression
20–28	moderate depression
29–63	severe depression

(Both the BDI, Beck & Steer, 1987, and the BDI-II, Beck et al., 1996, are published by the Psychological Corporation.)

3.   *Mania Rating Scale* (Bech et al., 1978) consists of 11 items that map into the patient's motor activity, visual activity, flight of thoughts, voice/noise level, hostility/destructiveness, mood level (feeling of well-being), self-esteem, contact (intrusiveness), sleep (average of past three nights), sexual interest, and decreased work ability. Each item is rated on a 5-point scale (0 = not present; 1 = mild; 2 = moderate, 3 = marked, and 4 = severe or extreme). The scale is used to assess the presence and grade of the individual items according to the patient's condition at the time to the interview. The items of sleep disturbance are less suitable for here-and-now rating and the item is judged according to the three days prior to the interview. The total scores are interpreted as: 0–5 = no mania; 6–9 = hypomania (mild); 10–14 = probable mania; 15 or more = definite mania. The scale has good inter-rater reliability and construct validity. See Appendix 5.6 for the Mania Rating Scale.

4.   *The Internal State Scale by* Bauer et al., (1991) consists of sixteen self-report 100 mm visual-analogue items to assess the severity of manic and depressive symptoms. The scale has four subscales: Activation, Well-being, Perceived Conflict, Depression Index and also a Global Bipolar Scale. The construct validity of the scale was supported by significant relationships between Activation scores and clinicians' ratings of mania and between the Depression Index scores and clinical ratings of depression. See Appendix 5.7 for the Internal State Scale.

HOPELESSNESS AND SUICIDALITY

As discussed in Chapter 1, manic depressive patients run a high risk of suicide. Hopelessness is an important aspect of assessment as it predicts suicide. Moreover, patients who are pessimistic about the future may not even stay in therapy unless hopelessness is addressed in the early sessions. In assessing suicide risks, any intention of suicide should be investigated further. No instrument should be used as the sole tool of assessing suicide risk or be used to replace expert clinical evaluation. Suicidal patients may deliberately conceal their intentions. Any instruments should only form part of the clinical assessment and should not replace the clinician's expert evaluation. Previous suicide attempts are also a powerful predictor of subsequent attempts. Hence therapists should always ask about previous suicide attempts, including the patient's intention to die, method of suicide and the seriousness with which the attempt was carried out. Any concerns about suicide should always be inquired into seriously and a second opinion sought if in doubt.

1. *The Beck Hopelessness Scale* (Beck et al., 1974) is a 20-item, true–false inventory. Nine items are keyed false and eleven items are keyed true. It measures the negative attitudes about the future as perceived by adults or adolescents. Like the BDI, it can be administered orally if necessary (see manual for instruction). Beck (1986) reported that hopelessness is a better predictor of suicide intention than depression. Beck et al. (1985) found that BHS scores of 9 or more were predictive of eventual suicide in a group of suicide ideators followed up for 5–10 years. Psychometric properties are reported in the Manual. The score interpretation guide is as follows:

0–3	normal range
4–8	mild
9–14	moderate
>14	severe

    (The Beck Hopelessness Scale, Beck & Steer 1988, is published by the Psychological Corporation.)

2. *Beck Scale for Suicide Ideation* (Beck & Steer, 1991) is a 21-item self-report instrument that can be used to detect and measure the severity of suicidal ideation in adults and adolescents. Oral administration can be done, if necessary, with the instruction in the manual. The BSI is a screening instrument. It is best regarded as indicators of suicide risks rather than as a predictor of eventual suicide in a given case. The authors stress that the scale is not to be used to replace expert clinical evaluation. Any intention of suicide revealed by the scale should be investigated further. Suicidal patients may deliberately conceal their intention. The authors recommend that no item in the BSI should be treated as the sole source of information in the assessment of suicide risk. Lastly the BSI has no mechanism to detect mental confusion or dissimulation.

    The scale measures a broad spectrum of attitudes and behaviours that clinicians routinely consider important in the assessment of suicide risk. The first 19 items measure gradations of the severity of suicidal wishes, attitudes and plans. Within each group, the statements reflect increasing gradations of severity (from 0 to 2). The last two items (asking about the number of previous suicide attempts and the seriousness of an intention to die during the last attempt) help the clinician to discover important background characteristics and should not be included in the BSI total score.

Administration: The first five BSI items serve as a screen for suicide ideation. If the respondent circles the zero statements in items 4 (no active suicidal ideation) and item 5 (indicating avoidance of death if presented with a life-threatening situation), then instruct the respondent to skip the next 14 BSI items. Otherwise the respondent is to rate the next 14 BSI items. However, every respondent is asked to rate item 10 and any respondent who has previously attempted suicide should be asked to rate item 21.

There is no empirical evidence to support the use of specific cutoffs for the total BSI scores. Any positive response to any BSI items may reflect suicidal intentions and should be investigated further.
(The Beck Scale for Suicide Ideation is published by the Psychological Corporation.)

SOCIAL PERFORMANCE

Social performance is defined by Platt et al. (1980) as the actual behaviour of an individual while performing or acting in a particular status or social position (e.g. a spouse, worker, parent etc.). It refers to how the individual fulfils certain key social roles which form the basis of social life. There is evidence that disturbed behaviour and social functioning may vary independently (Creer & Wing, 1974; Weissman & Paykel, 1974). Social performance may persist long after the psychiatric episode is over (Paykel & Weissman, 1973; Hirsch et al., 1979). Gotlib and Lee (1989) followed up a group of depressed women for 7–10 months and reported that even though there were significant reductions in depression at follow-up, the sample reported significantly fewer social activities, fewer close relationships, poorer quality in those relationships and more family conflicts compared to non-depressed psychiatric and normal community controls. Moreover, there is evidence that depressed patients functioned less well when compared with other groups suffering from chronic physical illnesses such as insulin-dependent diabetes or severe arthritis (Hammen, 1991). Lam & Wong (1997) and Lam et al. (in press), using the MRC Social Performance Scale (Hurry et al., 1983), examined the social functioning of two samples of manic-depressive outpatients. They reported that a significant proportion of manic depressed patients had serious problems in the various domains even though none of the subjects was in an acute episode. The most affected areas were: employment, intimate relationship, social presentation and coping with emergency. Note that both samples were outpatients and none of the subjects in either samples was in an acute crisis. Hence there is evidence that the social functioning of manic-depressive patients is impaired.

Gitlin et al. (1995) reported that subjects' social functioning is important as it can in turn affect the duration between episodes. Clinically, it is often noted that a manic episode can be very detrimental to the patient's inter-personal relationships, work and finances. Part of the overall goal of therapy is to promote a better level of social functioning, and problem areas can form specific therapy goals. Hence it is important to assess the patient's level of social performance independently of psychiatric or mental state. By assessing how the patient is functioning in the various areas of life, the therapist often gains a better overall view and puts the individual in a wider social context. Our experience is that the assessment of manic-depressive patients' level of social functioning often gives us a more complete picture. Often it reveals aspects of problems not necessarily disclosed by patients spontaneously.

In assessing social performance, it is important to avoid the pitfall of being influenced by the unwarranted assumption that the values and norms behind certain roles are fixed or absolute. There should be no idealised conception of normality or fixed norms of social roles. The person's own social milieu and life stages should be taken into consideration. The roles of being a worker or parent may vary according to age, sex, social class and even within the person's subculture.

There are various schedules that enable the systematic assessment of social performance. The Social Behaviour Assessment Schedule by Platt et al. (1980) and MRC Social Performance Schedule by Hurry et al. (1983) are semi-structured interviews. The Social Adjustment Scale (Weissman & Bothwell, 1976) is a self-report instrument, later modified by Cooper et al. (1982) for the British population. All these schedules map into similar areas of social functioning. In the context of the pre-therapy assessment of social functioning, we recommend using a semi-structured instrument with the patient as the informant. A semi-structured interview approach allows the rater to be sensitive to the patient's social milieu, life stages, race and social class. Having the patient as the informant has the advantage of getting the patient's own perspective on how they are faring in their various social domains. Weissman (1975) reviewed the techniques of assessing social adjustment and commented that non-psychotic depressed patients are reasonable informants. Furthermore, interviewing a close relative or friend may lead to resentment from the patient, particularly those who value autonomy.

We have used the MRC Social Performance Schedule by Hurry et al. (1983) and found it appropriate for patients suffering from manic depression. The MRC Social Performance Schedule is an observer-rated scale based on a semi-structured interview that provides a quantitative assessment of social performance in the last month. The patient is the informant. The schedule covers eight areas of social performance: Household Management, Employment, Management of Money, Child Care, Intimate Relationship, Non-intimate Relationship, Social Presentation of Self and Coping with Emergency. The interview is directed towards actual behaviour and performance in each area and is rated on a 4-point scale: 0 = fair to good performance, 1 = serious problems on occasions but can sometimes manage quite well, 2 = serious problems most of the time, and 3 = not able to cope at all. For each area, examples of serious problems are given. A very stringent threshold is set for serious problems. For example, serious problems in Household Management means shopping has to be done by someone else, and meals are not provided or inedible and the house is filthy unless someone else cleans it. An overall score is obtained by totalling the scores. In the original paper, the authors reported a better than chance inter-rater agreement. Lam & Wong (1997) also reported good inter-rater reliability using a sample of manic-depressive patients. See Appendix 5.8 for the MRC Social Performance Schedule.

RESOURCES AVAILABLE TO THE PATIENT INCLUDING FORMAL AND INFORMAL SOCIAL SUPPORT

Cobb (1976) defined social support as possessing 'information leading individuals to believe (they) are cared for and loved; esteemed and valued; and that they belong to a network of communication and mutual obligation'. There are several functions of social support. It can provide esteem or emotional support by expression of positive affects and sense of like-mindedness. It can also mean instrumental support, when more practical, tangible help is given. Informational support can be crucial when the person is facing a novel problem that needs to be resolved. Social company is another important aspect of support so that the person feels less isolated. Lastly motivational support to maintain hope and to sustain a belief in a chosen course of action is important in the context of chronic situations.

When assessing social support, it is important to assess both the structural and functional aspects of social support (Cohen & Willis, 1985). For the structural aspects of the network, the size and density of the network is important. Density refers to whether the people in the network come from the same source or different diverse groups. If all the people in the network come from the same one or two sources, the density of social support is low and can be limited to a similar kind. In any case, if the patient loses the source which provides the main network which comes from the same group of people, it is harder to reestablish and obtain social support from a totally new network. A social network could further be divided into informal and formal networks. An informal network is the patient's natural network of family, friends, colleagues and acquaintances. A formal network consists of the patient's professional contacts, e.g. general practitioner, psychiatrist, community psychiatric nurse, social worker and therapist. Care should be given to the presence or absence of significant relationships and to the quality of these relationships. In assessing the patient's social network, the frequency of contact, strength of ties and reciprocity are important. The expectations of each party in the network and whether these expectations are fulfilled should be enquired into. The satisfaction and dissatisfaction of each close relationship should be assessed. Not everyone in the network is equally supportive. There is no direct relationship between the size of a social network and the amount of social support available. The functional aspects of support could be broadly divided into emotional and practical support. In some cases, there may be over-provision of certain types of support, particularly in the context of a recurrent mental illness. Some carers or close family members can be over-protective and patients may resent it. Similarly, certain kinds of social support can only be provided and accepted if it comes from someone close to the person such as a confidant or spouse.

No published instrument can replace a detailed assessment of social support and social relationships by the therapist. Various instruments have been published (Henderson et al., 1981; McFarlane et al., 1981; Sarason et al., 1982; Surtees, 1980; Power et al., 1988). We have used the Significant Others Scale by Power et al. (1988) to assess the quality and quantity of social support. The Significant Others Scale by Power et al. (1988) is a self-report instrument that enquires into the functional supports of up to seven important relationships. Furthermore, the instrument enquires into the ideal (expectation) and actual support. The scale can be a useful start in assessing both the quality and quantity of social support. See Appendix 5.9 for the Significant Others Scale.

Chapter 6

INTRODUCING THE MODEL TO THE PATIENT

BASICS OF THE MODEL

When therapy actually begins, the key first task is to help the patient understand and, hopefully, accept our basic model. This is of course outlined in Chapter 4, but in this chapter we will be discussing how to facilitate client acceptance. This phraseology is important: our goal is not simply to present the model in a *didactic* manner, but to develop a model *collaboratively* with the patient. This being the case, it is important to note that models developed with different patients could vary, depending on each patient's own views; this point may be worth emphasising, because it bears on a fundamental aspect of the CBT approach.

In this chapter, we will first discuss the use of written information in developing a collaborative model of the patient's difficulties. Our goal is to be authoritative without being authoritarian; the patient is encouraged to ask questions and express doubts about the information provided, with the goal of facilitating real commitment as opposed to polite verbal agreement. We have already discussed the various assessment tools used in our approach, but this chapter also discusses the use of some of these tools in educating the client. Finally, some examples are offered of situations in which clients do not accept the model, and ways of dealing with this are discussed.

USING INFORMATION SHEETS

The use of an information sheet is generally routine in our therapy programme. This sheet (See Appendix 6.1) is generally given to the patient during the first or second session, and the patient is asked to take it home, read it over, and return with questions and comments. The leaflet is presented as a platform for discussion, and patients can then be asked what they found to be useful or interesting in the leaflet, and what aspect of it they found difficult to apply to themselves. The key message is that patients do not have to accept everything in the leaflet to take part in therapy; often points of disagreement can pinpoint good areas for exploration. In our experience, some patients find the leaflet to be tremendously helpful, and have no trouble applying the model to themselves, while others will question it on many points. For example, some patients may doubt that they actually suffer with the illness at all, or they may be hoping that their past episodes will not recur. For other patients, any reference to biological causation may be problematic, perhaps preferring to construe their problems as 'emotional' or 'only requiring counselling'. These reactions should be noted by the therapist, who may need to take account of them in planning therapeutic interventions, as they can predict the client's reaction to certain ideas. Careful handling is often required. After all, one cannot 'prove' that a patient is a manic depressive, or that episodes of illness will always recur. A good strategy may be to enunciate the possible views of the illness and 'agree to differ' on certain points. As therapy proceeds, evidence bearing on these disputed points can be accumulated, but in the meantime, therapist and patient can look for points on which they can agree, with a view to developing a mutually acceptable model.

Such a model will generally have certain characteristics. First of all, it will be a *diathesis–stress* model. This necessity grows out of the nature of our therapy; it assumes that stress can trigger episodes, because that in turn implies that reducing stress can reduce the number of such episodes. Second, it will involve careful study of the different phases of the illness, such as the role of variations in mood and the recognition of prodromes. Thirdly, it will emphasize the *interrelationships among thought, emotion and behaviour*, and the relationship of all of these to the *environment*. This is of course part of standard cognitive therapy, and is important because it offers a model of how the various symptoms of manic depression can be controlled by non-pharmacological means. Finally, the therapist should generally make clear his or her belief in the utility of mood stabilisers and other psychiatric medications, and we have prepared a leaflet on this subject (See Appendix 6.2). Some patients may be doubtful about this point, and if they are, it is best to avoid confrontation, and to return to the issue when more evidence has been gathered.

Carla is 27 and is recovering from her second manic episode. She arrived for her second session having read the fact sheet, and the therapist has just asked her what she thinks of it.

CA: Well, I was a little puzzled by the fact that it said that, in many cases, manic depression had a genetic basis.

TH: Why is that?

CA: No one in my family has ever suffered with anything like what I have. I know my mother used to get depressed sometimes, but she never ever got high. Sometimes I wish that she had. The whole idea of a genetic illness bothers me.

TH: There's something about having a genetic component to your illness that bothers you?

CA: I definitely want to have children some day. And I want to make sure that they have a better start than I did.

TH: If there was a genetic factor involved in your problems, what would that mean to you?

CA: I've always told myself that I would give my children a fresh start. I never liked my childhood, and I never felt that I was much like either my mother or my father. My mother always seemed to be depressed and complaining, and my father was never around. When I do have children, I want them things to be different.

TH: And if there's some genetic factor relating to manic depression, that would mean?

CA: That they would be repeating my problems. I would find that very difficult to live with.

TH: Suppose I told you that I had some sort of genetic disorder, and that I really wanted to have children – what advice would you give to me?

CA: I don't know – I suppose I'd tell you to learn as much about the problem as you could, to find out how the illness was treated and how you can manage it. It's easy to advise someone else about that. But I hate the idea of having a long-term illness myself, and I also don't like the idea of taking medication over a very long term.

TH: What don't you like about it?

CA: I hate the idea of having to take something to manage my moods; I feel I ought to be able to do that myself. I know I needed some help in the short term, but I feel that taking medication in the long term means there's something really wrong with me.

TH: I think we have to learn more about your history, and also about how we can best manage your problems in the present. Hopefully we can help you have more control over those problems.

CA: That's what I want.

TH: And if taking medication was part of having that control?

CA: I'd have to think more about that.

Throughout therapy Carla and her therapist had to wrestle with the issue of the role of medication in long-term management of her problems. Carla was finally able to see that both psychological and medical methods could help her manage her mood, and she found that this helped her to gain a greater sense of control.

Carla was very loath to think of herself as suffering from a medical illness. The opposite viewpoint is also sometimes observed: patients may 'over-medicalise' themselves, believing that only medical interventions can help them.

Rebecca, a housewife in her 40s, was referred for therapy by her psychiatrist, who was worried by the restricted life that she seemed to be leading. She was very reluctant to depart from any of her daily routines and avoided any activity that might be seen as challenging. When discussing the information sheet, she commented that, since manic depression was an illness, she was not sure that psychological therapy had anything to offer her. When the therapist explored these issues with her, a paradox emerged: her very routinised and restricted lifestyle was, in large measure, an attempt to avoid stress and possible relapse. Rebecca did take this point on board, but these early comments indicated a theme that would recur throughout her therapy, as will be seen below.

Having introduced these ideas about manic depression and its management in the first or second therapy session, the therapist must next help the patient to understand their relevance and learn to apply them in his or her own life situation. This is of course the role of therapy as a whole, but a useful start can be made during the process of assessment (see Chapter 5). Two useful tools are the Problem List and the Life Chart: their roles in educating the patient will be discussed in the next two sessions.

THE PROBLEM LIST

The creation of a problem list is of course standard cognitive therapy practice. One function of this procedure is the promotion of a therapeutic alliance: the patient sees that the therapy is focused on goals relevant to him or herself, instead of merely goals chosen by the therapist. In addition, it helps to reinforce the practical, problem-focused nature of cognitive therapy. However, in addition to these two functions, the problem list should be used whenever possible to begin teaching the patient about the model. Particular problems can be used in specific ways:

Self-critical thoughts. Many of the thoughts which manic-depressive patients bring to the therapy are self-critical, especially if they enter therapy in a depressive or euthymic phase of the illness. Some of these thoughts may represent the standard negative automatic thoughts of cognitive therapy for depression. These will in due course be dealt with using standard CBT techniques (Beck et al., 1979; J. S. Beck, 1995), but during the initial few sessions the therapist should help the patient to understand the link between these thoughts, dysphoric emotions and particular behaviours, whether of avoidance or overcompensation. A related type of automatic thought may focus on issues concerning a history of chronic mental illness, such as concerns about stigma or about losses caused by the illness. Such problems may require complex interventions (see Chapter 11), but initially they can also be used to explore the links between thoughts, behaviour and emotions.

Will is 27 and works in construction. He highlighted shyness and inhibition in social situations as one of his main concerns. Here the therapist explores what this means to him:

TH: Now you've listed social situations as a major problem. Perhaps you could tell me a bit more about how they are a problem, and what sort of help you'd like with them.

WI: Well, I always feel out of place; I don't feel that I fit in.

TH: Can you give me an example?

WI: OK, last week my girlfriend and I went to the pub. We met some of her friends there, and they were all laughing and drinking, and one of them, Doug, always has a lot to say, and always makes everyone laugh. I never feel comfortable saying anything, and I feel as if, when I do say something, nobody pays any attention.

TH: Do you feel this problem relates in any way to your illness?

WI: Yes, I do. During my first breakdown, I suddenly got very talkative and outgoing. I felt that I was the life and soul of the party. I remember being in a pub talking to some people and having a great time. But now I recall the incident, and I feel as if they might have all just been humouring me, being polite, and that probably I was talking a load of rubbish.

TH: And these thoughts affect you now?

WI: Definitely. Whenever I feel like saying anything, I have a lot of doubts. I remember those times, and I don't want to be patronised, or to feel that I'm just talking rubbish.

TH: So tell me if I understand this correctly. You're in the pub, you see everyone talking and joking, and you're thought is something like, 'I'd like to do that, but I might just be talking rubbish.' Is that sort of it?

WI: Definitely.

TH: And how does that make you feel?

WI: Depressed. Like I can't trust myself to take part in things.

TH: And that affects how you act?

WI: Definitely. It makes me really hesitant about saying anything. I just sit and smile politely, and agree with people.

By exploring this example further, the therapist clarifies the interrelationship of thoughts, emotions and behaviour. The role of the social setting, and of the views of both the patient and his friends about his illness, are also important and should be made explicit. The specific situation, and the issue of social anxiety, will be explored further, and hopefully both cognitive and behavioural approaches can be used to help Will with his problem. But in addition, the exploration of this example helps the patient to understand the cognitive model.

Grandiose thoughts and behaviour. Patients are often more ambivalent about the manic symptomatology associated with their illness. On the one hand, they may fear the consequences of the illness, the various risky behaviours and the damage to interpersonal relationships. On the other hand, some of the symptoms may in themselves be highly seductive, and patients may have had little chance to discuss this fact. These perceived positive aspects of the illness may create difficulties in treatment, and this may need to be acknowledged in the initial interviews. At the same time, the relationship between enjoyable grandiose thoughts and destructive behaviours can also illustrate the cognitive model:

Raymond is in his late 40s and works as a chauffeur. Although his salary is not high, he had few expenses and had managed to save a considerable amount of money. He had suffered with bipolar illness and been maintained successfully on lithium for many years. However, because of some kidney problems, he was switched to carbamazepine. Following this he went high and ran up enormous bills on two credit cards. Raymond focused on avoiding the repetition of this experience as one of his major goals:

TH: So what actually happens when you're about to buy something? What goes through your mind?

RA: There's a feeling of 'I've just got to have it!'

TH: Can you give me an example?

RA: Well, look at this raincoat. It's a really nice coat, as you see, and a good buy, and it's very good quality, so it's lasted. So you think of all these things, and you know you can buy it on your credit card, so you just go for it.

TH: And what do you think about the credit card balance?

RA: You feel that it's so big already that another few hundred pounds really doesn't matter. The funny thing is, after you've bought it you sort of know that you shouldn't have, but then you put it out of your mind and go on to the next thing. Sometimes you buy something else, just to show yourself that you're not really worried about the previous purchases.

TH: So the thoughts are of how nice the item is, and what a good buy it would be … ?

RA: That's right.

TH: And the behaviour is to go ahead and buy it.

RA: Yes.

TH: Would you go to the shop specifically to buy it?

RA: No, you tell yourself that you're just 'window shopping'. You look at a few things and find fault with them, and then you tell yourself you are a really discerning shopper, and then you see something really nice, and you feel you have to buy it.

TH: And there is a real pleasure in making a really good buy?

RA: Definitely. This is a wonderful coat, I just wish I wasn't still paying for it three years later.

This dialogue illustrates the links established between particular situations and the thoughts, emotions and behaviours that occur in them. The therapist might choose to inquire further, until these links were absolutely clear to the particular patient. It is also important to acknowledge the positive aspects of the experience; if the therapy is to work, the patient will often have to make the decision to renounce certain positive experiences.

THE LIFE CHART

Early in the therapy, patient and therapist begin to take a history of the patient's illness. This is summarised in the form of a 'life chart', as discussed in Chapter 5. Such a history is of course standard CBT practice, but in this case the life chart can also help the patient get a clearer view of the costs and benefits of illness. If patients are to enter into collaborative work regarding the control of their illness, they must be ready to give up perceived benefits, and it is therefore important that they should understand the effects that therapy might have. For example, our approach emphasises the importance of having a regular lifestyle and attention to the sleep–wake cycle, but it is worth noting that many people, and not simply those with bipolar illness, could object to living in a style that might seem to be boring and conventional. The literature on habit change suggests that most people experience some difficulty in developing a more healthy lifestyle (Rollnick et al., 1992). The life chart can also help the patient to understand the relationship between lapses in medication use and relapse of illness, assuming there has been such a relationship in the particular case. Such an approach has been used to improve compliance with other psychotropic medications (see Kemp at al., 1996a). However, one caveat is necessary: the therapist must beware of appearing to 'sell' any particular change. The inquiry should be open, so that possible changes in the patient's behaviour are arrived at by mutual agreement.

Alicia is 31 and works as a graphic designer for a large design company. She had her first manic episode in her late 20s. Here she talks about what happened after she was discharged from hospital following that episode and how it affected her relationship with her boyfriend, Roger:

TH: How would you say your mood was after your discharge?

AL: About here (indicates middle level on chart).

TH: And that lasted how long?

AL: About a year.

TH: (Draws line) How did you feel at that time?

AL: Well, at first I was glad to be out of hospital. Work was OK, and I was taking the medication they gave me, the lithium, but after a while life began to seem grey, boring.

TH: Grey and boring?

AL: That's right. I would go to work every day, and most nights I'd just sit at home. Roger had been wonderful through the admission, he'd visited me every day, and afterwards he was always around at my house, and he began to get on my nerves.

TH: How so?

AL: Well, he wanted to take care of me. He always reminded me about my medication, and he was always nagging me about getting enough sleep. He'd say, 'Let's watch the telly, and I'll make you a nice cup of herbal tea.' After a while, I just wanted to punch him for being so dreadfully nice and understanding. We'd go out at the weekends, and go to clubs, but it just wasn't the same.

TH: How do you mean?

AL: Maybe it was the lithium, or maybe it was just something in me, but I just didn't feel like myself. I've always loved going out, looking my best, flirting with all the guys, knowing that they fancied me. And I loved being witty. If some guy I didn't fancy tried to chat me up, I could always say something clever, and I could always make my friends laugh, but I seemed to lose all that. I just felt … heavy …, it's hard to explain, like I did put on a bit of weight, and I had to watch my diet really carefully, but also my mind felt heavy, slow, I didn't get the same buzz out of clubbing, and out of work. And Roger was getting to me more and more. I felt like he was turning me into an old woman – I kept waiting for him to buy me a shawl and some knitting.

TH: So what happened?

AL: Well, we kept arguing, and finally we had a real blazing row, and I threw him out. But I didn't feel any better, any lighter, if you know what I mean. I began to feel worse. I couldn't get up in the morning, I couldn't work. I'd just stare at my computer, and my ideas didn't flow, and the work I did was real crap.

TH: What did your employers feel about your work?

AL: Well, I got it done on time, usually, but it got harder and harder. And they began to be more critical. There was one big account where I worked for days on the presentation, and they looked at what I had done and just gave it to someone else. I was crushed. I just stopped going out, because I felt so boring and unattractive. Finally I just stopped all my medication to see if that would help.

TH: And your mood at this point?

AL: Here. And that lasted for about 6 months.

TH: (Draws on chart). And then?

AL: Then I began to get high again.

TH: Can you tell me what was happening around that time.

AL: I remember that I began to feel better. It was spring, and I felt well, really well for the first time in a long time. I remember that there was a lot of work on, and I think that I started to get behind, but I didn't really worry about it. I felt that all I needed to do was work a bit harder, and I would catch up. And I remember that I got back into clubbing again, and had a really good time. At the time, I felt fine ... but looking back, I guess it wasn't really all fine. I think I got a bit slapdash with my work.

TH: It sounds like you were doing a lot of different things at the same time.

AL: I was, really.

TH: How did you keep up?

AL: Well, I didn't sleep very much. I used to be up all hours. And my mind would be racing. I'd get a lot of ideas for work, and I'd scribble them down on bits of paper, and sometimes I couldn't understand them afterwards.

This portion of the life chart suggests some of the problems that will probably continue to trouble Alicia. She associates many positive experiences with the 'high' state, and many negative experiences with medication and the type of lifestyle that seems to be associated with staying well. These areas will clearly require a great deal of work. The therapist can clearly focus more on her account of her relapse, and illustrate the interaction of work pressures and excessive activity, and how these in turn might precipitate relapse, as an example of the diathesis–stress model of illness. The key point is to elicit evidence for the model from the client's own experience.

PROBLEMS IN ACCEPTING THE MODEL

It is important at this point to comment on one very important fact: that many patients will have great difficulties in accepting this particular model of their problems. In some cases, these problems may well prevent effective therapeutic work. This may seem surprising: if patients have willingly entered into therapy, one might think that they are ready to accept that they have an illness, and that that illness can be treated, at least in parts, using psychological methods. However, most therapists have seen patients who claim to want help, but who find it difficult to accept a cognitive–behavioural model of illness. Patients may enter therapy with their own wishes and hopes, sometimes unarticulated, such as that their illness will disappear and not recur, or unarticulated fears, such as that any change might make their situation worse. Such beliefs can constitute a barrier to therapy; sometimes these barriers can be overcome, but some-times one must accept, for whatever reason, that a particular patient is not suited for this particular approach. Early problems in accepting the model may be revealed in the patient's reaction to the Information Sheets or Life Chart, as discussed above. We will now discuss some particular examples of such barriers to therapy and suggest possible ways of dealing with them.

The patient who denies illness. Some patients may present for therapy with very mixed feelings about their particular diagnoses. They may resent the medical model, feel stigmatised (see Chapter 11), or not perceive many aspects of their illness as a problem. For some patients, the limitations and problems which they perceive as being associated with their illness may seem very painful; therapeutic empathy is important here, as is a focus on the positive possibilities for change inherent in our model. Other patients may be unwilling to admit even the possibility they may suffer with manic depression. The only approach in such cases would be to find some issue which the patient would be willing to work on; even if that issue is not connected with bipolar illness, it might provide a starting point for some sort of therapeutic approach. In such cases, the therapist must strive to develop some shared therapeutic goal; such a goal can sometimes provide a fulcrum to effect therapeutic change, but this can be difficult.

Joanna is an unemployed woman in her mid 30s. She is interested in writing and other creative pursuits, has enrolled in a number of writing courses but never completed one, and likes to write poetry and attend poetry readings in pubs. Her insight into her illness is mixed—she admits that she has problems 'organising herself' and that she 'sometimes gets depressed', but rationalises her two hospital admissions as 'times when I needed a rest'. She has been will-ing to take medication when hospitalised, saying, 'Sometimes I need something to calm me down'. However, she is not compliant with long-term maintenance medication, saying that lithium dulls her 'creative edge'. Likewise, she denies that she has an 'illness':

TH: So, if I understand what you're telling me, the doctors have told you that you're ill, but you find this hard to accept.

JO: That's right.

TH: Why do you think they describe you as having an 'illness'?

JO: Well, doctors aren't very creative, are they? They live in a very cut and dried world, they're basically dull people, and they want everybody to be as dull as they are. They haven't a clue about people like me.

TH: As I understand it, you have accepted treatment at times. How does that fit in with your beliefs about doctors?

JO: They've got their uses. The last time I was in hospital, I'd had a very creative period. I'd been writing for weeks, the ideas just kept flowing, and I'd also been going out a lot, drinking, having affairs, and I got really wound up and bad tempered. They gave me these drugs that slowed me down, and I really hated how they made me feel, but I knew I needed them for a while. I don't see that as illness, I think it's the way I am. And that's something I don't want to change.

TH: But there are some ways in which you'd like to change?

JO: Well, I admit that sometimes I need to be more organised. I'll start things and not finish them, sometimes I have really good ideas, but I just can't seem to sit down and get them on paper. And I find it really hard to do the boring things—you know, the hoovering, the washing up, stuff like that.

Clearly autonomy issues were very important for Joanna; she and the therapist needed to explore the costs and benefits of various types of intervention, so that she would not feel that they were being imposed on her. She entered into an initial contract for a series of sessions focusing on scheduling, but found it very difficult to keep activity schedules. When she did complete the schedules, it was clear that she lived a very erratic life, missing sleep, drinking heavily, and socialising to excess. Her therapist did suggest a trial of maintenance medication 'to help her sleep', and she was finally willing to take a low dose of lithium for a few months, and admitted that this was somewhat helpful. She did complain, however, that lithium reduced her creativity, a reaction that has been observed in many creative people (Jamison, 1993); this is likely to make her future compliance erratic and might require careful negotiation between her and her doctor. Another helpful intervention involved encouraging her to experiment with meditation: this helped her to relax when she was feeling 'wound up'. However, she remained very resistant to seeing her condition as an illness, and her pattern of life became only marginally less chaotic.

The patient who is excessively reliant on the 'medical model'. Paradoxically, an excessive concern with illness and medication can also be counter-therapeutic. Patients may feel that, because bipolar disorder is an 'illness', the only possible treatment must be medical, that psychological or 'lifestyle' factors cannot have any impact. Such patients may have a personality type opposite to the ones discussed previously, in that they can be dependent and afraid of taking control. The dichotomy between medical and psychological treatments is of course a false one: there is evidence that psychological approaches can have an impact on 'physical' illnesses, ranging from diabetes (Surwit & Schneider, 1983) and asthma (Kinsman et al., 1982) to cancer (Greer et al., 1979). It may be worth while to make this point to such patients.

Rebecca is a housewife in her mid 40s. She has been married for the past 15 years: a shy and withdrawn woman, she has always been dependent on her husband for his support, and has been very subservient to him. Ten years ago she had her first manic episode: during that episode she became very angry with her husband, behaving much more assertively and putting their relationship in jeopardy. After that episode she was very fearful of having another one, especially because she was afraid that her husband might leave her. Since that first episode she has been very compliant with medication and has felt very dependent on her psychiatrist, wanting extra appointments and seeking additional support. She had one further hypomanic episode, but this was a minor one, treated by raising her medication. In between these episodes she is almost chronically dysphoric, with few pleasures in life. She concentrates on housework and 'keeping herself busy', and has few friends or social contacts.

TH: Now I see on your activity schedule that it says, 'shopping', and your mood rating goes up, and then down. Can you tell me why that is?

RE: Oh, that. Well, I was very upset then. I thought I might be going high.

TH: Can you tell me what happened?

RE: David and I went to the supermarket, and he got angry at me. I guess I was spending too much money.

TH: Why do you say that?

RE: That's what David said. He shouted at me, 'Why do you always buy so much food!' It's because I want to make nice dinners for him—cooking nice meals is one thing I enjoy. But I guess I'm just too extravagant. After he said it I felt all hot inside; I thought I was going to go high. I didn't say anything, but when I came home I took one of my chlorpromazine and went to bed. And I felt better, except for the next two days I felt low and tired.

TH: Have you seen this pattern before?

RE: Yes, a few times. If I do something wrong and David finds out, I'll often feel that I want to shout at him. But I can't. If I do, he'll tell me that I'm going high, and I'm always afraid that he's right. I can't shout at him … I just can't.

TH: So there are a fair number of times when David thinks that you've done something wrong.

RE: Yes.

TH: Do you always feel that you've done something wrong at those times?

RE: Yes ... Well, I have to, don't I? I can't manage without David.

TH: Why do you say that?

RE: If I go high again, David might leave me. I just can't risk it.

TH: It sound like you feel that if you get angry at David, that means you're going high.

RE: I do feel that way.

TH: And at those times, you also feel you need medication?

RE: Yes. I feel that it will keep me from going high.

TH: And after that, you sometimes feel low for a while?

RE: Yes.

Rebecca found it very hard to be assertive with her husband, or with anyone else. She was also very afraid of feelings of anger, fearing that they were a sign that she was going high. Further exploration revealed that her husband, while supportive, was also rather domineering. Issues of dependency and self-image were obviously important in this case, but Rebecca was very wary of discussing them. She was also wary of learning assertiveness skills, feeling that she had to agree with her husband's wishes. However, in the course of therapy she did learn the technique of stating her point of view before acquiescing with her husband's wishes, and she reported that this helped to alleviate her low moods to some extent. Behavioural work was also useful in helping her to develop more activities on her own, and this also helped improve her self-image. She remained, however, very wary of anything that reminded her of 'going high'. In her case, it is possible that a marital approach might have been useful, but it also seemed that her husband was very reluctant to consider such an approach, perhaps because Rebecca's illness helped him to retain a dominant position in the relationship.

CONCLUSION

Once the therapist has carried out a thorough assessment and socialised the patient to the model, the initial phase of therapy is completed. At this point the therapist should have a clear idea of the patient's problems, goals, strengths and vulnerabilities, and the patient should have some idea of how the therapy is going to proceed and what it is intended to accomplish. The chapters that follow will deal with some of the specific techniques that will be employed during the next phase of therapy.

Chapter 7

GOAL SETTING

INTRODUCTION

Goal setting is introduced to clients as an important and ongoing part of the cognitive–behavioural therapy (CBT) intervention. Client and therapist would be expected to set treatment goals following initial assessment and to review these as treatment progresses. Through the process of therapy it is likely that additional goals will also emerge, which will then need to be discussed within sessions and their appropriateness evaluated. Goals are identified in relation to illness but also in terms of specific targets relevant to work, leisure or family issues. Goals can relate to areas that have previously been neglected by the clients. Thus a primary focus on work 'at all costs' can be associated with dysphoria and the prodromal stage of depression. It can then be difficult to access pleasurable activities and even when these are attained it can be useful to have as broad a range of alternatives available as possible.

It is explained that within the CBT approach it is essential that gaols for treatment are those of the client themselves rather than externally imposed. This is not to say that the first ideas of the client are always accepted as the target for treatment but rather that the agreed goals come from a constructive dialogue between client and therapist. Likewise, potential areas for goal setting deemed appropriate by clinicians may not be immediately acceptable to clients. Some may find the prodromal symptoms of mania seductive and appealing. Great tact and sensitivity is required therefore in addressing these issues. There is a reliance on collaborative working and discussion of longer-term dysfunctional outcome and compromise on both sides may be required. Some of the areas which goal setting might cover are described in the following section.

TOPICS FOR GOAL SETTING

Symptom Reduction

Most clients will have goals in terms of symptom reduction. These may relate to symptoms of either depression or mania. Targets in these areas will be around the client gaining greater control of hypomanic and depressive symptoms through the use of behavioural and cognitive techniques. At a goal-setting stage the likely techniques are described in summary terms, but are then introduced in detail as each technique is applied. In this book specific behavioural and cognitive techniques are described in Chapters 8 and 9.

Some people may set an initial goal which is unrealistic. For instance, at the present state of knowledge it would not be reasonable to expect an appropriately applied CBT programme to remove all symptoms of mood fluctuation in clients with a long history of relapse. It would however be reasonable to target increasing control over symptoms, and reducing risk of relapse. Thus the specific goals in this area may be a compromise between what clients might ideally wish for and what clinician and client together might realistically achieve. Common areas for goal setting in relation to symptom reduction would usually include: (a) greater awareness of prodromes; (b) management of arousal; and (c) development of healthy routines.

Sarah had a 10 year history of bipolar illness. She was 40 years old at the time of referral and was continuing to experience recurrent episodes of hypomania in spite of complying with the pharmacological treatment prescribed by her psychiatrist. Although these hypomanic episodes did not usually require hospitalisation they had led to her losing her job on several occasions and her current position was under threat following a recent episode in which she had been verbally aggressive with her manager and verbally abusive to a customer.

TH: We have discussed the problems that hypomania has caused in your work and social life. Would you have particular goals for therapy in this area?

SA: Yes. From the pattern of work problems recently I would like to catch myself before things go too far.

TH: So does that mean you would like to be better at noticing warning signs?

SA: Usually when I have had a bad phase I can look back afterwards and see how it came on, but at the time I don't notice.

TH: The warning signs are called prodromes and can be different for each person. So one job we could do is to work on a list of things that happen in your prodromes.

SA: OK. But how does it help to have a list?

TH: As well as developing the list we can work on ways to cope with the prodrome symptoms at an early stage to prevent them escalating.

SA: So that might help me avoid some of the trouble I have had at work?

TH: Yes. Usually if people can act early on in response to prodromes they have a much better chance of avoiding those sort of difficulties.

Her goals were focused around the issue of early identification of prodromes for these hypomanic episodes and in particular developing an action list for strategies to employ when these prodromal signs were identified. This clear symptom focus was indicated by Sarah's own preferences and also by information from symptom history and current state, indicating that outside these periods she was usually able to run her affairs in an orderly and structured manner without exposing herself to undue pressures which might exacerbate her clinical condition.

Medical

Cognitive behavioural therapy for bipolar illness endorses the important role of medication in the treatment of bipolar illness and hence goals in terms of compliance with pharmacotherapy may need to be set. These goals will vary according to the individual client. As noted in Chapter 2, compliance with medication regimes can be quite low, especially when clients have difficulties with side effects. In other clients there may be evidence of 'over-compliance' such as continuation on a high dose of antidepressant in spite of excessive fatigue when there is little evidence of therapeutic benefit. The issue of compliance would be likely to be discussed on the basis of the educational phase of the treatment programme in which the roles of lithium and antidepressant medication are discussed.

The main aim here is for the optimal regimen for the individual to be developed. This means that compliance is to be an active process in which the client engages in ongoing discussion with the prescribing clinician to achieve maximum therapeutic gain with minimum side effects. Goals within therapy will be likely to include providing support and information to facilitate this active relationship between client and prescribing clinician. In some cases the issue of finding a GP or psychiatrist with whom mutual trust can be formed can be discussed explicitly. In addition to educational information and cost–benefit assessments of previous drug regimes this would probably include targets regarding preparation for meetings with their psychiatrist so that the client is able to convey pertinent clinical issues in an effective manner. A constructive relationship between client and prescribing clinician also allows for appropriate requests for PRN (take when necessary) medication when this is required to alleviate a developing prodromal state. In the contrasting situation of the client assuming a stance of passive acceptance of whatever is prescribed there is clearly a risk of later resentment over side effects or lack of efficacy and subsequent non-compliance.

Brian is a 30 year old man with an 8 year history of bipolar illness. When he first became ill he was admitted to hospital under Mental Health Act Section. He has not had any further hospital admissions but continues to feel very strongly that this first admission was unwarranted in spite of evidence to the contrary from family and medical team. The most important consequence of his feelings in relation to this was that he only occasionally had contact with the psychiatric team responsible for his care. His medication, although regularly prescribed and usually taken, was rarely reviewed in detail due to his low attendance rate at such meetings. He himself felt dissatisfied with the treatment which resulted from this process, but remained wary of increasing contact for fear of being re-admitted.

BR: So why do want to see me so often? Is it to keep a check for the other doctors, so they can get me back into hospital?

TH: No. It is important at least at first to meet quite frequently to work on ways of helping you keep yourself as well as possible. One aspect of that is working on what your goals might be for progress in therapy.

BR: My main goal is to keep out of hospital. I hate it in there, especially when they bring me in against my will. The police come to the house, the kids are crying, the neighbours have a good old look at me being taken away. How is all that supposed to make me get better?

TH: So you would like to avoid compulsory admissions to hospital?

BR: Yes, but I also want to feel well more of the time. Most of the time I feel drugged up to the eyeballs.

TH: So it sounds as though looking at ways of discussing medication issues with your psychiatrist would be helpful.

BR: Well I try to stay away from him.

TH: Why is that?

BR: I'm afraid he'll want to admit me if I talk through problems with medication.

TH: I suggest we spend some time looking at the costs and benefits of having more involvement with the psychiatric team. Would you see your doctor more if it might help you stay out of hospital and feel better?

BR: Well yes, but how would that work?

TH: Let's agree to spend some time looking at that now.

After discussion Brian identified, as important goals, avoiding re-admission to hospital under section and optimising mental state. Once these gaols were identified it was possible to investigate the steps that might be involved in attaining them. A detailed analysis of his approach to the medical team was made and the cost and benefits of alterations were considered. It was eventually agreed that increasing attendance at review meetings would be of likely benefit in terms of the goals described as the better his medical treatment was the more likely he was to stay well and away from hospital at other times. To avoid repetitions of his early experience of being an unwilling and passive recipient of medical treatment much time was spent on discussion of drug treatments and their various benefits and side effects. Armed with this information Brian was able to prepare himself well for his review meetings and to raise the issue of changes in medication to address his current chronic problems of low mood. These changes were made as a result of his active involvement in his own treatment and led to his feeling more positive with regard to future contact due to experiencing a constructive outcome in terms of his own goals.

Functional

Goals in this area centre around one fundamental question. What is it that the person is not currently able to do, but would like to be able to achieve? These goals may relate to many areas but would include family, academic interests, job performance, other relationships. These may involve building on previous success, but may also require taking steps to repair damage in previous periods of ill health. One relatively common issue is that of over-functioning within work at the expense of other areas such as relationships and recreation. This may in itself be a risk factor for future episodes. When such goals are set it is important that the therapist supports the client in having realistic aims. These may range from at the one extreme introducing one extra activity per week for a depressed individual to return to full employment in an individual in a currently euthymic state at the other.

Cost and benefits of over- or under-ambitious goal setting in this area will be discussed to allow appropriate goals to be set by guided discovery from the client rather than using an instructional approach. Targeting functional goals at an early stage is likely to enhance engagement as these goals will aim to add to the person's range of experiences/activities. This will probably be seen as being rather in contrast to their goals around avoiding relapses of hypomania, which may be regarded as a 'loss' by some clients.

Jim is a 40 year old man whose bipolar illness was currently relatively well controlled. In spite of mood fluctuations he had been able to maintain his clerical job with the local council and was currently considering an offer of promotion which would mean greater salary but also longer working and greater responsibility. His main goal, however, was in terms of family. His marriage failed after his first manic episode in his late twenties. This required admission to hospital prior to which he had behaved in a sexually promiscuous manner making inappropriate sexual suggestions at work and visiting prostitutes, which was normally completely out of character. He had no similar episodes subsequently but it was not possible to effect a reconciliation with his wife and they finally divorced when he was 30 years old. At that time he had a 2-year-old daughter to whom he was very attached and with whom he had regular contact for the first year. After a second hospital admission in his early thirties contact with his daughter ceased and he had not seen her for some years. His goal was to rebuild his relationship with his daughter now that he felt that he was coping relatively well with his mental health problems.

TH: So Jim. What do you highlight as your main goal at present?

JI: Seeing Jessica again. Getting to know her and showing her that I can be there for her now if I get the chance.

TH: What do you mean by 'be there' for her?

JI: You know like any dad would. See her regularly, take her to places, talk about stuff.

TH: How do you think your ex-wife would feel about that level of contact?

JI: I don't know. She probably wouldn't be happy at first. I haven't plucked up courage to speak to her yet.

TH: When did you last see or speak to your daughter?

JI: When I got ill it was all such a mess that we had no contact for 3 years after the divorce. I seen my ex-wife several times since then but not Jessica.

TH: So it is about seven years since you have seen Jessica. That's a long time for a child. How do think she will have changed?

JI: Well in lots of ways I suppose. She will be at secondary school, she'll have friends, she'll be turning into a young lady almost. I just want to see her.

TH: How were you thinking of approaching this goal?

JI: Well I know where she goes to school. I thought I might meet her after school someday soon and take her for an ice cream in the park and talk things through.

TH: How do you think her mother would react to that?

JI: She would probably hit the roof I suppose. Actually she might get the police onto me, saying I'm a madman like she did before.

TH: So it sounds to me that your ex-wife will need some convincing that you are well enough to be getting into a father role again first. Is that right?

JI: I suppose it is. I just want to see Jessica, but I will have to show her mum that I am stable and trustworthy first.

TH: How might you show her that?

JI: I suppose I could contact her and talk this through. See what she thought would be an acceptable way to begin some contact with Jessica.

TH: OK. So you are saying that the first step would be to arrange to meet your ex-wife to see if the two of you can come up with a plan. Is that right?

JI: Yes. Then we can sort things out before I have contact with Jessica. I still remember the rows we used to have. I don't want any more of those in front of her.

Clearly this raised issues of what was best for himself and his daughter, whether she would wish to have such contact and if begun how it might be maintained. It transpired that at this time he had not spoken to his ex-wife for several years and that she was not aware of his current situation. It was agreed that a first step would be to contact her to request her opinion on whether any contact would be appropriate and to inform her of his current situation. She responded in a guarded manner to this first communication but did agree to meet him to discuss matters in relation to his daughter. Initially he reported frustration over the time it took to arrange this meeting and that its outcome was inconclusive. However, by managing this and thus providing evidence of his current coping skills the situation improved to the point where by the time of writing he was visiting his daughter at her home for one evening per month. This was still limited success in relation to his goal of having a full father–daughter relationship, but he was able to agree that in the current situation this was a realistic outcome given the prior history of the relationship and that success in maintaining this could later open up the possibility of greater contact.

Cognitive

In addition to reduction in specific clinical symptoms goals in this area will focus on the client gaining greater control over their emotional/cognitive processes. The appropriate applications of these techniques will therefore aim to reduce the extent of the 'highs' of hypomania but also the 'lows' of the depression that follow. It is useful for clients to understand that the focus for therapy is on both of these areas and not just on the removal of the 'highs'. Clients are often bemused by what they regard as the obsession of mental health professionals to damp clients' mood, but to be less interested, as they see it, in addressing problems of low mood.

These techniques are described in detail in Chapters 8 and 9. The main focus is on helping clients to increase their own skills in controlling and changing unhelpful thinking patterns. This includes both the over-positive thinking associated with mania and the negative automatic thoughts which are characteristic of depression.

Emily was a 35 year old woman who was first diagnosed with manic depression in her early twenties. Since then she had had a couple of episodes of mania but her illness was predominantly characterised by periods of dysphoric mood. These were not of sufficient severity to require admission or indeed to cause particular alarm amongst the clinical staff responsible for her care, but was prioritised as a primary difficulty by Emily herself.

EM: The main thing I want to sort out is these periods of feeling really down.

TH: Can you say a little about how these affect you?

EM: They just make everything really hard to do. I don't enjoy myself. I have to try twice as hard to keep going with my job and no-one seems to care.

TH: Why do you say that no-one seems to care?

EM: Well when I get high everyone is interested. My family, my doctor, everyone. They all want me to take treatment, get help, get into hospital. But when I feel down no-one seems bothered.

TH: What sort of help would you like when you feel that way?

EM: I just want to be able to make myself feel better. I'd like someone to talk to and I'd like to be able to help myself more. I'd like the right sort of help, not hospital or lots more drugs though.

TH: I think that it would be useful to work on ways of coping with these periods of low mood that help cut them short. How would that be?

EM: Yes OK. What sort of thing?

TH: We could work together to track patterns of thinking and behaviour that might be associated with you feeling low. Once we have identified these we can come up with some plans to help you make changes in them.

EM: Well OK. I'll give it a try anyway.

The goal that derived from this was to attempt to implement appropriate cognitive–behavioural strategies in an effort to elevate mood to within the normal range. A combination of structured activity scheduling and challenging of negative thoughts through guided discovery was employed. Over the course of treatment this led to significant improvements in mood. She still described herself as feeling rather flat on occasion, but this was less frequent and when it did occur she felt that the techniques she had learnt were effective in minimising its effects.

Support Services

Goals in this area will be around the appropriate use of support services when required, including mental health team, social services and thera-pist. It also includes friends, relatives, help lines and community support services. Effective goal setting in this area obviously requires that the ther-apist has knowledge of support services available in general and also has details from the client's own account of what informal supports have been of benefit or indeed have been harmful in the past. Research on expressed emotion in people with affective disorders indicates that, as with earlier research into psychotic client groups, exposure to high emotional tone and critical comments is associated with risk of relapse. Thus the mere avail-ability of friends or family may not be sufficient. More detailed discussion of the forms of interaction between the client and these individuals will be important in agreeing goals which are likely to be beneficial for the client. This will include assessment of previous use of such support and outcome of this use. The appropriate and planned use of services tailored to clients' needs should be discussed as a means of optimising independent func-tioning rather than removing autonomy. A goal in this area would be the reduction of hospital admission by early and appropriate use of commu-nity services. Impediments to service use should be identified at this stage, in particular any negative experiences which the client may previously have had in relation to services so that plans to avoid repeating this can be set in place at an early stage.

Sid is a 50 year old man who until 5 years ago had been a very successful busi-ness man. He had run several large companies and was used to being in con-trol of the people around him. Although he had had periods of depression and hypomania, he had prior to this period had only one hospitalisation and other-wise continued working whilst receiving appropriate medication. However, when his wife died 5 years ago he was first depressed but then subsequently experi-ence a prolonged episode of mania. During this period he worked longer and longer hours, developing increasingly speculative business schemes which even-tually led to his being declared bankrupt. He then could not find further employ-ment and eventually required hospitalisation with depression. His mental health over recent years had been variable with several admissions. However, when-ever he was discharged he would stop medication and refuse contact with psy-chiatric services as he was intent on recapturing his former status.

TH: So what are you plans now that you are out of hospital?

SI: I need to get back into business. I've still got some contacts in my old line and I'm sure I could get enough capital to get things moving again.

TH: What was your old line?

SI: I ran a group of heavy engineering companies. They are in the hands of a multinational now but I can build something up again. I haven't forgotten how to do it you know.

TH: I recall you said previously that you had had a few business ventures in recent years.

SI: Well, I started a couple of things off but they all came to a dead end.

TH: Why was that?

SI: I got them off the ground OK. I enjoyed the planning process but once things were up and running I seemed to get unwell.

TH: I expect you had to put a lot of time and effort into these ventures.

SI: Yeah. Each one I put in 12 hour days 6 days a week at least. I felt I was really doing something again.

TH: My feeling is that the hard work and stress involved may have been associated with you becoming ill again. What do you think?

SI: I don't know. Maybe. But I've always been able to do it before. Why not now?

TH: It may be that your threshold for the effects of stress and fatigue is not quite as high now. Also all that work meant that you found it hard to meet with your doctors to keep a check on medication.

SI: Yeah, I was busy and I didn't want to waste time chatting when I could be getting on with things. I could have done with help on the medication side, though, I remember once running out of lithium and then not being able to restart it because I couldn't fit in a meeting with my psychiatrist to get the prescription.

TH: My suggestion is that we try to look for ways to work within your resources. Then you might be able develop a working routine that does not harm your health and allows you to keep in touch with your mental health team.

SI: How will we do that?

TH: I suggest we spend some time discussing possibilities for work that require less time and financial risk for you in the first instance.

SI: Well, my cousin has already offered me an office job in his firm. I didn't really fancy it because I like to be my own boss.

TH: Well, how about giving it a try for a limited period to see how well you feel. In recent years the business ventures have tended to last a few months, so why not try this for a similar period while we monitor how you are feeling?

SI: OK, I'll test it out for a few months anyway.

Detailed work was done within the therapy sessions on trying to come to agreement over reasonable goals to set. He initially felt that only recapturing control of his former company would be adequate. However, as the therapy progressed more realistic goals of sustaining a more modest form of employment initially and maintaining therapeutic contact whilst doing so was agreed on. This was initially set out as a 'scientific' exercise on the basis of the ineffectiveness of the previous approach, to test whether this worked better in terms of the career goals which he had for himself.

As noted above the process of goal setting is a dynamic one. In addition to consideration of the five general areas above there are a number of other issues in relation to goal setting that are worthy of consideration.

CURRENT VS. LONGER-TERM GOALS

For most clients it is possible to make a distinction between current immediate goals and longer-term goals. It would usually be appropriate to try to address the current goals first. These will usually be the client's own priority and thus there will be likely to be high levels of motivation towards achieving goals set in this area. The process of goal setting and goal attainment set out for these immediate goals can then be used as a model for planning towards longer-term goals later in the therapy process. Immediate goals might centre around either internal or external areas. Internal issues might include symptom management, elevating or lowering mood state, specific problem solving, physical health issues. External issues might be legal matters consequent on behaviour when ill, housing situation, financial issues, development of recreational activities. Longstanding goals again can have internal or external components. Internal might include variable levels of commitment to treatment, fluctuating self-esteem, social skills problems, personality issues. External might include long-term unemployment, relationship problems, family issues, consequences of destructive behaviour whilst ill, stigma issues

STEPWISE APPROACH

With all goal setting it is important to break down the process of achieving the particular goal into manageable steps. Clear operational description of these steps will be important in maintaining motivation and sense of progress for the client. If this is not done there will be a risk that clients will make efforts to reach each goal too quickly and experience failure or indeed feel overwhelmed by the task in front of them and thus withdraw.

IMPORTANCE OF MAKING GOALS ATTAINABLE

Goals reported by the client may be unrealistic or unattainable. Perfectionism is a factor in bipolar illness and can impact on the goals and aspirations which clients have for themselves. This should be identified in the goal-setting process, otherwise there is a risk that the process itself can become self-defeating. If clients settle on goals which are beyond their current power to attain, then this can risk either hypomanic overcompensation or feelings of helplessness and depression.

Graham apparently had a very clear idea of his primary goal. He had until 3 years ago been involved in computer sales and wished to set up his own computer sales operation within the next 4 months. However, on assessment it was clear that this was unlikely to be possible so quickly. He was still experiencing significant mood fluctuations, he had only recently been discharged from hospital following a manic episode and his symptom history indicated that previous attempts to set up his own company had been associated with a rapid decline in his mental health.

TH: So you want to set up your own sales operation?

GR: Yeah. When I was employed as a salesman before I learnt all the tricks. I think its time I earned some money for myself.

TH: Have you tried to set up this sort of thing before?

GR: A couple of times. But I got high.

TH: Would there be any risk of that this time do you think?

GR: I don't know. I feel good. I feel ready. What's the problem?

TH: Well, you say that when you tried this before you became manic and I am concerned that this may happen again.

GR: What is the alternative? I don't want to sit around all day doing nothing.

TH: I notice that from your record sheet your mood is still quite variable. Can you see that?

GR: Well yes I suppose I have ups and downs. I feel pretty up today though.

TH: What about waiting a little until your mood is more stable? Then the risk of problems developing once you started work would be much lower.

GR: I could wait a bit I suppose. But what then?

TH: Then we could look at ways of re-starting work but staying well also. One way of doing this may be start off with a part-time position rather than leaping right in at the deep end.

Within therapy therefore time was spent in analysing the cost and benefits of this goal and again guided discovery was used to generate intermediate goals that were more likely to be attainable. The goals identified in this way included a target period of two months of relative stability of mood, which when achieved would be a trigger for the next step of investigating part-time work in his chosen field. This approach did not rule out later attempts to try for his initial goal, only that this be based on a number of realistic steps which would indicate if and when his initial goal was an appropriate target which would not be likely to put him at high risk of relapse.

IDENTIFYING IMPEDIMENTS REGARDING GOAL ATTAINMENT

Once goals have been set it may become apparent that the client is having difficulty in reaching them. The ongoing process of review and monitoring should allow this to be picked up at an early stage and addressed. If goals are not being achieved it would first be necessary to check that they were realistic. An analysis of whether the client had made attempts at the chosen goal and what the consequences of their efforts were would be important in this. If goals were set too high then re-setting on the basis of information gained from initial efforts should allow goals to be better targeted. In addition it is important that the therapist avoids the temptation of instructing the client in what goals to choose and aim for. Whilst it may seem to the therapist that certain goals are obviously important, unless the client shares this view and has a sense of having identified his or her own priorities, such goals are unlikely to be attained. Such resistance is often more likely than a direct challenge to the therapist's suggestions and should be used as a trigger for a review of how goals identified fit in with the client's own priorities.

CONCLUSIONS

This chapter has identified the importance of goal setting within therapy. This needs to be a collaborative process and goals identified will usually fall within the five areas discussed above, namely: (1) symptom reduction; (2) medical; (3) functional; (4) cognitive; (5) support services. Within these areas there will be both short- and long-term goals. Identifying appropriate steps towards manageable goals can be one of the most important aspects of therapy. The process of achieving success experiences by aiming for achievable goals is likely to be motivating for engagement in other aspects of therapy.

Chapter 8

COGNITIVE TECHNIQUES

INTRODUCTION

Many of the cognitive techniques employed with bipolar patients during the depressive phase of their illness are similar to those used with patients suffering from unipolar depression. However, there are specific cognitive techniques which can be used with bipolar patients, particularly when they are relatively stable (relapse prevention techniques), moderately depressed or hypomanic. We shall focus on these. Some bipolar patients, particularly those who have experienced frequent relapses, are scared of mood fluctuations, even normal day-to-day mood swings. Hence it is important to teach them to distinguish between a normal and abnormal mood range. Techniques of mood monitoring are outlined. The importance of accessing and challenging the dysfunctional thoughts that arise both in depressed and manic mood states cannot be over-emphasised. Techniques are outlined in detail in the context of manic depression. Methods of discovering and dealing with the more fundamental underlying unhelpful assumptions are also discussed. The last section in this chapter deals with the difficulties some patients may have in accepting that manic prodromes are an early stage of an illness episode, as opposed to a normal 'happy or self-confident' mood. A hypomanic mood state is often welcomed by patients, particularly after they have been suffering from a depression for some time. A retrospective 'cost-and-benefit' analysis to examine the consequences of such experiences is often helpful. A cognitive and behavioural delaying tactic can then be discussed.

However, we cannot emphasise strongly enough that the success of any cognitive therapy intervention relies on the quality of the therapeutic relationship. It is particularly important when dealing with patients whose illness has features of irritability and elated mood to develop a rapport built on trust and empathy. This helps patients to feel less criticised when they are slightly high and the therapy is aimed at containing the patients' emotional states and more extreme behaviours. Techniques such as an appeal to 'delaying cognitions' and 'delaying tactics' as described below will have a greater chance of being accepted if the patient feels he/she can trust the therapist.

MOOD MONITORING

Mood monitoring is recognised as being a key component. Because mood fluctuation in these patients is often associated with periods of illness, they can become anxious, fearful and over-cautious in relation to what would otherwise be deemed as normal mood states. This is particularly the case for patients who have experienced frequent relapses. Tiredness, sadness and feeling 'fed up' as a result of normal everyday life are interpreted as precursors to a depressive episode and viewed with alarm. Similarly feeling good and enjoying an everyday event can be viewed unnecessarily as the onset of a manic episode. As a result of these interpretations, some manic-depressive patients often severely restrict their activities and treat normal mood states as pathological. Conversely, patients in the early stages of their illness often refuse to accept obvious symptoms of hypomania as anything other than a normal feeling of optimism and are reluctant, if not totally unable, to accept that they may be demonstrating early signs of relapse. As a result they may allow a hypomanic state to develop into a full manic episode.

Goodwin and Jamison (1990, p. 732) make a salient point when they point out that 'closely related to the discrimination of moods is the slow, steady process involved in patients' learning to unravel what is normal personality from what the illness has superimposed upon it—turbulence, impulsiveness, lack of predictability and depression'. Therefore accurate mood and activity rating is a key element of therapy, the final aim being to enable the patient to devise a range of activities and mood states in which they can confidently operate without excessive fear or danger of becoming ill.

Mood can be rated using a mood and activities diary. A mood and activities schedule (Figure 8.1) is a 24 h recording sheet with space for brief hourly activity recordings accompanied by an associated daily numerical rating of mood state. Mood rating differs from that used by unipolar depressives in the range of mood rated. It is important to discriminate normal mood swings from abnormal swings. Patients suffering from manic depression require a range that will encompass both elated and depressed mood. We recommend using a range that extends from -10 to $+10$ with -5 to $+5$ designated as the normal mood range. The advantage of using a 24 h activity chart to rate mood is that it allows small discriminations of mood fluctuation, in either direction, to be identified and immediately tied into particular activities as well as recording more extreme changes of mood. Figure 9.1 in the next chapter is an example of a completed mood and activities schedule.

As with all homework tasks, when presenting a rating chart to a patient it is necessary to present a rationale that makes sense to the patient in order

WEEKLY MOOD AND ACTIVITY SCHEDULE

Name _____

Mood rating
(–10 to +10)

DATE	M	T	W	Th	F	S	S
6–7 a.m.							
7–8 a.m.							
8–9 a.m.							
9–10 a.m.							
10–11 a.m.							
11–12 a.m.							
12–1 p.m.							
1–2 p.m.							
2–3 p.m.							
3–4 p.m.							
4–5 p.m.							
5–6 p.m.							

Name _____

WEEKLY MOOD AND ACTIVITY SCHEDULE

DATE	M	T	W	Th	F	S	S
6–7 p.m.							
7–8 p.m.							
8–9 p.m.							
9–10 p.m.							
10–11 p.m.							
11–12 p.m.							
12–1 a.m.							
1–2 a.m.							
2–3 a.m.							
3–4 a.m.							
4–5 a.m.							
5–6 a.m.							

Figure 8.1 An example of a mood and activity schedule

to promote good compliance. It is useful to demonstrate how to fill it in during a therapy session. This will ensure that patients are clear about what is required and also will help dissipate a commonly expressed fear about 'not doing it right'. Patients can also be taught to relate normal mood fluctuations to activities surrounding them. For example, going on holiday allows a normal happy mood. However, if the mood is going up and up without obvious events to relate it to, then patients should be wary and careful that they are not entering a prodromal stage. They can then look out for early warning signs.

Sarah had been coming to therapy for a few weeks; she had filled in her activities chart regularly and her mood had been relatively stable. Both she and her husband had always been committed Christians and were quite involved with their local church.

SA: I have had a very good week this week. Take a look at my chart and you will see.

TH: I notice that you have been staying up later in order to spend more time in the church.

SA: Yes, I am sure the sermon last week was specially for me. The vicar said things that made me think that I had a special role to play for God in the church. I was so excited. I think it is important for me to show my gratitude by spending much more time at night praying .

TH: I notice that your mood rating had gone up to +6 on Sunday. Is that unusually high for you? And I notice that right now it is +7.

SA: Yes it is but it's nothing to worry about, it is only because of the realisation that I have this special responsibility in my church. I just feel so good and excited about it. If you remember I had a +6 when I went to my daughter's carol service last week which I enjoyed so much and that was okay.

TH: On that occasion you did not stay up at night and your mood went down to −1 the next day because of an argument with your husband. What has your husband got to say about your role in the Church?

SA: Oh, he is just a bit boring. He thinks it is not sensible of me to stay up at night praying.

TH: Why is that?

SA: Because if I lose too much sleep, I can get ill.

TH: So is he worried about you?

SA: I suppose so. I do know not sleeping enough can cause me problems.

TH: So your mood at present is unusually high and not coming down and you are not getting your usual amount of sleep and your husband is worried about you. But you are thinking that you have a special responsibility, are feeling on top of the world and spending more time than usual praying at night.

SA: Yes, that's it.

Sarah's mood rating suggests a dysfunctionally high mood level, which is of course a warning sign. Such extreme mood states generally produce characteristic changes in cognitions; the therapist must be on watch for these.

COGNITIVE CHANGES IN DIFFERENT MOOD STATES

Biased thinking is one of the hallmarks of extreme mood states and results in an idiosyncratic negatively biased view of self, the world and others. Beck describes this phenomenon as the *cognitive triad*. When depressed, the self is seen as defective and/or worthless, the world is seen as making exorbitant demands on the individual and the future is characterised by failure (Beck et al., 1979). The bias results in a reduced ability or total inability to take in information that is positive or in some way conflicts with the depressed person's view of the situation and merely focuses on the negative components of the situation. In depression cognitive changes can be subtle or profound and are often a combination of both (Goodwin & Jamison, 1990). Depression can also slow patients' thinking processes down so that they feel they are wading through mud. Patients can describe being beset with doubt and indecision, so much so that in one patient's case she described being unable to decide when to change gear when driving her car. There can also be a significant magnification of ordinary fears; patients describe fearing the breakdown of their life as they know it. These fears may be grounded in real experience as patients have often suffered many losses throughout the course of their illness. The negative thoughts of people with manic depression when depressed often cluster around the concept of, 'I am no longer able to,' or 'I can't do it'. For example the thoughts 'I used to be able to do this but can no longer manage it', 'I am incapable of doing this' and 'I will never be able to do this again,' are common ideas expressed by these patients. Patients will often make unfavourable comparisons with others. These thoughts are generated by a low self-esteem which has invariably been exacerbated by the illness itself.

Patients in the early stages of a manic episode will report a series of changes. In terms of the cognitive triad they experience themselves as competent and in control, the world as bright and people too slow or not understanding of their view and the future as encouraging and full of opportunities; these changes are the opposite of the 'cognitive triad' referred to above. They may experience an increase in creative ability and self-confidence, often accompanied by an increase in activity. Patients not only experience a change in their style of thinking and their interpretation of events but also in the number and frequency of what are often described as 'racing thoughts'. In the early stages patients may notice an increase in the number of particular types of thoughts, especially creative ones. They may then become excited by this enhanced creativity and increase the speed and time that they work. 'The ideas and feelings are fast and frequent like shooting stars, and you follow them until you find better and brighter ones. But somewhere this changes, the fast ideas are far too fast, and there are far too many; overwhelming confusion replaces clarity' (Jamison, 1995 p. 67). Patients tend to become over-optimistic, overestimating their abilities, believing their future plans will all come to fruition and seeing the world as a truly benevolent place. Any negative aspects of situations are either not recognised or played down. Patients become unable to see any negative consequences in their actions, and there is a minimisation and dismissal of problems. Other patients may complain of an increased irritability, restlessness, agitation and suspiciousness, with associated paranoid ideas. This group often find an elated state somewhat aversive and therefore may be more amenable to self-monitoring and early intervention than the former. They may became irritated with other people whom they perceive to be operating too slowly, not understanding their view and behaving critically towards them in ways that are unwarranted. In some cases, the manic state may come to resemble paranoia, with anger towards those whom they may perceive as thwarting them.

During the early stage of a manic stage, some patients become unusually friendly and deliver inappropriate remarks and even inappropriate praise of the therapist. Another consequence of this style of thinking is that patients come to believe that they are no longer ill and do not need to take their medication. Excessive criticism of others, including their therapist, may be an early sign of mania, giving the impression that the patient knows better than the therapist how therapy should be conducted. In the later stages of mania, judgement becomes significantly impaired. Patients are unable to distinguish workable from unworkable ideas and they lose the ability to plan in a constructive and coordinated way. Also in the later stages of a manic episode patients can became significantly deluded and believe they have God-like powers or in some cases that they are an envoy of God or supernatural being. At this stage cognitive strategies will have a much reduced chance of being effective.

Common beliefs that appear in hypomanic states are ones associated with an overestimation of talents and abilities and over-personalisation of the behaviour of others. This may present in ideas about romantic involvement based on flimsy evidence or somewhat paranoid ideas about other people's jealousy of the patient's 'exceptional talents'. A common cognitive error made by patients at these times is one of selective abstraction, when undue attention is paid to one detail in order to form an illogical opinion. For example a patient might be attending to a piece of positive feedback from a boss at the expense of more critical feedback to make the assumption that they could do the job better than their superiors, or selecting certain remarks out of context and concluding that a friend or acquaintance loves or admires them. Failure to recognise such a change in thinking style as indicative of the beginning of an illness episode is common with patients who have only had one previous attack and have not yet learned the more subtle danger signs. Patients who have had the illness longer and experienced more episodes of elated mood may have become more aware of these signs.

However, with bipolar patients who have experienced many previous episodes the sense of being damaged and stigmatised may be worse. Being sensitive to genuine fears as well as being able to discern exaggerated ones is a key feature of therapy with patients with a severe mental illness such as manic depression.

COLLECTING AUTOMATIC DYSFUNCTIONAL THOUGHTS

One of the cognitive components of an extreme mood state is the occurrence of automatic thoughts. These thoughts are conscious ones; pop up spontaneously; are usually brief; can be in shorthand form; and are associated with extreme emotions. They may be in verbal form, visual images or both. They are not formed as a result of reflection, are often distorted to some degree or another, but nevertheless seem totally plausible to the patient. A key part of the therapy is teaching the patient to collect and challenge these automatic thoughts.

Even small changes in mood in either direction can result in the occurrence of automatic thoughts and it is important to note mood change as a trigger for identifying them. In the early stages of therapy it is sometimes easier for patients to identify mood changes than to collect these dysfunctional thoughts. Mood change may well be a response to a particular situation or trigger event. This event may appear to be insignificant and barely discernible, at first appraisal; however, it will have special significance to the patient. Careful questioning and examining of the circumstances surrounding the mood shift is intended to uncover not just the details of the event, but also its significance. This applies equally to a depressed or an elated mood.

Jane came to therapy and said she had felt a bit high and excitable on Friday and that the feelings had continued all weekend. Initially she was unable to explain why it had happened.

TH: Think back to when you were last feeling more stable. Did you wake up feeling high on Friday morning?

JA: No, I was all right then.

TH: So when did this feeling of excitability start on Friday?

JA: Well I was all right until lunch time, and then my sister rang up.

TH: What was the phone call from your sister about? Do you think it may have had anything to do with your feeling high?

JA: I was overjoyed. She is getting married in six months time and she said she wanted me to be her bridesmaid. I was shocked, I had thought she would not ask me.

TH: So were you very pleased at her request?

JA: I was delighted. We have always been a bit strained with each other. It made me think she did like me after all. I started to think we could be really good friends after all and I started to plan what I would wear. I must look brilliant so everyone will think what a wonderful sister she has got.

TH: So you started making plans in your head?

JA: Well not at first, I was really pleased initially but as the days wore on I have become really frantic. I have always felt like she didn't care about me, always leading her own life and having her own friends. But things have begun to change. Now we can be best mates, go everywhere together. She must have realised how important I am to her. Now, my life is changed, I won't need to worry about being lonely, she will always be there for me.

In this example careful questioning uncovers the source of Jane's elated mood, that she had always believed she did not matter to her sister and her sister asking her to be her bridesmaid had made her feel very happy and she has now started to believe that her life will change as a result of it. Note that Jane describes her belief that her sister did not 'care about her' as a feeling. This confusion is common in the early stages of therapy and will be pointed out by the therapist.

Initially it is key to help patients identify their automatic thoughts. Marking them in sessions is the first step. As automatic thoughts are expressed they are picked up and fed back by the therapist. It is enough, in the early stages, to just reiterate thoughts or even words. During a summarisation the patient's attention is drawn to the automatic thoughts and the therapist writes them down and encourages the patient to do the same. The patient is encouraged to have their own note book in which to write down these thoughts and other important aspects of therapy. In Jane's case her thoughts about her life changing and her sister always being there for her may well be exaggerations of reality; if so, they will be fed back to Jane as examples of thoughts she has when feeling high.

The patient's ability to collect these thoughts will vary right from the start. Some patients come into therapy very aware of their thinking processes and are well able to pick out salient automatic thoughts, whereas others are unaware of them and need considerably more coaching in this skill. It is important whenever possible to implement this strategy when patients are in a low mood state or relatively stable, as they are more inclined to see the rationale of collecting automatic thoughts at such times than when in an elated mood state. Once the strategy has been learned it can hopefully be transferred for use in an elated mood state.

The next step is to alert patients to the impact of these thoughts on their mood state. Questions such as 'so when you thought that how were you feeling?' or 'When you say that to yourself how does it make you feel?', are good starting points. Educating patients about the relationship between their thoughts and their feelings is a process that also continues throughout therapy. It is vital that the patient understands this relationship as it is the main rationale for them to work in a cognitive way.

This process is equally if not more salient in an elated mood state and as patients are often more compliant with therapy in a depressed phase, it is important to teach them the skill of thought identification and challenge so that the process can be adapted to thoughts generated in a hypomanic phase. Depressed thoughts such as 'I am no longer able to do this' are clearly related to behaviours and levels of functioning. Patients with these beliefs will not even be attempting to do things and the importance of the relationship of these thoughts to their failure to try things needs to be amply demonstrated. In short, the next stage is to illustrate to the patient the impact of mood and negative predictions on their behaviour and current functioning. This process also continues throughout therapy.

Once a patient is able to do collect their automatic thoughts, relate them to specific experiences and recognise associated mood states, then he or she can be introduced to the thought record. Greenberger and Padesky have designed one which not only has a section for collecting evidence against the thought but encourages the patient to ring the 'hot' thought (Greenberger & Padesky, 1995). This can prove an invaluable device to ensure that the therapist is working with relevant thoughts. Initially the patient is requested to fill in the first three columns only. Some patients are able to do this right from the start of therapy whereas others are hesitant, often out of a fear that they will not 'get it right'. Stressing the point that it is a device that the patient will need practice to use beneficially and that part of the next session will be to iron out difficulties with it can help patients feel more inclined to have a go. In the next session the chart is examined and challenges attempted and the information added to the other columns as a demonstration to the patient.

Strategies for dealing with the cognitive elements of mania may follow similar lines to those for depression. First patients need to learn to identify thoughts that are associated with their early signs of mania. Patients are taught to recognise an exceptionally elated mood by use of the 24 hour activities sheet. The thoughts that accompany these mood shifts are collected and considered as ideas to be treated with caution in the same way as thoughts associated with excessively low mood.

There are some types of thoughts that are often associated with hypomanic and manic states, such as unrealistically positive assessment of abilities. Patients who experience enhanced self-esteem may compare themselves very favourably with people in superior positions to them across situations, especially related to fields of endeavour. This may not only apply to the formal work situation but to other more socially defined situations as well. Patients express beliefs such as 'I can do it better than others', 'My ideas are superior', 'I could do it in half the time'. 'I am indispensable', 'Without me it will all fall apart'.

When patients are high, these beliefs are frequently expressed in absolutist terms and fail to take into account any conflicting evidence or situational factors. A problem for the therapist is that patients who are hypomanic often do experience an actual increase in their ability to think creatively and to work more productively. They experience a reduced need for rest and an associated increase in activity levels. This enables patients to present convincing evidence for their need to carry on as they would wish. However, they have failed to account for the fact that they are draining their personal resources without replenishing them, as well as adopting strategies that will feed their mania and lead to the possibility of a full-blown manic episode.

Some patients become significantly more driven and take on more work or tasks than they can reasonable hope to accomplish. The result is that they work longer hours as well as trying to speed up the rate at which they work in the belief that this is the way to success. This strategy can result in initial success which makes it difficult for patients to believe that it is an illness sign and may well lead to ultimate failure incorporating exhaustion and possible manic episodes. Some patients really throw themselves at work in order to make up for lost time as illustrated by the example below.

Jamie is a 34-year old artist. He lived on his own but had a girlfriend and a circle of friends. He had four episodes of mania and depression in the last year. Prophylactic medication did not seem to have much effect.

TH: You said that last week you could not relax and were very anxious.

JA: Yes. I could not relax or socialise with my friends.

TH: When was the last time you were like this?

JA: I was like this for the whole week. Yesterday I was with a group of friends but I could not relax.

TH: Can we try doing it like an 'action replay'? What time of the day was it and where were you?

JA: It was in the afternoon. I was at a friend's house having afternoon tea with a group of friends.

TH: When you were anxious and could not relax, what went through your mind?

JA: I thought 'I am wasting my time'. 'I should be working.' 'I have a lot to catch up.'

TH: How did you feel as you had these thoughts?

JA: I felt anxious. I made an excuse and went back to my studio. I did not leave until 3 o'clock in the morning.

TH: How do you feel today?

JA: I am still anxious and my mind seems to be going round and round a bit more.

TH: Was this what happened in the past when you were discharged from hospital?

JA: Yes, I simply worked all the hours God sent in order to make up for lost time.

CHALLENGING AUTOMATIC THOUGHTS

Challenging becomes a test of the therapist's ability to help the patient reframe their ideas without getting into a conflict or 'power struggle' with the patient. Working with patients with manic depression it is important to recognise the difference between upsetting thoughts that are linked to depressive realism and automatic negative thoughts that are the result of a distorted perception driven by a lowered mood state. Being able to empathise with these patients is dependent on a therapist's recognition and acceptance of the patient's unpredictable and diminished world. The trick is to gain a balance between recognition of the unfortunate aspects of the patient's world and an objective view of their negative outlook and predictions.

Challenging automatic thoughts is conducted in a very systematic way. In a session where challenging automatic thoughts is going to be a main focus, then all the thoughts surrounding and associated with the ones initially identified are elicited and written down. Then by a process of collaboration the thought to be worked on is selected. This thought must be a concrete automatic thought relevant to the patient's fundamental problems and associated goal list but amenable to a relative straightforward challenge (see J. S. Beck, 1995, for a full discussion). Thoughts that are most relevant are associated with high levels of emotion. The patient rates the degree to which they believe the thought. Once the key thought is isolated the process of challenging can begin. By a process of Socratic questioning the patient's reasons for believing this thought are discussed and written down. This continues until all the evidence is collected. At this point the therapist moves towards the other perspective in a small step. Take too big a step and the patient will resist. Manic-depressive patients who are currently depressed have often had long-term experiences of failure and things going disastrously wrong and have plenty of substantive evidence to support their perspective. Working with these patients it is important not to diminish the reality of their experiences or belittle the extent of their disability. Many of them have been significantly damaged both by the illness itself and the impact it has had on their self-concept and their lives in general.

Similarly, when challenging an over-positive idea it is important to be sensitive to the patient feeling criticised or undermined as often this will be their experience in the world outside therapy. These discussions must be sensitively conducted as a patient may quickly feel criticised, unfairly judged or that he/she is not being taken seriously as a person of ability but merely being viewed as a patient. Patients may feel put down and restrained by members of their family who are only too aware of the damage over-optimistic thinking can do. A key factor is not to present the ideas as ones to be challenged but ideas to be examined for validity.

The next stage is to collect as much evidence as possible to help the patient gain a different view of the thought. With a concrete thought this is not too difficult as there should be concrete evidence to refute it. An example of such a thought could be 'I don't need any further help'. Evidence to refute this can be drawn from past experience. In this instance it would also be important to look at the consequences for the patient of holding such a prediction. These thoughts may have some truth in them and this must be acknowledged. The aim is not to totally refute the idea but to help the patient see it from a different perspective. Some thoughts are more amenable to a more complete challenge; for example the thought 'People in the shop were looking at me, thinking I looked odd' can be examined in a more straightforward way than the thought, 'Having a mental illness means I am unlikely to find happiness.'

In spite of previously deciding to employ a manager especially to prevent her from taking rash decisions when she is high, Mary has now become convinced that she can make her business work without him because he has advised against her taking out a large loan to expand the business. She came to therapy complaining that both her manager and her family were against her current plans and she wanted help to convince them she was right.

TH: So you are feeling good again and have developed plans to expand the business?

MA: Yes, but I am going to have to sack my manager, we don't really see eye to eye and he is consistently over-cautious. I can make the business take off if I can go ahead with my plans. I intend to take out a big bank loan to fund the expansion. But I cannot convince either him or my family about it. They are so sceptical of my abilities, I need your advice about how to convince them I am right.

TH: Why do you think your family are being so cautious?

MA: They say I'm a bit high, and when I'm high they don't take my decisions seriously. They don't understand that even though I am a bit high, I'm not manic, and I've had some of my best ideas when I've been high.

TH: So you accept that you are a bit high at the moment?

MA: Yes, but I don't think that matters.

TH: Can you give me an example of a good idea that you've had when you are high?

MA: The last time I was high, I took on two excellent contracts and made a big profit on one of them.

TH: So, if I'm understanding you, you are aware that you are a bit high, you've been working long hours, you feel that the business is going well, so you've decided to take out a big loan and expand the business. You've taken other decisions when you've been high, and they've worked out well, so you feel confident that you are right?

MA: Yes, that's right.

TH: OK, but maybe we should look at your reasons for taking this decision to see if we can understand your manager's and family's reluctance. Have you sought any other opinion on your plans for expansion?

MA: No, but I have been given a loan by the bank to do it. They would not give me money if they didn't think I was doing the right thing.

TH: How carefully did the bank examine your plan?

MA: Well, I talked it over with my account manager.

TH: How thoroughly did the manager examine your plans? For example, did he examine all the figures, and how carefully did he do it?

MA: No, he didn't actually look at the figures. But he trusts me because we're doing well at present.

TH: In the past, has the bank ever refused you any money?

MA: No.

TH: And in your experience, has the bank ever loaned you any money for schemes that went wrong?

MA: Well, they did lend me some a few years ago on one deal that wasn't very successful. But in business you have to take certain risks.

TH: So the bank might lend some money even if there was the risk of things going wrong.

MA: I suppose so.

TH: Now I understand that you've made some very good decisions when you've been high. Have you ever made any decisions that didn't work out so well?

MA: Well, I did have some cash flow problems after I paid my workers those big bonuses. But I was able to sort that out.

TH: You've mentioned that you've taken on certain jobs when you've been high. Have all of those jobs been profitable?

MA: I suppose that some of them have gone wrong. But that's the nature of business.

TH: So some of the jobs you've taken on haven't been successful, and some have. And it seems the bank can't be relied upon to ensure that your plan is bound to be successful.

MA: I suppose so.

TH: I also wondered that looking back, you sometimes may think those good ideas you had when slightly high were not so good after all?

MA: Oh yes.

TH: If that is the case, what can we learn from it?

MA: Not to be in such haste.

TH: I wonder if there is any value in having second thoughts.

MA: You mean 'if it is a good idea, it will still be a good idea in a week's time?'

TH: I was wondering about that.

MA: I see.

TH: Just suppose for the moment that this scheme were to go wrong. Would that be a big problem for you?

MA: Yes. I should leave it for a week and then look at it again. I will also consult people if I think it is worth it in a week's time.

The therapist further examined the risks and benefits of the scheme. In the end, Mary decided to postpone asking for the loan and to seek some outside advice.

Another way of dealing with automatic thoughts is to look for explanations that are an alternative to the one given by the patient. Once again Socratic questioning is the way forward. For example when examining the thought 'people were laughing at me in the shop' other aspects of the situation will be examined, such as what they were doing prior to their laughter, to ascertain if there was something else that the people were laughing at. Finally it is important to stress to the patient the necessity of continuing to challenge these automatic thoughts as one of the most salient ways of coping with daily mood fluctuations.

In the case of Jane, challenging the thoughts about her life undergoing total change because her sister asked her to be her bridesmaid had to be done with considerable sensitivity, as the therapist quite rightly predicted that underlying her elated mood was a significant lack of confidence in herself. The therapist was careful not to challenge the thoughts in a strident way, but instead used a process of questioning about her sister's past relationship and behaviour towards her to reveal a caring but ambivalent relationship between the two women.

TH: Now, if I understand you, you said that you used to feel that your sister didn't care about you. That must have been hurtful to you.

JA: Yes, it was.

TH: What do you think made you believe that she didn't care about you?

JA: Well, she never used to telephone me, and she almost never would come to visit.

TH: So, before this last telephone call, when was the last time you spoke to your sister?

JA: Hmm... . It must have been about three weeks ago. I think she phoned me one evening after work.

TH: I see. And how long did you talk to her for?

JA: Not very long ... . Maybe about half an hour.

TH: So these two phone calls were about three weeks apart, and the last one lasted half an hour. Do you remember what you talked about?

JA: Well, she asked me about what I was doing, of course, but I didn't talk much about that. She was always telling me about all her friends, and what she was doing, and how well her job was going. I used to feel that she wasn't really interested in me at all.

At this point the therapist might be tempted to challenge this last idea, but this could be premature and dangerous. It is very possible that Jane's sister doesn't care very much about her, that her telephone calls are relatively infrequent, and that her decision to have Jane as her bridesmaid was born out of a sense of duty. Instead, the therapist chooses to gather further data.

TH: And was this fairly typical? What I mean is, did your sister generally telephone you every few weeks and talk to you for about half an hour?

JA: I suppose so.

TH: How often did you see each other?

JA: Well, the last time was at Easter. She invited me to visit her. But I felt kind of ill at ease. We went to a party with some of her friends. All of them seem to be so successful, so well off. I just felt as if I didn't fit in.

TH: When did you see her before that?

JA: She came to visit me at the beginning of January. But she only stayed overnight. I couldn't help feeling that she wanted to get away. But that's all changed now.

The therapist continued to explore the relationship between the two sisters, forming the hypothesis that much of Jane's sense of estrangement grew out of feelings of inferiority to her sister. This was not explored directly, as the therapist felt that it might be too threatening at this time. Instead, Jane's attention was directed to how often her sister did contact her. It was suggested that relationships can have different degrees of closeness, and that Jane's sister had maintained a considerable degree of contact with her. Jane expressed the idea that this was not as much as she would have liked, and she and the therapist also looked at practical barriers, such as time commitments and the distance between their two homes, which might have reduced the amount of time which they could spend together. The therapist explored the possibility that Jane's sister could value her and also maintain other relationships, and also that as Jane gained more self-confidence, she would be able to deal more equally with her sister's friends. In fact, the wedding was a difficult time for Jane, but she was able to weather it successfully with her therapist's help.

RE-FRAMING THOUGHTS AS SYMPTOMS

This is one of the most important cognitive strategies for dealing with periods of hypomania or mild depression. Automatic thoughts may be elicited and then reframed as early symptoms of a hypomanic episode, not as thoughts to be considered in their own right. Some patients may have specific identifiable thoughts that they know signal a change in mood state that is illness related. For example one patient knew that as soon as he started to feel anxiety when leaving his home associated with the thought that the people who lived in the flat across the road from him knew where he was going, he was becoming paranoid and ill. Another patient associated becoming more protective towards and suspicious about the whereabouts of her husband with the early stages of a manic episode. Patients with ideation that is paranoid may find it easier to re-evaluate these thoughts as symptoms than patients who believe they have become more attractive, powerful and creative. On the other hand, patients who have had many depressive episodes may also be able to recognise certain negative thoughts as signs of lowering mood state: one patient reported that, in the early stages of depression, she would worry that her pet dog had not had a satisfactory quality of life, while for another worries about cancer or some other fatal illness often appeared when he was becoming depressed.

TACKLING GRANDIOSE IDEAS

Grandiose ideas can be dealt with in a similar way. However, the ability of the patient to discern them as unhelpful is more difficult and needs considerable prior discussion. Although patients who have had prior experiences of mania are often desperately keen to avert another episode, this is not always the case. Some patients are quite addicted to their manic states and almost encourage them, even though they are also aware that they can be destructive. Patients like this have an ambivalent relationship with their elated moods and need more work to enable them to reframe their experiences and optimistic thoughts as symptoms. The key point when dealing with grandiose ideas is to enable the patient to reframe them as symptoms. This task is best done as a retrospective exercise. Some people feel their manic states are part of their personality and define them as a person in some way. These patients are understandably loath to contain them, although most patients who form a commitment to therapy do so because part of them recognises a need to contain the extremes of their emotions to enable them to lead more productive lives. It is this desire which may be hidden in hypomania that is the therapist's strongest ally.

This work can be done best when the patient is no longer manic or deeply depressed, but in a more stable mood state. Patients identify the thoughts that are associated with early signs of relapse by being encouraged to recall their most recent episode of illness and the thoughts that were associated with it. Thus, it is important not just to elicit the more extreme grandiose ideas but the initial thought shifts that occur in the very early stages of a manic episode. Patients will often describe these ideas in a general way, reporting that they felt more able to do things than usual, and more confident in their ability to complete tasks they would previously have believed to be out of their sphere of competence. As their mood becomes increasingly elated these ideas often become elaborated on to encompass over-positive comparisons with other people, beliefs about superiority, an increase in the amount of creative ideas and over-optimistic estimations about what can be achieved. There is often an underestimation of the negative consequences of their behaviour.

Joe worked for a supermarket on the till and had managed to stay in employment throughout a depressive episode. However, as he got better his mood became mildly elated and he began to compare himself with his boss. At a later stage when he was more stable the incident was examined in detail.

JO: I began to feel like a new person. I was in work and I overheard my manager discussing plans to re-organise the shop. Quite honestly I thought her ideas were really boring. I thought afterwards that I could come up with much more exciting ways of setting up the store. In fact I nearly butted in and said so.

TH: Could you explain in more detail what happened?

JO: Well, I started getting up at 5:00 feeling bursting with energy and started working on some ideas for changing the store. I thought they were excellent. I did not bother to go into work because I felt the job at the till was boring and I was sure I could get promoted. I recall thinking that when the boss saw the designs she would realise how much better my ideas were than hers. I felt for the first time in ages like a real person and that I could make something of my life.

The therapeutic task here is to help the patient recognise the extent of the change in his beliefs as a result of his upturn in mood and to consider them with a degree of objectivity. Firstly the thoughts are highlighted by being fed back to the patient.

TH: So when you started to feel better you developed more confidence and you started to believe that your ideas were better than your boss's and that she would realise it.

JO: I certainly did, although now I can see that was silly, but in some ways I do think I have ideas that would be useful.

TH: Do you have thoughts like these often? Are they around when you are feeling a bit low?

JO: No, I don't have them often and definitely not when I am feeling low.

TH: So these thoughts about your job being boring and your ideas being better than your boss's occur only when you are feeling confident?

JO: Yes.

TH: And when you are feeling low you never think that but when you are feeling a bit better you think you may have something to offer but not that you are much better than your boss?

JO: It does seem that what I think about myself depends on how my mood is. I sometimes wonder which is the real me.

TH: What is important is to recognise which of these thoughts are related to an elated mood state that could be dangerous for you.

JO: The ones about being better than my superiors at work, which I don't think even when I'm not depressed, I obviously need to watch out for.

Once these thoughts are identified they may be automatically evaluated as symptoms by more experienced and/or insightful patients, particularly if they occur in the presence of other emotional and behavioural symptoms, and dealt with accordingly.

A further difficulty of dealing with the subtle cognitive changes that occur in the very early stages of hypomania is that they can easily be interpreted by both the patient and the therapist as being a normal upturn in mood. Indeed one of the problems most frequently reported by patients is that they cannot tell when a 'good mood' is normal and when it is a precursor to a manic or hypomanic episode. Naive therapists who have only seen a patient in a depressed phase are often eager to see an improvement in their patient and fail to recognise early signs of mania. An ongoing task of CBT with this patient group is to help them distinguish between a normal sense of wellbeing, for example in response to good news, from early signs of mania. One way is to examine the degree of mood change and conse-quent cognitive interpretation relative to the trigger event. Also patients often have themes that regularly occur in manic episodes. Some examples of common themes are about religious significance or in the case of one patient the 'need for a spiritual journey' or the tendency to develop unwarranted romantic ideas about someone. A careful examination of the prodromes of previous episodes can be helpful here (see Chapter 9).

COSTS AND BENEFITS OF BEING HYPOMANIC

Many of the techniques outlined above can apply equally to either hypo-mania or depression: we have chosen to highlight the former because this is an area in which less has been written. However, the idea of a cost--benefit analysis is generally not appropriate in dealing with depression, since few patients feel that there are any benefits to the depressive state. Hypomania, on the other hand, does have positive aspects. Hence, it can be seen as analogous to other states which can be both maladaptive and tempting to the patient, such as the abuse of alcohol or drugs, cigarette smoking, or non-compliance with some unpleasant medical regime. Interventions in these areas often include the technique of reviewing costs and benefits (Rollnick et al. 1992; Kemp et al. 1996a).

As an introduction to this procedure, it can be suggested that the best way to gain control over an episode is to be well prepared. As well as a detailed examination of the changes in thinking that took place just prior to the last episode, the costs incurred by the patient as a result of manic episodes need close scrutiny. There are often benefits to an elated mood, especially for someone who has recently suffered from a depressive episode. In this case it is often difficult for both patient and therapist to consider what appears to be a great improvement in the patient's mental state as a significant sign of a manic episode. Therefore it is particularly important to have a carefully worked out barometer of the patient's mood and behaviour so that a bandwidth of 'normal behaviour and feelings' can be established.

It has been suggested that one of the benefits of being hypomanic is that it is a defence against depression in many respects (Lyon et al., 1997). Thus, it can be seen as artificially enhancing self-esteem, enabling patients to function effectively sometimes for the first time for a considerable length of time. An episode of hypomania often increases the time that patients can give to active work or endeavour by diminishing the need to sleep. Patients often feel more capable, attractive and energetic. These feelings may have been long absent and are deeply pleasurable. Sometimes apparently manic behaviour can be masking a depression. We have come across a patient who said that one of his ways to cope with failing to achieve a task was to take on more tasks which were even more demanding until he could not cope and then sank into a deep depression. Examining his cognitions helps to understand his apparent over-ambitious goal-directed behaviour.

When treating someone who has been depressed for some time it is a relief to observe their mood improving in a significant way, so it is easy to collude with the patient in not recognising it as an early sign of mania. However, close family members and friends will not be so seduced. For them manic episodes are often more difficult to deal with and significantly more destructive to their relationship with the patient and their lives in general than episodes of depression. Relatives become much more cautious in viewing the patient's often sudden upturn in mood with optimism. In fact patients will often complain that their close family members are out to 'spoil their good feelings'. Furthermore, even in a hypomanic episode patients can engage in destructive activities such as spending excessive amounts of money, developing romantic beliefs and fantasies about inappropriate people, taking on excessive amounts of work and becoming exhausted as well as being irritable and belligerent with family and close friends.

A technique is to encourage the patient to set a homework task which will look at the benefits to themselves of being hypomanic and also the costs incurred derived from all previous episodes and past experiences. The information is condensed in a session and transformed into a form that can be easily accessed by the patient, for example into one or more flash cards. This is best done when the patient is stable for use in the early stages of a hypomanic episode; however, it can still be used with patients in an elated mood, especially if the therapeutic alliance is a good one.

Mary ran a successful building business; she was trained as an engineer and this plus a strong commitment to work and a personality incorporating much charm had served her well for many years. However, when hypomania began to appear she became over-generous with her workers, overpaying them and failing to keep a tight check on the firm's finances. She was joyful and exuberant and attendance at therapy sessions became erratic; often she would phone at the last minute to cancel claiming she had something 'essential' to do. She also became somewhat over-confident about what her workers could achieve and began to lose contracts. On receiving an unfavourable statement from her accountant she plummeted into depression, saying she had ruined everything and proved herself to be a failure. Once she was stable an analysis of the aspects of her hypomania that she had enjoyed were discussed, along with the costs incurred by her business and by her own resources. These were placed on a flash card along with an ongoing behavioural plan incorporating measures to protect her business, including regular meetings with her accountant and employing one of her trusted employees to liaise with the other workers in the event of further episodes of elated mood. With help from the therapist she was able to use these strategies along with some delaying thoughts to keep the business together in a further episode of hypomania.

DELAYING TACTIC

It is important to help patients to learn to delay the acting out of their excessively optimistic plans. The basis of the techniques employed when patients are in an elated mood is the use of distancing and delaying tactics. These strategies enable the patient to step back or distance themselves from the situation in order to explore the situation in more detail. This almost invariably involves the use of delaying thoughts and other delaying strategies in order to allow time for patients to make observations about the impact of the passage on time on their beliefs and to ascertain the objective reality of their ideas. Patients in the hypomanic stage invariably find it difficult to 'reality test' their ideas, so therapists need to have prior agreement for using delaying thoughts and tactics which are derived when the patient is more stable. In short most of the ground work is done when patients are relatively well, when the irrational thoughts can be examined in several ways and delaying behavioural and cognitive strategies can be agreed upon.

Excessive activity can be restrained by a series of previously devised questions that patients ask themselves. For example one patient devised the following questions: 'Why do I need to do this now?' 'What will happen if

I leave it until tomorrow?' 'What happens when I get over tired?' She says it is something to do with the questions that makes her 'think twice'. When patients present in an elated mood global cognitive tactics of delay such as 'If it's still a good idea in two weeks time then it is a truly good idea', 'If he's still attractive in two weeks time then he is genuinely attractive' can be employed with a rationale that is acceptable to the patient.

Examples of some useful questions are as follows: 'Would there be anything to be gained from waiting a while before formally leaving the course?', 'Would you lose anything by delaying?', 'What would your most trusted friend say of this decision?', 'If you were advising him in the same circumstance what advice would you give?', 'What is the minimum time you would be prepared to take before closing this option down?', 'What would it be useful to do in the meantime to ensure that you are making the right decision?', 'How would it be if you did those things and we met up again in a few days to discuss it again?'

The delaying strategies and reasons for the delay must be arrived at in the session, written down on a card and kept in some accessible place, so that if the patient gets the urge to act he can use the card as an aide memoire as to why he should take this delaying course of action.

Joe became elated later in the year and once again began to plan to tackle his boss in an inappropriate way.

JO: I told her that I would not be coming into work at the moment as I have something more important to do.

TH: How did she respond?

JO: She was not pleased but I have to work on my new designs which will exceed anything she has ever even dreamed of.

TH: I will be interested to hear about your ideas but first perhaps we could think about the work we have done on what to do when these creative thoughts come so forcefully. It may well be that your ideas will be very beneficial to the organisation. But I am thinking that it may be important not to alienate your boss meanwhile. This was a concern you yourself expressed a few weeks ago. You wrote it down on a card. Perhaps we could look at it now.

JO: It says I would try not to stay off work unless I was ill and not to discuss my thoughts with my boss for 10 days to give me some leeway to clarify my ideas without upsetting her. It also says I have to work less than 6 hours a day and to ask myself questions about the consequences of acting on my feelings straight away.

TH: Do these seem like strategies to employ at this point? You also state on the card that you consider holding onto your job to be of prime importance.

JO: This is true, but I won't find it easy.

The therapist and Joe then discuss ways in which Joe can return to work and keep quiet to his boss.

Joe is asked if he has spoken to interested others about his plans and if so what was the response, has he had similar plans or thoughts before and if so what was the outcome? He is asked about any disadvantages to the thoughts and plans. Finally he is asked to account for the validity of the plans.

Patients will present with varying degrees of acceptance to the idea that to wait before taking action is advisable. Some patients may believe that success in their venture depends on immediate action and will be very loath to consider waiting before taking action. It is during an intervention such as this that trust and rapport play a key role. If the patient trusts that the therapist is working in his or her best interests, he or she will be more inclined to consider employing this sort of strategy. An in-session assessment of the advantages and disadvantages of taking such an action immediately against implementing a conservative plan of waiting and seeing are discussed, with particular reference to past events where impulsive actions led the patient into difficulties. The plan of waiting must be detailed and specific and mutually agreed upon. It must have a specific time period, during which the patient agrees to take calming action such as cutting down on stimulation as much as possible. After this a revaluation of the patient's beliefs about the outcome of the action is conducted if possible in a later session.

At the same time it is important to set the patient some 'calming down' strategies as 'homework', such as having a relaxing bath or a good night's sleep with a possible increase in their medication to ensure a reasonable restful night.

DYSFUNCTIONAL ASSUMPTIONS

In recent years, writers including Teasdale and Epstein have discussed the concept of two parallel, interacting systems of information processing; a rational system and an emotionally driven experiential one (Teasdale, 1993; Epstein, 1994). In relation to cognitive therapy this could be described as the conflict between what a patient feels to be true against what he knows to be true. In short that there are two ways of knowing and the experientially derived knowledge, what we feel to be true, is often more compelling and more likely to influence behaviour than is abstract knowledge (Brewin, 1989). Underlying assumptions are most often related to knowledge that we 'feel' to be true rather than that we 'know' to be true. For example a person may feel they are stupid or to blame when there is objective evidence that this is not the case.

In our experience, manic-depressive patients are often imbued with issues related to autonomy in the sense that they define their self-worth in relation to their achievements rather than how lovable they consider themselves to be. Consequently they are often driven and perfectionistic people with assumptions related to these areas. Assumptions such as 'unless I set myself the highest standard I will be second rate' lead to perfectionist strivings which are doomed to fail and can lead to further episodes of depression. Many manic-depressive patients may well have been functioning well for periods of their life and after being ill and unable to function for some time become frantic about 'catching up' or 'making up for lost time', as in the case of Jamie cited above. These patients are inclined to overwork and become anxious and or guilty if they take time out to relax or socialise; often wearing themselves out, slipping into very unbalanced routines and risking the possibility of depleting their resources and therefore relapse. The underlying assumptions are that they must achieve as before in order to prove they are still worth while and that if they work hard enough they can get back to where they were before they got ill.

Alan was a solicitor who had risen rapidly in his firm to become a senior partner. He was intelligent and worked exceedingly hard and had been rewarded as a result. His parents, themselves high achievers, encouraged him and he grew to believe that his worth as a person depended on his success in his work. Following a relationship breakdown he threw himself further into work to distract himself from his loss. Initially he received ample praise for his extra endeavours which inspired him to further feats of endeavour. He felt that he could show his previous girlfriend and the world that he didn't need her to succeed. He took on more and more cases, staying late at work and arriving early in the morning to cope with the extra work load. Eventually, he found himself unable to sleep and he developed a hypomanic episode where he became unable to work in any organised or structured way. Following on from this episode he became depressed and questioned his worth as a person because he had allowed his work to get out of hand. After he had recovered and returned to work he came to therapy to deal with his compulsion to overwork in order to sustain his self-esteem.

The identification and challenging of assumptions in bipolar patients is similar to that of unipolar patients. Assumptions can come from the realms of behaviour (if I do …), emotions (if I feel …), or thoughts (if I say …). Underlying assumptions are beliefs that underlie automatic thoughts. They can take the form of a rule for living or a conditional statement that incorporates an 'if … then' component. They are less accessible to conscious thinking and can often be discerned initially by observations of recurrent behaviour patterns. They take the form of 'if … then' statements which are often not articulated but can be observed from a patients 'should' statements (e.g. I should always work hard and never fail, I must always put others first) and overly repetitive behaviours or rigid coping strategies. These behaviours often overlie a belief that if they deviate from the pattern then some unacceptable consequence will ensue. Socratic questioning involving the use of informational questions which move from the concrete to the abstract will help uncover the salient underlying assumptions. Therapists also need to be aware of the idiosyncratic use of words and listen to the emotional intensity of these rules. Words such as 'I have to do well' may mean 'I have to be perfect and always the best'.

Many patients have interpersonal schemas which involve predictions and expectations about the response of others to certain of their behaviours, feelings or thoughts. For example, 'If I am not the best, people will look down on me', 'If I make a mistake, I am second rate and people will dismiss me.' Once an assumption has been identified it is written out and the next step is to construct a new more adaptive assumption that can be tested out. Once again using Socratic questions a discussion ensues to formulate a new rule. Here therapists tend to appeal to pragmatism to highlight how these rules are unhelpful. Examples of suitable questions are: 'Is it reasonable to believe this?', 'What are the advantages and disadvantages to holding this belief?' The disadvantages may include procrastination or stopping the person from being truly creative and learning from experience. 'Does this rigid belief prevent me from achieving life goals?' 'How can this rule be changed to fit more closely with the real world?' 'Is it realistic to expect anyone not to make any mistakes?' For example, a rule that says 'I must always perform at a very high standard in order to be adequate', does not allow for circumstances that interfere with the person's ability to perform, such as illness or conflicts of interest where a compromise would allow the best solution. Furthermore, failure to perform at best at these times leaves the patient feeling they have failed and at risk of feeling inadequate generally. Further questions such as 'What would you have to change in order for this rule to work?' move the patient along to the next stage, that of testing out the validity of the new rule.

Once a new more workable rule has been formulated the patient is encouraged to act 'as if' the new rule were true. This inevitably means acting against the old, strongly held rule, and this can create high anxiety. Patients often have negative predictions attached to infringements of their rule and these need to be identified before the behavioural test is set in motion so that data can be collected by the patient about these predictions. Behavioural experiments are set up collaboratively in a therapy session to try out the new rule. For example a patient with perfectionist standards who has formulated a new rule that says, 'It's good to do well but it is not always practically possible and doing something less well does not render me a failure' will need to drop his standards by performing a particular task adequately or even 'poorly' and to monitor his levels of anxiety and the outcome of his predictions. Setting up these behavioural tests is often difficult as patients are very anxious at the prospect of changing deep-seated behaviours. The experiments need to be constructed with maximum collaboration with the patient, testing out at each stage of the process any discomfort felt or resistance demonstrated by the patient, which is ironed out so that as far as possible the experiment is set up to succeed. Finally, as with all homework, it is crucial to obtain feedback on the experiment at the beginning of the next session. Failures can then be examined and rectified. Repeated trials of behavioural tests of the new rule will reinforce it as gradually the patient learns new more adaptive behaviour patterns.

Chapter 9

BEHAVIOURAL TECHNIQUES

INTRODUCTION

Behavioural approaches are central to the management of manic depression. In particular, the individual with a manic-depressive illness has usually had extensive experience of a chaotic lifestyle varying between periods of extreme lethargy and damaging overactivity. Although the 'highs' associated with these extremes can be subjectively pleasurable, their consequences are usually damaging. As Healy & Williams (1989) have proposed, life events tend to lead to manic-depressive episodes through disruptions to sleep, routine and circadian rhythm. Also, the American Psychiatric Association (1994b) have recommended regular social and sleep routine as part of their treatment guidelines for manic-depressive illness. In combination with the lethargic effects of depression the 'highs' of mania can present the individual with many episodes of failing to cope. Enabling the individual to develop their skills in managing and planning their routines can both protect from the extremes noted above and enhance self-esteem by building up experience of success with planned and completed tasks and goals. It is important that any efforts made to change routines and behaviour patterns are undertaken in a collaborative manner. Individuals may well have developed quite specific routines which fit their personal inclinations but have costs in terms of mental health. Evidence with respect to this must be identified in terms of the individual's own experience through guided discovery. More directive or controlling approaches on the part of the therapist are likely to meet with significant patient resistance, leading to unsuccessful psychological treatment. Once evidence has been discussed which illustrates the costs and benefits of current routines, a further aspect of this approach is a recognition of the need for collaboration in terms of goals for changes in routine or behaviour. Even if the patient identifies a need for change it is important that any targets set are achievable. This may mean that initial changes are relatively modest, but may serve as a basis for further changes at a later stage in therapy. Trying to change too much too early will again run the risk of causing resistance or leading the patient to feel overwhelmed and drop out from therapy.

Jane is a patient with strong religious convictions who is in a stable relationship of 8 years standing. She described during the period prior to her admission to hospital that she felt increasingly elated and sensual. Thoughts began to focus on her sense of her own attractiveness and increasing sexual needs which led her to seek casual sexual relationships with other men. Contrary to her usual character she began to frequent local clubs, started binge drinking and became involved in a number of short-term relationships. This changed behaviour was accompanied with a conviction that such behaviour was her right and thus she had enormous difficulty in appreciating her partner's objections. Her partner eventually left her, after which she experienced a period of increasing chaos in her domestic routine followed by a period of depression which was sufficiently severe to require hospitalisation.

MOOD AND ACTIVITY SCHEDULES

All individuals complete mood and activity schedules during the course of therapy. In the first instance these measures are used to assess the current range and pattern of activities in which the individual is engaged. In particular the therapist is concerned with how well patients are able to structure their week and the extent to which patterns of activity vary over time. Some patients present with quite disorganised routines, others in contrast have very demanding routines, sometimes in an effort to 'catch up for lost time' due to previous periods of illness or hospitalisation.

Celia is an artist in her early forties who has had numerous hospital admissions. She has an acute sense of her illness interfering with her life. She describes this in terms of her illness 'returning me to square one' each time she feels she is making progress. After a recent hospital admission she spent her first day following discharge at work in her studio, completing a 10-hour day in an effort to catch up for time lost whilst in hospital. This reflected a general pattern that when well she found that she got progressively more tense when spending time with friends or trying to relax because she wasn't doing anything creative.

TH: From what you are recording and saying it seems as though work is top priority at the moment.

CE: It is, I don't feel I want to waste time on other things. It's just too precious.

TH: Can you say any more about time being precious in this way?

CE: Well, I have wasted a lot of time being ill and now that I am well again I want to catch up. It is so frustrating because before my admission I was very productive.

TH: I remember at that time you were working for around 16 hours per day on your project. Is that right?

CE: Yes, I often wish I had the energy to do that now.

TH: Was there any down side to all that energy?

CE: Well no, not at first. I was just painting more and more, better and better.

TH: What about later on, did it continue in that way?

CE: Well no, I suppose not. Later on I couldn't stop even when I wanted to and when I was working I couldn't focus in the same way on any one task. I found myself rushing from one thing to another.

TH: Were you getting much done at that point?

CH: I thought I was at the time, but looking back there was not a lot to show for the final weeks.

TH: What is your most important target in terms of your work at the moment?

CE: To keep working while I am well, to get as much done as I can.

TH: Is that why you are working long hours again?

CE: Yes, of course.

TH: What would you say if I suggested you spend less time working?

CE: No chance.

TH: OK, well lets look at the activity sheets. The number of hours is increasing and your mood ratings are elevating. These are the sheets you completed before admission: can you see any similarities?

CE: Well, some. Maybe my mood is a little hyper at the moment.

TH: I suggest as an experiment we monitor how your mood is when you work for shorter periods and do more non-work activities such as seeing friends. You see at the moment it seems you work harder and harder, but this puts you at risk of being ill and having a long time away from your work. What if we could show that working less could help you keep well and productive for longer?

CE: Well, I suppose then it would be worth sticking with. OK, let's give it a try.

In therapy it was possible to identify a vicious circle in which this 'need to create' in combination with making up for lost time led her to working progressively longer hours which eventually led her to a point of collapse, which on numerous occasions had triggered a relapse and further hospital admission. Identification of these patterns with the patient provided a basis for discussion of alternative routines which, although they involved shorter periods of work in each day, actually were likely to be more productive in the longer term due to a reduced chance of interruption through relapse and hospital admission.

The mood and activity schedule used is adapted from the measure traditionally employed in CBT for depression (Beck et al., 1979). Whereas the original measure has space for entries on an hourly basis between 9 a.m. and 8 p.m., the current measure accommodates entries made for each day in hourly slots throughout a 24 h period. This permits ratings to be made outside 'normal' waking hours when people in the prodromal stages of mania may be active. No specific provision is made for pleasure and mastery rating to avoid making ratings overcomplicated. As discussed in Chapter 8, this allows for a mood rating ranging from −10 extreme depression to +10 for extreme elation. This mood variation information has proved clinically useful, particularly in combination with concurrent information on activities and activity changes which might be associated with particular mood shifts. An example form is presented in Figure 9.1.

INTRODUCING MOOD AND ACTIVITY SCHEDULES IN THERAPY

The importance of the mood and activity schedule is discussed with reference to the diathesis–stress model presented in initial sessions. Stressors acting through life events, disruption of social routines or sleep deprivation are identified as potential triggers for biological vulnerabilities (such as circadian rhythm instability) which can lead to prodromes. Hence the development and monitoring of routine core activities can potentially protect against the progression towards prodromes. Core factors within activity monitoring are identified as sleeping, eating and planning, as discussed in the following subsections.

Sleep

Many people with a diagnosis of manic depression tend naturally to have quite variable sleep habits even when well. Sleep may itself be an activity that is primarily determined by external demands rather than internal cues. Some people with a diagnosis of manic depression may have less conventional jobs/life styles in which periods of work and 'normal' leisure time overlap. Thus artists who like Celia above, work long into the night or people employed as shift workers may find that development of a regular sleep pattern is impeded by shift changes and the difficulties of daytime

WEEKLY MOOD AND ACTIVITY SCHEDULE

Name

Mood Rating
(−10 to +10)

DATE	M	T	W	Th	F	S	S
	−5	+4	+1	−5	−5	−5	−1
6–7 a.m.	Asleep	Got up 6.30	Asleep	Asleep	Asleep	Got up 6.30 Dogs breakfast	Asleep
7–8 a.m.	Got up 7.50	Dogs breakfast Left for work 7.30	Dogs breakfast Left for work 7.30	Dogs breakfast Left for work 7.30	Dogs breakfast Left for work 7.30	Argument	Got up 7.30 Dogs
8–9 a.m.	Made dogs breakfast	Work 8.30	Work 8.30	Work 8.30	Work 8.30	Work 8.00	Breakfast
9–10 a.m.	Washed and tidied	Work	Work	Work	Work	Work	Read papers
10–11 a.m.	Read Watched TV	Work	Work	Work	Work	Work	Went to garden centre
11–12 a.m.	Took dogs for a walk	Work	Work	Work	Work	Work	Into town for lunch
12–1 p.m.	Read Went to local pub	Work	Work	Work	Work	Left work 12.45	Housework
1–2 p.m.	Had lunch at pub	Lunch 1.45	Lunch 2.00	Lunch 2.00	Lunch 2.00	Shopping	Housework
2–3 p.m.	Watched TV	Work	Work	Work	Work	Local pub	Local pub
3–4 p.m.	Watched TV	Work	Work	Work	Work	Housework	Read

	Day 1	Day 2	Day 3	Day 4	Day 5	Day 6	Day 7
4–5 p.m.	Watched TV	Work	Work	Work	Work	Meal	Made tea
5–6 p.m.	Watched TV	Left work 5.50	Left work 5.50	Left work 5.50	Left work 5.50	Walked dogs	Dozed
6–7 p.m.	Watched TV	Visited mother – had tea	Visited mother – had tea	Hospital appt	Packed up	Washed up Dozed	Read
7–8 p.m.	Watched TV	Drove to school meeting	Drove home	Drove home	Went home TV	Watched TV	Watched TV
8–9 p.m.	Washer hair Walked dogs	Home	Played with dogs – watched TV	Fed/walked dogs	Read	Ironed	Ironed
9–10 p.m.	Watched TV	Bed	Bed	Read	Bed	Pub	Pub
10–11 p.m.	Pub supper	Asleep	Asleep	Bed	Asleep	Supper	Pub supper
11–12 p.m.	Argument Bed 11.30	Asleep	Bill in from pub	Asleep	Bill in from pub	Asleep	Argument Bed 11.30
12–1 a.m.	Asleep	Bill in from pub—wants to talk	Fitful sleep	Asleep	Fitful sleep	Bill in from pub —wants to talk	Asleep
1–2 a.m.	Asleep	Argument	Argument	Asleep	Argument	Argument	Asleep
2–3 a.m.	Asleep	Fitful sleep	Fitful sleep	Asleep	Fitful sleep	Fitful sleep	Asleep
3–4 a.m.	Asleep	Asleep	Asleep	Asleep	Asleep	Asleep	Asleep
4–5 a.m.	Asleep	Asleep	Asleep	Asleep	Asleep	Asleep	Asleep
5–6 a.m.	Asleep	Asleep	Asleep	Asleep	Asleep	Asleep	Asleep

Figure 9.1   An example of a completed mood and activity schedule

sleeping. Most people will experience at times a need to delay sleep due to other factors, but this will usually be an exception rather than a rule. However, when this pattern of external factors becomes more intrusive or frequent, changes to sleep routines can become excessive. If also, the focus is on external cues, the individual can become less sensitive to cues for fatigue and also less aware of associations between fatigue/sleep disruption and their symptoms of manic depression.

Once the pattern of sleep has been identified from the monitoring sheets session time is devoted to identifying realistic routine targets. These will aim for both minimum sleep periods and for sleep times with reduced variability. In practice for most individuals this will mean aiming at around 8 hours sleep and going to bed between 11 p.m. and midnight. It should also be noted that targets may also be required when the individual is in a depressed phase, as sleep times may then escalate as a means of 'switching off' from the depressed mood. This can serve to exacerbate low mood and again introduction of a more regular sleep pattern has benefits in terms of accelerating recovery.

Figure 9.1 provides an example of a completed mood and activity schedule which indicates a pattern of disrupted sleep routines in a patient who was beginning to report increasingly 'fragile' mood. As can be seen mood ratings also indicate persistent low mood in association with this disruption. Further details of this example are provided in the Sleep Routines section later in the chapter.

Making these apparently simple changes may be difficult for some patients. Therapists need to be sensitive to reasons for resistance to such changes and listen to the patient's viewpoint. This should include a clear recognition of the patient's individuality and specific efforts to tailor increases in sleep duration and regularity around their other needs and goals. Thus the actual patterns may vary widely depending on the individual patient and there may well need to be compromises made in terms of other external demands on the patient. However, as long as this allows the patient to sustain a regular and reasonable sleep pattern it will be an important contribution to maintaining psychological health. The use of the monitoring sheets can also serve to highlight the importance of sleep for the individual when competing demands are made. Thus when work or holidays etc. are approaching during which reduced/disrupted sleep appears likely, time is allocated to planning means of moderating the impact of this and to developing coping strategies if difficulties should develop.

Eating

For many people with manic-depressive illness developing a routine of regular balanced food intake can be difficult. During phases of elation food can be regarded as an unnecessary distraction from the exciting projects and ideas with which the person is engaged. In contrast during periods when the person is feeling depressed the effort and planning required to achieve this goal can seem at best daunting and at worst overwhelming. A target is to help people achieve eating at regular periods on three occasions throughout the day. Initially there may have to be some discussion of how this might be achieved in relation to other priorities. Emphasis is again placed on the diathesis-stress model as a rationale for investing effort in this area. The role of nutrition in general health and the role of general health in protection against illness is discussed, particularly in the context of manic-depressive illness. This is associated also with the importance of regularity and routine in protecting against the elated periods of manic-depressive illness in particular.

Planning

In addition to specific activities within particular days, the mood and activity schedules are used as a basis for looking at patterns of activity over longer periods of time. This information can provide a picture for each individual of the degree of balance across activities which they have during treatment. It will indicate whether they are overly task orientated or conversely avoidant of constructive activity. In individuals who are very work orientated there may be a total absence of pleasurable or hobby activities. This can make tackling of prodromes of depression difficult as self-reinforcing activities will have to be identified for such individuals rather than focusing on building up activities which are already present. Identifying this issue prior to such prodromes generates the possibility that a gradual introduction of non-task activities might be made whilst the individual is well as a preventative measure, again as part of a collaborative process. It can be used to assess where particular sources of stress come from the person being treated and how much randomness there is in their normal routine in terms of both stressful and reinforcing events. In the planning stage clients work with their therapist on mood and activity schedule blanks to identify specific activity areas for the next week/fortnight. This will not usually involve planning the whole week out in detail but in targeting specific periods for particular activities which have been identified as missing or unbalanced from the preceding series of unplanned sheets.

Planning targets a number of areas:

Making Time for Pleasurable Non-task Activities

If there is evidence that the person is not engaging in sufficient pleasurable non-task activities this is identified during the planning session. Targets are then set for remedying this problem and such activities are entered into the Mood and Activity Schedules for the forthcoming period. A problem-solving approach is applied to identifying and including these activities. In periods of low mood inclusion of such activities is especially important and the effects of inclusion on mood can be demonstrated behaviourally by additional records of daily mood. Mood ratings are usually taken for each day on the record sheet, the patient rating the day as a whole between 0 (very low mood) and 10 (very high mood). This record of mood built up over several sessions will help to identify the extent to which mood responds to particular activities and the extent to which it naturally varies over time. In patients with experience of numerous episodes of manic depression they can come to believe that they can have no influence over their mood—'It just happens, I have 7 months of depression and then 3–4 weeks on a high and there is nothing I can do about it.' Information from the mood and behaviour records can demonstrate that even during low periods they can affect the extent of low mood and that by developing a repertoire of mood-enhancing activities during their periods of low mood they can moderate the effects of this low mood which can in turn reduce both the likelihood and likely severity of the expected manic phase. In patients who have had a long period of chronic depression it can again be important to learn to identify mood changes in this way. The individual may have come to feel helpless in the face of this depression and believe that their mood never varies. Identification of shifts in mood ratings can help to challenge this and subsequently to enhance the rationale for planning of positive non-task activities since mood can vary.

A converse problem can be that in elated mood such non-task activities can begin to dominate the weekly routine. In this situation targets are planned for moderation of this behaviour with a focus on setting normative targets for task behaviour to avoid escalating work or domestic difficulties.

Jim was experiencing a period of depression. Although he was usually a keen road runner and general 'fitness fanatic' he was currently taking no interest in this. He was finding his work tasks harder to complete and was working progressively longer hours to try to 'catch up'. Activity and mood schedules revealed that breaks during the day were rare and that working hours were extending into leisure time, whilst progressively more time was being spent sleeping. On discussion he reported that he 'felt slow' and that therefore there was 'no point' in running as he could not perform to his usual standard. Jim is an intensely competitive individual for whom sport was the only acceptable form of relaxation.

TH: I see from your mood and activity schedules that you seem to be working longer hours than usual.

JI: Yes, well I have to. I feel everything takes so long and if I don't put in the extra time I will never keep up.

TH: It also looks as though you have not spent much time with your running club recently. Is that so?

JI: Yes. I don't have the time. I'm either working or I am just too tired.

TH: I can see why that might get in the way, but are there any other reasons why you haven't been out running in the last few weeks.

JI: I'm not sure. Possibly … You see, when I feel like this I can't make the grade. I'm used to being up there with the other top runners on our road runs but I don't think I could do that at the moment so there's no point.

TH: So are you saying that at present you feel slow, then you work harder and longer, and you then feel more tired?

JI: Sounds right so far.

TH: Then because of this you find recreational activities harder and do less of them?

JI: Well what is the point of hammering yourself for no reward?

TH: Good question. It seems that you are describing a vicious circle in which feeling low and tired makes work harder to perform and that this can lead you to drop the sports activities which you normally used for relaxing and for managing stress.

JI: OK. Maybe so, but what can I do about it?

TH: Well, we could make a start by looking at other non-work activities in addition to running. Have you ever done any other sports or followed any other interests?

JI: I used to swim but I stopped that some months ago. I also used to enjoy going to the cinema but somehow never have time for that now.

TH: What would you think of trying to plan a couple of swimming or cinema trips in for the next week, if you feel too tired for competitive running?

JI: But what about the vicious circle you mentioned. Won't things just get worse?

TH: The first step in breaking the circle will be to have a range of relaxing activities which you can do to manage stress. This should help you to avoid getting progressively more tired and stressed each day at work. I suggest we try this over the next two weeks and check it out.

Targets were set for reinstatement of his running and for inclusion of other less competitive sports to be engaged in when feeling 'slow'. Specific goals for these activities were identified as reducing stress levels and 'forcing' limits to time spent working, rather than focusing on performance during activities themselves. This intervention proved acceptable and facilitated improvements in mood and anxiety levels, leading to work becoming more manageable and allowing Jim to defer a request for sickness leave which he had discussed with his GP when these problems were developing.

Planning to Avoid Unnecessary Crises

Mood and activity schedules can provide useful information on amounts of task-related activity as noted above, but also on the form this activity takes. Whilst individuals may be spending long periods of time at work for instance, this may on further discussion be found to be largely non-productive. Thus if the individual is arriving early and leaving late, but procrastinating over important tasks whilst there, problem solving around reasons for this can provide a useful means of pre-empting possible escalations of work problems and avoiding the negative consequences that these would have on mood for the individual. Under these circumstances more detailed planning within the work routine of specific task targets would run in tandem with setting reasonable limits to working time, with a view to providing opportunities for pleasurable non-task-orientated activities.

Yale was a senior teacher in a busy inner city comprehensive school. She was very committed to her pupils and concerned about helping them to fulfil their academic potential. During the pre-exam period she reported feeling quite elated, working extra hours to provide a range of revision classes to her pupils. However, after the exams she began to worry increasingly and to defer marking and administrative tasks which progressively built up to the point that she again had to work excessive hours to catch up. This over-activity/inactivity cycle was clearly demonstrated in record sheets, along with an absence of non-task activities in both phases of this cycle.

TH: Looking at your mood and activity schedules it seems as though your pattern of working has been varying a lot over the last few weeks. Have you noticed that yourself?

YA: I certainly have. I just can't cope at the moment. I either can't be bothered with anything, or I'm in such a panic that I feel guilty if I spend any time doing anything but work.

TH: That sounds very tough for you. Do you have any ideas why things are different at the moment?

YA: I'm not sure. I have lots of deadlines to meet, but that isn't really unusual. I just feel I have no energy. Everything feels too hard to begin, except when I am in a panic when I try to do everything at once.

TH: What do you do apart from work?

YA: Not a lot. I don't have time for anything else.

TH: It sounds as though you have a lot of different demands on your time at work. Do you think all the tasks you have to do are equally important or urgent?

YA: Well, no, I suppose not. But I feel so rushed I don't have time to sort out which is which.

TH: Do you think we could spend some time on that now?

YA: OK then. Where do we start?

TH: It is often useful to make a start by sorting tasks into A and B lists. The tasks on the A list are 'must do now' tasks, the B list has the tasks than can wait a while.

YA: Right, but how will that help me?

TH: It sounds as though at the moment it might be a good idea to focus your energies on the A list tasks so that important things don't get missed, but you are not overwhelmed with a whole number of things you are trying to do at once. That should also leave some space in your week for doing other things apart from work.

Discussion within therapy sessions centred on both the introduction of constructive non-task activities for the purposes of mood enhancement and distraction from ruminations regarding exam results for her pupils and the setting of manageable targets for work tasks. An analysis of task priorities was undertaken as the pattern identified was one of 'avoidance of all tasks' or 'all tasks must be done'. Identification of priorities led to lower task targets per week and opportunities for constructive activity away from work. Yale reported over three sessions that instituting these changes reduced her sense of being overwhelmed by her responsibilities and led to a generally more stable routine of work and leisure activity.

Learning to Prioritise Allocation of Time

This is a further area in which review of a series of mood and activity schedules can be most helpful. It can indicate the balance in activities, but also the appropriateness of the amounts of time allocated to specific tasks. Thus the person may have a balance between activities at work and in the home, but within the home find that most of their time is isolated from the family, or alternatively working on 'new projects' with little time for relaxation or communication with other family members. Again identification of these issues by review of previous sheets then leads to planning for greater balance on future sheets. This will include assessing with the individual a limited number of priority areas to be included as a rule for each week and a subsidiary list of more optional activities.

USEFUL BEHAVIOURAL STRATEGIES

Relaxation Training

Relaxation training can be a useful behavioural technique for the management of overarousal and also for addressing anxiety symptoms which can commonly be associated with mood difficulties. This can take many forms but is usually implemented clinically through training in progressive muscular relaxation. Once this has been identified as an appropriate form of intervention for the client then it would be usual to set aside most of one session to take them through in vivo training in the use of this technique. Usually a shortened version of the Bernstein and Borkovec (1973) procedure is used in which the patient learns to employ the 'tension and release' cycle across the following muscle groups: left and then right arms and hands; face area including forehead; upper body; stomach and then legs. It will normally take around twenty minutes for the person to successfully relax each of these areas, after which a period of several minutes will be spent visualising a relaxing scene before relaxation is ended. These sessions are either taped at the time and the client provided with a copy or they are provided with a pre-recorded tape after the initial session which covers the same topic. Targets for learning this skill will be based on daily practise which can be identified in the mood and activity schedules.

Sleep Routines

As noted above sleep is an important target area for behavioural intervention in this client group, in particular because of the association between sleep disruption and deteriorating mood control. The specific targets vary, dependent on current mood state.

In the person with current low mood there will be a risk of excessive sleep, using sleep as an escape, and increasing levels of fatigue and low mood as the person sleeps longer into the 'normal' day. Under these circumstances targets need to be set in terms of maximum sleep duration and times of wakening, with an additional ban on sleeping during the day to avoid shifting of excessive sleep to later in the day. Often it can be helpful to encourage clients to commit themselves to particular tasks in the hour or so after waking to ensure compliance. It can be helpful to implement these targets along with mood monitoring to provide the individual with objective evidence of the 'responsiveness' of mood to such changes.

In the person whose mood is becoming elevated or whose mood is developing components of agitation and irritability the focus tends to be the reverse. In these circumstances sleep can be regarded as 'time wasted' or 'an unnecessary distraction' or merely 'impossible'. Work can therefore first be targeted on identifying what form the person's sleep routine is taking at the present time. Often they will report waiting until exhausted before trying to sleep, delaying sleep until tasks are completed or relying on alcohol to facilitate sleep. Some of these problems can in themselves be associated with excessively long working hours, failure to take breaks or allow a 'wind down' period and high levels of stimulant consumption, in particular caffeine during the evening. In developing a sleep hygiene protocol it can therefore be important to set targets which begin in the early evening. Thus caffeine to be banned/restricted after 7 p.m., work to be continued no later than 7.30–8 p.m., and regular use of relaxation techniques as part of wind-down procedure, can all be components in this area. Also target times for sleep are important, as it will often be noticeable from activity records that these can vary widely, again interfering with the stability of social rhythm associated with greater mood stability.

When mood has become elevated to the point that behavioural techniques are not readily effective, then it can be useful to assess whether medication changes (such as short-term hypnotic prescription) are appropriate to help reinstate sleep pattern and aid mood stabilisation. In such circumstances the target would be to return to non-pharmacological approaches for this area as soon as was clinically feasible.

Karen is in full-time employment and lives with her partner who is currently unemployed, although he has previously worked in quite senior management positions. She recently reported feeling that her mood was increasingly 'fragile', that she was beginning to notice concentration difficulties and that she was feeling more than usually irritable. There was no obvious single cause apparent on discussion. However, review of her recent mood and activity schedules indicate that her routine had been progressively disrupted since her partner ceased employment. His habits had changed since unemployment, as he began to stay late at his local pub, returning at around midnight, leading to Karen rarely going to bed before 1 a.m. even when she was not going with him. This led to her having only 4–5 h sleep on most nights, with occasional very early nights to 'catch up' which were in themselves often disrupted by her partner's return.

TH: You were saying that your mood is currently feeling more fragile. Has anything happened since we last met that you feel might be important in relation to this mood change?

KA: No, not really. Just the usual work routine.

TH: Looking at the activity schedules, the daytime recordings are as usual, but it looks as though sleep times are more variable than is normal for you. Is that so?

KA: Well, yes. I suppose so. Since Bill stopped working he just does what he likes. That normally means chatting to his mates at the pub until after closing time then coming home and waking me up. That makes me really angry, especially when I see him sleeping in late the next morning.

TH: We talked in earlier sessions about the evidence that sleep disruption can be associated with worsening of symptoms in people with manic-depressive illness. Do you think the changes in your sleep pattern are affecting how you feel?

KA: Well, now we look at it in detail, I suppose so. I've got so many things going on at the moment I can't say I'd noticed until we focused on it.

TH: How would you feel about setting some targets for your sleep routine to see if this helps with your mood?

KA: What sort of targets?

TH: Well, to aim for specific regular periods of sleep and to set these periods as 'top priority' for you. It might be helpful to discuss these targets with Bill so that he understands how sleep is important to your health. Do you think you could do that?

KA: It's worth a try. I'll talk with him tonight.

Having identified this pattern, targets were set to identify ways of protecting herself from the changes in her partner's routine. By assertively discussing this with her partner and making clear the role which these changes had in relation to her mental health, an agreement was reached which led to her being able to regularise her own sleep routine towards a target of 7 hours sleep, which she had identified as 'satisfactory'. Achievement of this target was associated with increasing stability of mood, which made maintenance of the target self-reinforcing.

Graded Task Assignment

Graded task assignment can be particularly useful when the patient is dealing with difficulties in low mood. Again information from the mood and activity schedule can provide a basis for working with the client towards identifying tasks which are felt to be important but which are currently avoided. There is usually an awareness of this avoidance which is often associated with feelings of guilt and, later, hopelessness, the avoided tasks seeming to become larger and more difficult. This may be in terms of household chores or in terms of work tasks or deadlines. In both cases session time will need to be allocated to first identifying problem areas. These will tend to be described initially in broad terms: 'I can't run the house any longer'; 'my job is impossible'; 'my bills or debts will never be dealt with'. These broad descriptions need then to broken down into the specific areas of difficulty for the person.

Thus if a difficulty is that 'I can't run the house any more' the question then becomes what tasks are difficult. This will lead to the generation of a list of specific tasks required to achieve the goal of 'running the house'. Once these tasks have been identified an assessment can be made of which of these are currently being performed. In addition tasks can be graded in terms of priority and how frequently they need to be done. The aim in the first instance is to leave the patient with a relatively short list of important but manageable tasks which they are realistically likely to be able to perform. From setting goals at an appropriate level the patient is thus able to get experience of success in contrast to the repeated failure associated with the global statement 'I can't run the house any more'. This experience of success facilitates greater levels of motivation in the depressed patient as they become aware that there are activities that they can manage even when depression is making life difficult for them. Although the development of this approach can require substantial time in initial sessions, once the patient becomes familiar with the process it can be self-sustaining once they have a clear understanding of the technique and may indeed generalise to a broader range of target statements than initially developed within therapy.

Sheila was currently depressed, but was still attempting to maintain her activities at a level which was consistent with how she performed when her mood was elevated. As a result she felt overwhelmed by the effort required to keep up with her household chores, which led to avoidance of tasks completely for extended periods of time. It became evident from the details of her household chores that her standards were extremely high to the extent that she felt that if she didn't virtually spring clean the household several times per week, she was failing.

SH: I just can't keep on top of the housework. Everything is too much. Its really getting me down.

TH: It looks as though you are trying to get through a lot each day.

SH: It's only things I normally do. I was managing fine until last month. I flew through the house. It was like a new pin all of the time.

TH: Has your mood changed in the last month?

SH: I suppose I felt good last month. Maybe a bit high.

TH: How would you describe your mood now?

SH: I feel pretty low really.

TH: What does feeling low do for your energy levels?

SH: It kills them. I sometimes feel I can barely get out of bed.

TH: That sounds very difficult. How do you feel when you think of your long list of tasks if you feel low?

SH: Just overwhelmed. I can't get started because I know I'll never finish them all. What's the point?

TH: So do you think it is realistic to aim to do all your tasks each day feeling like that?

SH: Well, they don't do themselves and they all need doing, so I don't know.

TH: OK, I appreciate what you are saying. Let me put it another way. Do you think that all of the tasks have to be done every day?

SH: I don't know.

TH: What I would like to do is to spend some time seeing whether it is possible to grade your tasks into those which need to be done every day and those which can be done less frequently.

SH: And what then? How will that help?

TH: You have said that you feel overwhelmed at the moment. It may be that having graded tasks there will be a more realistic daily list of tasks, which you would have a reasonable expectation of attempting even when feeling low. The non-daily tasks can then be planned in for when your mood lifts, or taken in stages during the week.

A graded task assignment approach was used to help identify important components of the jobs required of her and to reduce the targets for activities which were less necessary to complete to maintain her home. This short list of central tasks was then broken down into constituent steps. Sheila's target was then to agree with the therapist the number of steps which she could currently realistically achieve in a week and to increase this in consultation with her therapist as changes in her mood permitted. The aim of the intervention was to reduce the feeling of being overwhelmed and to encourage practice in achieving less 'perfectionist' standards.

Problem Solving

Problem-solving approaches can be used within graded tasks assignment or separately from it. The solving of problems is clearly a crucial activity in everyday life which many people with a manic-depressive diagnosis are usually well able to perform. However, particularly in the depressed stages of the illness a more structured approach may be required to address problems that may seem overwhelming or insoluble. The first task within the therapy session is to obtain a clear description of the nature of the problem to be solved and details of where, when, how and in what context the problem occurs. Having obtained information on the nature of the problem, time is allocated to brain storming possible solutions. It is important that this is focused on facilitating the generation of possible solutions by the patient, rather than those provided by the therapist. It is often useful to have solution lists which are initially over-inclusive and even to wilfully include inappropriate solutions to 'free up' the patient's thinking. Socratic questioning can then be used to select likely candidates from the lists of solutions, which are then looked at in more detail. Once the patient has chosen a particular solution, possible difficulties in implementing the solution are identified and ways to address this discussed. If more than one individual is involved in the solution it is of course important that agreement from all parties is obtained prior to setting the problem-solving solution as a homework task.

Time Delay Rules

This and the next section (Sitting/Listening Targets) are based on the work of Newman & Beck (unpublished manuscript). Impulsive and damaging decisions are a feature of mania and can often be identified prodromally. The patient may become preoccupied with a particular plan involving a business venture or a change in personal relationships which has struck them as foolproof. This increased generation of ideas in tandem with decreased editing of the possible pitfalls is often associated with increasing grandiosity. In session it can therefore be all too easy for the therapist generating alternative viewpoints to be drawn into a confrontational situation which may in fact serve to further polarise the patient's view. Time delay rules can therefore be very useful, particularly if these have been set up early in therapy. The patient is asked to agree, usually when in a non-manic state, that there may be times when acting without caution on their ideas may be potentially harmful, this usually being done with reference to previous acts when unwell. A verbal or written contract can then be agreed in which the patient agrees to hold off from implementing such ideas for at least 24/48 hours (whichever is most appropriate). The signal that such a time delay needs to be brought into operation can be agreed to come from the therapist or other trusted people in the patient's life. When this is brought into action the therapist is not required to actively dispute the particular idea, but suggest that if it is as good as the patient suggests, it will still be good after the time delay, but if it is not any limitations to the idea will be given time to surface. There is therefore 'nothing to lose' for the patient in complying with this rule and it is often the case that such delay is sufficient for destructive behaviours to be averted. It may well be important during the delay period to employ cognitive strategies such as 'testing the strength of the idea' identified in the chapter on cognitive techniques.

Sitting/Listening Targets

This approach is again more relevant to the prodromal stages of mania/hypomania than to the onset of low mood. In the prodromal stages of mania people tend to become increasingly active both behaviourally and cognitively. They experience an increasing number and frequency of ideas, in association often with increased verbosity, making listening to others and partaking in the turn-taking aspects of conversation very diffi-cult. Targets can therefore be set for the person to try to resist this impulse to overactivity at an early stage. When they notice that they are beginning to experience motor overactivity, the aim is to sit down and use the energy to focus their listening skills. It seems that this type of behavioural response taken early on in the prodromal phase can be helpful in reducing the escalation of overactivity and the fragmentation of social rhythms. It is, however, much less likely that this form of behavioural self-control is usable when mania has escalated through the prodromal phase; thus early detection is again a priority.

Stimulus Control

This technique is employed to help the patient to identify stimuli which are associated with risk of relapse. This is again most successfully attempted by means of guided discovery, in which the patient's own prior experience of the relationships between particular stimuli and relapse is extracted and used to generate a current list. Although there will of course be a large degree of individuality in such lists there are some things which are common to most and hence useful to look for:

(1) *Increased/excessive alcohol use.* Can be associated with mania or depression. One patient described alcohol as being an anaesthetic for depression and a source of energy in mania.

(2) *Excessive caffeine consumption.* Often part of a vicious circle of sleeplessness in mania or hypomania.

(3) *Risky behaviour*
   (a) *Street drugs.* The urge towards sensation seeking can lead to illicit drug use which would in more normal moods be out of character. Contact with friends who are in the habit of using street drugs can obviously be a risk factor associated with temptations to re-start drug use. In the cases of stimulants such as amphetamine, they can in themselves trigger a prodromal manic phase in vulnerable individuals.
   (b) *Sexual promiscuity.* In terms of stimulus control the issue is again one of identifying situations in which this behaviour is made more likely (alcohol, stress, visiting ex-lovers etc.) and setting targets to avoid them.

(4) *Financial controls.* Whilst most people with a manic-depressive diagnosis are usually capable of managing their own personal finances there is likely to be risk attached to their having unsupervised access to large sums of money, either in work or domestic situations, when in prodromal phase. Impulses towards gambling/investing/spending will be high at this time and such access will risk feeding the individual's sense of grandiosity. Their agreements to having financial controls during these stages are important and should ideally be agreed with the individual when well, to be implemented as there is agreement on the beginning of a prodromal phase.

Tim is a successful lawyer working for a large city legal firm. He has had two periods of hospitalisation due to mania but also recognises more frequent prodromal phases when his mood lifts to 'above normal' levels. When in these states he has in the past spent large sums of money on impulse. He states that at these times it seems foolish to wait for purchases, as 'nothing can go wrong', so that he would spend up to and beyond his credit limits on an array of credit cards and loan facilities for items which he had little interest in when his mood stabilised. A pattern was identified in which this increased spending tended to fuel his elevated mood which could then lead to further and more rash spending sprees. Of his own initiative he reported having signed over all access to credit cards to his wife to protect against this process and arranged for bank accounts to be in joint names so that he could not commit large sums to projects without reference to her. This appeared to work well in delaying acting on the initial impulse to spend and ensuring a shared approach to significant financial decisions.

(5) *Work stress.* Long hours, excessive pressure and extensive travel requirements can all be associated with onset of prodromal symptoms. It is therefore important that the individual acts to moderate these areas are far as is possible. Again it will often be the case that the 'thrill' of these pressures can lead to their being actively sought by that person, hence 'giving them up' will often involve a sense of loss. It can be important to work with the patient to analyse the extent to which exercising reasonable control does in fact often enhance work output and performance, Successful identification of this issue can allow the patient to derive reinforcement from work performance rather than focusing on 'busy-ness' as an indicator of success.

(6) *Physical context.* The streams of ideas and plans which accompany mania can be present to an extent in the pre-prodromal phases of the illness. The patient may well therefore have adapted their physical environment to collude with this process. Hence their bedroom may have become a place for sleep/work/listening to loud music so that the usual time for sleep may mark another period of 'stimulation'. As with the focus on sleep noted above, it can be important that changes are made to the physical environment which reinforce the regularising of routine. Thus 'bedroom is for sleep only' can be an important part of a sleep hygiene routine, leaving work and hobbies etc. physically outside this space.

(7) *Reduction of stimulation (interpersonal or environmental.* In prodromes of mania the control of external sources of stimulation can be important in the avoidance of full relapse. This might include staying indoors, not talking to people, listening to soothing music and focusing on yoga/relaxation or other idiosyncratic calming activities.

Safe Thrills

It is important that the implementation of behavioural techniques is associated with the gain of positive activities as well the supervision of other, sometimes pleasurable, activities which have been associated with pro-dromes in the past. Thus whilst the patient may be able to see the patterns of risk discussed above from their own history, as individuals they will often retain a need to experience challenge, and indeed the thrill of risk taking. A task during therapy can therefore be to identify ways in which such thrills may be obtained in a way which is not likely to constitute a sig-nificant risk. Thus engagement in sports pursuits, adventure games, com-puter simulations of racing flying etc., may all be ways in which the individual can experience some degree of thrill but within safe limits. Acknowledging the need for compromise in this area can be important in encouraging compliance with the general intervention. There is otherwise a significant risk that the patient will drop out of therapy and seek stimu-lation in a uncontrolled manner through the behaviours noted above to which substantial risk of relapse is attached.

MONITOR DURING THERAPY FOR OCCURRENCE OF BEHAVIOURAL INDICATORS OF PRODROMES

Reference to the information recorded in Mood and Activity Schedules can help to indicate when prodromal manic or depressed behaviour is beginning to develop. For mania this tends to be seen in increases in goal-directed behaviour, decreasing sleep, increased sociability and excitability or restlessness. For depression a behavioural pattern of withdrawal from people and activities, interrupted sleep, difficulty in getting out of bed and feeling of fatigue can be seen. As described in detail in the following chap-ter this information can be used to implement an action plan with both behavioural and cognitive components to help reinstate core activities and help reduce the likelihood of these prodromal symptoms developing into a full relapse.

CONCLUSIONS

This chapter has described the importance of activity schedules and mood monitoring in the cognitive behavioural approach to bipolar disorder. These forms are used as the basis for collaborative changes to structure and routines within the client's daily life to protect against excessive mood fluctuations. These changes include both restricting behaviour which can fuel prodromes, such as lack of sleep, excessive use of alcohol, and consis-tent overwork, and extending recreational and social activities where these have declined. Specific behavioural strategies for moderating the effects of depression (combating inactivity) and mania (combating hyper-activity/ impulsiveness) have been discussed. The overall behavioural element to the psychological treatment of people with bipolar illness is significant and applies to both poles of the disorder. These behavioural changes are facilitated by the client's own record sheets, which provide rapid feedback of the efficacy of changes in activity implemented after discussion between client and therapist. Changes made are not therefore imposed, but evolve out of the client's own descriptions of coping difficulties. Implementing these changes can thus be then viewed by the client as 'taking control' which can enhance the collaborative nature of further more cognitive interventions in later stages of treatment.

Chapter 10

SELF-MANAGEMENT AND COPING WITH PRODROMES

Self-management involves patients increasingly taking a more active role in controlling and managing their illness. In manic depression it involves developing a good routine, particularly a regular sleep-and-wake cycle, good coping strategies for stress and appropriate use of formal and informal networks. The idea of detecting and coping with prodromes is particularly important in self-management. It may arrest the progression from prodromal stages into full-blown episodes. Moreover, to actively control and manage manic depression, patients need to learn about the illness and have a collaborative partnership with the professionals. This enables patients to have an active role in deciding about what medical and professional input is appropriate at various times. Patients should be involved in making decisions about medication, particularly long-term prophylactic medication which may highlight many issues relating to suffering from a major psychiatric illness. Self-medication can also be an option at an early stage of an episode, in the hope of putting out the 'sparks' before they develop into a 'fire'. In addition to medication, patients need to actively monitor and regulate their mood via their cognition and behaviour. The cognitive behavioural techniques described in Chapters 8 and 9 are particularly useful skills for patients to acquire to maximise their taking control and managing their illness. Cognitive therapy sits comfortably with the idea of self-management. The ethos of cognitive therapy is to teach patients skills in order to enable them to manage their illness. Similar to self-management, the idea of monitoring and regulating is also a *sine qua non* of cognitive therapy.

Most of the ideas of self-management rely on good clinical sense. However, there are empirical studies on detecting and coping with bipolar prodromes that can guide clinical work in coping with bipolar prodromes. There are also special techniques in helping patients to systematically detect and cope with bipolar prodromes which have not been discussed in the previous two chapters on cognitive-behavioural techniques. Hence in this chapter, Detecting and Coping with Bipolar Prodromes forms the first main section. Other Areas of Self-management forms the second main section.

Before we go into the details of self-management, we would like to point out that self-management as a 'lifestyle' approach has been rightly advocated by many professionals and sufferers of manic depression. However, some aspects of self-management may sound very daunting. This is particularly the case at the early stage of the illness when most patients may find being diagnosed with a severe mental illness upsetting. Associated with this upset is the fear of the unknown. Patients may respond to this fear very differently. Some patients may be scared and want to be taken care of at the initial stage of the illness. Others may want to take control immediately and clinicians need to be sensitive about patients' fear or over-enthusiasm. At different times, patients may want to take more or less responsibility. Clinicians need to be sensitive to this and never preach self-management as a 'religious' principle.

DETECTING AND COPING WITH BIPOLAR PRODROMES

The word prodrome comes from the Greek word 'prodromos' which indicates the forerunner of an event. In medicine prodromes are defined as the early signs and symptoms that herald a full episode. Molnar et al. (1988) defined prodromes as the interval from the time that the first symptoms were recognised to the time when the symptoms reached maximum severity. Prodromes can be strikingly different to that of a full-blown episode or can be similar to the full-blown episode but of less intense quality. Many of the common bipolar prodromes such as not being interested in sleep, more goal-directed behaviour, loss of interest and worrying are similar to the symptoms of a full-blown mania or depression but are of less intensity.

Two methodological issues need to be considered in discussing bipolar prodromes. Firstly, the decision of where the prodromal phase ends and the full-blown illness begins can be difficult for an illness that may not entail a dramatic onset. Mania is less of a problem in that respect as often it is more acute. However, a depressive episode may gradually become worse over several weeks or months. The issue is further complicated by two clinical observations. As discussed above, some common bipolar prodromes can be quantitatively but not qualitatively different from the symptoms experienced in a full bipolar episode. They are similar to the full-blown episode but of less intensity. Some patients also never recover fully from an acute episode and suffer from residual symptoms. When there are residual symptoms and the prodromes are similar to symptoms of a full-blown episode but of less intensity, it is even harder in these circumstances to define when a prodromal stage becomes a full-blown episode. The second issue relates to whether a checklist-based interview or an open-ended interview should be used in the study of bipolar prodromes. Several studies of bipolar prodromes have been published. Some studies used a predetermined list of prodromes. Others just asked patients about their prodromes in an open interview. Examples of the former include Smith & Tarrier (1992), who used a 40-item checklist, and Altman et al. (1992) who used the British Psychiatric Rating Scale (BPRS). Examples of the latter include Joyce (1985), who rated patients' ability to describe in detail the sequence of development of their own symptoms, Molnar et al. (1988) and Lam & Wong (1997), who asked bipolar patients to report prodromes spontaneously. There are several potential disadvantages of using a predetermined list. A predetermined list may lack some of the more idiosyncratic 'relapse signatures of prodromes' and not measure all the changes in the cognitive, affective or behavioural aspects of a prodromal stage. Patients may also endorse prodromes indiscriminately. There is an increased risk of patients endorsing as prodromes items that are similar to a full-blown episode. Furthermore, most of the available scales such as the BPRS measure the general psychiatric symptoms which are not specific to bipolar illness. The advantage of a predetermined list is that it can be sent to patients to complete. An interview approach also demands more manpower and is more expensive. However, the open-ended interview approach allows subjects to report symptoms that are more prominent in their recall and can accommodate more individual differences. In the context of therapy, we advocate an open-ended recall approach so that patients can anchor their prodromes in a meaningful personal context. Targeting prodromes that can be recalled spontaneously and putting them in a personal context may make more sense to patients when therapists work with them to detect and cope with their prodromes constructively. Traditionally the detection and treatment of prodromal symptoms has been important in clinical medicine. We also advocate the early intervention at the prodromal stage in manic depression.

Working with Patients to Define their Patterns of Prodromes and Cope with Them

Clinically therapists can work with manic-depressive patients to map out their patterns of prodromes and work out coping strategies to tackle these prodromes. This is normally a task at a later stage of cognitive therapy when the patient's mood has been relatively stable and they are familiar with the cognitive model of emotional disorder. Furthermore, they are usually quite skilled in the application of cognitive-behavioural techniques to tackle symptoms.

To define the individual's pattern of prodromes, patients are asked from their experience what sort of things in their behaviour, thinking or mood may lead them to think they are going into either a manic or a depressive episode Patients are prompted to produce prodromes that map into the three domains of mood, cognition and behaviour. They are also asked to anchor their prodromes in a social context, e.g. in their social interaction with others and comments from other people. Then the patient puts the prodromes in the early, middle and late stage by a card-sorting technique (Perry, 1998). The therapist then discusses with the patient ways of coping with mania prodromes, using cognitive and behavioural techniques. The cognitive model of emotional disorder of how thinking, behaviour and mood can affect each other is used. Furthermore, the idea of avoiding stimulation, engaging in calming activities and prioritising are important elements. Medical appointments and self-medication can be seen as good coping strategies. In doing so, therapists rely on Socratic questioning and guided discovery rather than prescribing coping strategies. To illustrate the technique, one case example of mania prodromes and one case example of depression prodromes are described respectively in this chapter.

Mania Prodromes

Peter was a 35-year-old accountant. He had been suffering from manic depression since the age of 28 and had had three manic episodes, six hypomanic episodes and two major depressive episodes. Peter had to give up work six years ago because of his mood swings. He attempted to go back to work three years ago, and within a week he developed a manic episode. The manic and hypomanic episodes bothered him more as he found them more destructive. He was taking lithium and carbamazepine and still had major mood swings. In this session, the therapist systematically mapped out his manic prodromes. At the beginning of the session, he said he felt a bit speeded-up inside and more energised but his thoughts were not going fast and he was not overactive. He described his mood as a little higher than normal and he was not depressed.

TH: What are the early warnings for you that make you think you are going high?

PE: One of the first things is sleep pattern, not sleeping well. I will go to bed about 10.30 p.m. and sleep for about 2 hours and then I find it hard to go back to sleep. I generally do wake up during the night but I go back to sleep. I usually just get up to have a glass of water and then I will try to get back to bed. If I can't go back to sleep then it indicates maybe I am getting high. I then get racing thoughts about what I am going to do next. I will then try to suppress those thoughts again.

TH: So far I've got not being able to sleep and racing thoughts. What else makes you think that you may be going high?

PE: Lots and lots of energy, which is quite nice in its own way but it is another indicator to me that things are not right. And during the following day I might do lots and lots of housework. On occasions I went out and dug the garden completely and did lots of low physical exercise. I also get agitated.

TH: Anything else?

PE: That's all I can think of for the moment.

In the above excerpt of a therapy session, the patient mentioned sleep problems, increased energy and engaging in lots of goal-directed behaviour as prodromes of mania. However, generally patients are encouraged to anchor their prodromes in their social surroundings and social network in order to make the prodromes personally significant and easier to detect for them. For example, some patients may say their irritability will show with their spouses at a very early stage. The comments of other people on the patient's behaviour are also used to anchor the patient's prodromes.

TH: These are good descriptions of your behaviour and mood. What about the people around you? Can you pick up clues, either from their comments or from your interaction with them?

PE: My family will pick up my agitation first before I do normally. They'll say 'You are short-fused, not agreeable. You are in a bad mood.' But I've started to pick it up much better myself now. Well, that's a fairly recent thing.

TH: What sort of things do you pick up more recently?

PE: The fact that I am snappy with people. Quite often what will happen now is that I will be very non-understanding at my daughter and I'll be critical of her.

TH: Does it happen quite simultaneously? Do you get snappy with people first or do you get critical of your daughter first?

PE: Pretty much at the same time.

TH: O.K. you talked about how your family might make comments about you in a bad mood. Anything else that they might pick up?

PE: I think both my wife and my daughter might pick up that I am going high probably before I do. My wife will say that you are a bit speedy at the moment.

Having anchored the prodromes in an individualised and social context, the therapist and the patient then proceeded to map into the later stages of prodromes of mania:

TH: How else might it develop if it goes further?

PE: By then I usually take some medication to stop me going any further.

TH: How would it develop if you did not take medication?

PE: Things that might happen in the past were that I had taken my plans further. I actually got out and spent a lot of money on things which were actually quite useless. If I get any higher because I do not have any medication, I do not actually have any recollection, just vague things, not clear memories. Another thing is, I just remember now, that I get more gregarious. I would go out and talk to people, which is not quite appropriate.

TH: Anything else you could remember?

PE: I think the most significant thing is that I get into arguments with my wife and my daughter.

We follow Perry et al. (1999) in mapping out the early, middle and late prodromal stages. Each individual prodrome is written on a piece of paper. The patient is encouraged to sort the pile of paper into three groups: the early, middle and late stages. Most patients find it useful to sort the pile of paper first into early and late stages and the rest go into the middle stage. Then the patient is given the early warning form to write down their three phases of prodromes. The therapist and the patient then further fine tune the pattern of prodromes to make sure there is no ambiguity in wording. Mood states are carefully defined to make sure the patient knows exactly what they mean.

TH: O.K. Peter, I have got quite a few early warnings now. What I am going to do is to write them down, each one on a piece of paper. Go through each piece of paper and see if you think what I have written down is correct.

(Patient looked at the prodromes and agreed they were right.)

TH: What I want you to do is to sort them into three piles. The first pile is the really early warnings. The last pile is really late early warnings, as if you were almost manic. Then the rest go into the middle pile, the middle stage of early warning.

Peter then sorted the prodromes of mania into three piles. After the three prodromal stages are identified, the therapist then asks how much time the patient has before they progress to the next stage. In the case of Peter, his prodromal stage only lasts four or five days before he gets into a full-blown manic stage: one or two days before he moves from the early stages to the middle stage and two or three days before he moves from the middle stages to the last stage of prodrome. Peter's three stages of mania prodromes and the length of each stage are:

Stage 1: Early stage of mania prodrome (1 or 2 days)
• sleep for a couple of hours only;
• family said you are on a short fuse;
• get into argument with wife;
• wife saying I am a bit speedy;
• doing lots of chores;
• lots of energy.

Stage 2: Middle stage of mania prodrome (2 or 3 days)
• racing thoughts after a couple of hours of sleep;
• loads of low-level exercise (e.g. digging the garden);
• critical of my daughter;
• too talkative and gregarious;
• talk to people inappropriately;
• snappy with people (which is really me being aware of me being short-fused with people, rather than people saying it).

Stage 3: Late stage of mania prodrome (swings into a full-blown manic episode within a day.)
• spend a lot of money and buy a lot of useless things;
• racing thoughts in the daytime.

The late stage is almost a full-blown stage for most patients. However, it is important to distinguish it from the full-blown stage. Sometimes patients find the transition into the full-blown stage quite blurry and usually move from the late stage of mania prodrome to a full-blown mania within a day.

TH: In the late stage of early warning, you have two things. Spend a lot of money and racing thoughts during the day. How is the late stage different from when you are really manic?

PE: I think when I am really manic, it's almost as if I am losing track of reality; that is very scary. I remember one morning I was so argumentative with a perfect stranger I was almost getting into a fight.

TH: So everything from early warning is so intensified and you almost lose track of reality?

PE: There are things I have no recollections of and there are things I have half memories of. I remember one evening I went out for a walk when I was quite high. But I thought I would go out for a walk and it would help me sleep. I have this half recollection of getting into a conversation with these teenage girls but I have no real recollection of what transpired.

TH: What else?

PE: Really what I have written down and everything is intensified.

Coping with Early Stages of Mania Prodromes:

TH: We talked a bit about how thinking and behaviour can affect mood, how important, as it were, to rein ourselves in even if the temptation is there. As we discussed, the whole idea is to monitor and regulate. From your experience what can you do at the very early stage that may stop your mood from spiralling up?

PE: I think I can try and re-establish sleep rather than giving in to the thing and getting up. I found from past experience it's a mistake to say I am not able to sleep and so I might as well get up because I start doing things. It's almost that I start to stumble if I do that. So one thing I can do is to get up for a short time for 5 minutes and then get back to bed, rather than getting up to do something else. The business of thinking that I can't sleep I might as well be doing something is a dangerous road to go down, I found from experience.

TH: Why don't you write it down? Write down whatever makes sense to you.

PE: Go back to sleep.

TH: Does it make sense to you? Do you have to jot down a couple of words to remind yourself about what we said?

PE: It's fine. It is fairly well established now.

It is important to adhere to the principle of collaboration and to ask Socratic questions so that patients can come to a conclusion about what are the appropriate coping strategies. If therapists rely on persuasion or prescribing coping strategies, patients may find their sense of autonomy offended and hence reject therapists' suggestions. The following illustrate how the therapist tried to understand the patient's experience and perspective. Then both the therapist and the patient work together to work out how to cope with the prodrome of being argumentative.

TH: What else can you do at that stage?

PE: With regard to being argumentative, I can hold myself back, not saying anything.

TH: How has it worked for you?

PE: Sometimes it does, sometimes it doesn't.

TH: Is there another way of dealing with it?

PE: I can put some physical distance. But it is quite difficult because I actually feel quite good about being argumentative at that stage.

TH: What is so good about being argumentative? (Therapist trying to understand the patient's perspective.)

PE: I see it as being very assertive. Other people see it in a different light. I see it being assertive.

TH: Do you feel assertive when you are not in the early stage of mania?

PE: Not always.

TH: On the occasions you feel assertive in your normal run of life, is that different to how you feel about being assertive during the early stage of mania?

PE: Yes, I feel in control.

TE: So it is feeling assertive and in control. That is the feeling you look out for. Is that right?

PE: Yes, yes. It feels like I can't stop. I can find more fault and more fault, whereas if I am just being assertive in my normal run of life, I can stop and calm down. I never thought of that.

TE: What enables you to calm down in normal circumstances?

PE: When I am not high? I think it's because I can keep a sense of proportion about what's happening.

TH: How do you do that?

TH: What's going through your mind to keep it in proportion? What sort of questions do you ask yourself?

PE: It will be 'Is it such a big deal? Am I making a mountain out of a mole hill?'

TH: Do you ask yourself these questions when you are a bit high?

PE: I think if I do, I succeed in not being high. Sometimes I do. Sometimes I don't.

TH: So maybe if we can ask ourselves am I making a mountain out of a mole hill, that will help to check these feeling of continuing to find fault. Is that right?

PE: Yes.

TH: Can we write it down?

Similarly therapists should discuss the pros and cons of certain coping strategies in order to guide the patient to come to a conclusion about whether certain types of coping strategies are dysfunctional. It often works better if the patient can see the pros and cons and then decide on the most appropriate coping strategies.

PE: Having lots of energy and doing lots of chores is quite a positive thing really. I have used it in a positive way in the past.

TH: Are there disadvantages?

PE: In a way when I am doing it I get down a slippery slope. So what I tend to do is when I am high, I make a list of things I should do. And if I am high and doing lots, lots and lots, I try to put the brake on it. Maybe I can tell myself not to do quite so much and I can do something in between, for example, reading, which is quite a calming thing for me. So I am not letting it snowball.

TH: That's really good. How do you summarise it?

PE: Keep tasks in proportion.

TH: Sounds like you prioritise and you do whatever is necessary without snow-balling.

PE: I do but it is a very seductive thing, because I get through so much by let-ting myself go.

TH: Sure, but what's the drawback?

PE: It's hard to stop.

TH: So what are you saying?

PE: It's something about not letting the whole thing snowball and losing control of what you are doing.

TH: By?

PE: By not giving into these urges to keep going.

TH: Can you summarise?

PE:. Prioritise tasks and do calming activities as well.

Coping with the Middle Stage of Mania Prodromes

TH: Moving on to the middle stage, what can you do to prevent yourself from snowballing? You've got 2 or 3 days.

PE: I don't have any strategies for combating racing thoughts. In a way they are quite seductive. I quite like them.

TH: Sure, but they are part of the slippery slope.

PE: In the past, I tried to read or watch TV. Sometimes it works, other times it doesn't. Sometimes I read for half an hour and go back to sleep. Other times, I could not go back to sleep.

TH: If it does not work, what can you do?

PE: Reading is a distraction and it sometimes works. Watching TV is another form of distraction, but it does not work so well.

TH: You said that you sometimes take medication. What medication do you take and when do you take it?

PE: I take Largactil between stage 1 and 2.

TH: This is something you agree with your psychiatrist?

PE: Yes, I take Largactil and that restores my sleep.

TH: When you wake up and you can't go back to sleep, would you be able to take some Largactil? I think what you said is important. You are right that sleep is very important and it prevents you from going down a slippery slope. We are really talking about two or three days here.

PE: Yes but it takes a couple of hours to kick in. The problem is the first night. First night it takes a couple of hours for Largactil to kick in. But it's all right and I can take some the second night, just to be safe.

TH: Perhaps it is particularly important to take some the second night, particularly if the other prodromes are there. Is it all right to take Largactil the second night?

PE: Yes, just to be sure.

TH: What about tackling racing thoughts in the daytime?

PE: Daytime is easier. I can do some physical activities to distract myself. I only do a couple of hours so that it does not become an obsessive thing.

TH: Good.

PE: I can also make an effort not to get into too much conversation with people. But that's difficult. I really enjoy talking to people.

TH: So what is the consequence of engaging in conversation a lot? Is this part of the slippery slope?

PE: I think the problem arises when I am not high and I have to meet the same people; I have been over-familiar with them.

TH: So what can you do?

PE: Ideally not to do it but I find it difficult. One solution is not to go out in the first place.

TH: The idea is to cut out stimulation. Is that right?

PE: Yes.

TH: Why don't we write it down?

Coping with the Late Stage of Mania Prodrome

TH: The really late stage, what can you do?

PE: I would be taking medication during the day.

TH: At what point do you go to see a psychiatrist?

PE: When Largactil does not work.

TH: Is it too late? How accessible is your psychiatrist?

PE: I can ask for my psychiatrist's number. In the past when I went to the emergency clinic, that has not been very successful.

TH: That sounds a good idea. Would you feel comfortable to ring your psychiatrist for an appointment when you start your medication in the daytime?

PE: Yes. I can try.

Notice how Peter kept saying that he quite liked certain prodromes such as feeling argumentative and seeing it as being assertive, having lots of energy and doing lots of chores, racing thoughts. The therapist understood what Peter was saying but kept helping Peter to see the drawbacks by asking questions. By being collaborative and Socratic, the therapist avoided having disagreement with Peter. Figure 10.1 shows Peter's completed Coping with Mania Early Warning Form.

Depression Prodromes

As mentioned above, some patients could not detect depression prodromes spontaneously. Some patients even went as far as saying that with depression you wake up with it. However, manic-depressive patients can be trained to monitor their mood and detect depression prodromes. Fairly soon after therapy has begun, patients are taught how to monitor their mood daily and by using the scale of −10 to +10 for their mood states, they learn to mark out the boundaries of normal and abnormal mood swings. They also learn to relate their mood state to external events in order to

Name: Peter X

Stage 1: My very early warnings of mania are: (1 or 2 days)

1. Sleep for a couple of hours only
2. Family said you are on a short fuse
3. Get into argument with wife
4. Wife saying I am a bit speedy
5. Doing lots of chores
6. Lots of energy.

Action:

1. Try to get back to sleep
2. Ask myself 'Am I making a mountain out of a mole hill?'
3. Prioritise tasks and do calming activities as well
4. Resist the temptation to do too much, and make time to relax, eat, etc.

Stage 2: My middle stages of mania prodrome are (2 or 3 days)

1. Racing thoughts after a couple of hours of sleep
2. Loads of low-level exercise (e.g. digging the garden)
3. Critical of my daughter
4. Too talkative and gregarious (talk to people inappropriately)
5. Snappy with people (which is really me being aware of being short-fused with people, rather than people saying it).

Action

1. Take Largactil
2. Physical activities for specific time
3. Cut out stimulation, e.g. not being too gregarious.

Stage 3: My late stages of mania prodrome are (a full-blown mania within a day)

1. Racing thoughts in the daytime
2. Spend a lot of money and buy a lot of useless things

Action

1. Extra medication during the day time.
2. Contact consultant psychiatrist.

Figure 10.1   Coping with early warnings of mania form

explain their mood fluctuations. Furthermore they learn to moderate their moods by their thinking and behaviour. Therapists should also take every opportunity to map out the details of individual patterns of prodromes whenever patients get into a prodromal stage. The following is an example of the therapist and patient systematically mapping out her depression prodromes and working out detailed coping strategies.

Natalie was a 36-year-old doctor, working as a general practitioner. Her first diagnosed episode of depression was when she was 26. However, she thought she was depressed at 14. The first episode of mania was four weeks after she came out of a depressive episode. Since the age of 26, Natalie had four episodes of mania (one of which happened when she was not taking any medication) and eight episodes of severe depression. Unlike Peter, she was more bothered and disabled by her depression than by her mania. Lithium and antidepressants did not help as prophylaxis. Natalie was relatively stable in her mood when she had a session of working on detecting and coping with depression prodromes. Her score on the Beck Depression Inventory was six.

TH: What sort of things might make you think you are swinging into a depression?

NA: If I sleep more than normal.

TH: Can you quantify it? What is sleep more than normal?

NA: If I come home and go to bed.

TH: Straight away?

NA: Yes, or at the weekend if I sleep more than an hour during the day.

TH: The implication being you do go to bed in the daytime during the weekend?

NA: Yes. I normally catch up with my sleep during the weekend and that's permissible. But if I find myself in bed for 4 or 5 hours, something is wrong.

TH: O.K. Which one comes first, oversleeping during the weekend or going straight to bed when you get home?

NA: The weekend. Then your structure is less.

TH What else?

NA: The whole tone of things changes.

TH: Can you quantify it more?

NA: Everything seems grey and drab. Enterprises that are going quite reasonably flip and everything seems negative.

TH: Are these two things together or do they come separately?

NA: Pretty much together.

TH: What else might make you think you are slipping into a depression?

NA: I wake up early. I normally wake up at quarter to six. So I wake up at 4 or 5 and I think about things. And paradoxically it is harder to get up, even if you have been awake longer.

TH: And for that hour, what goes through your mind?

NA: You tend to think very negatively. You think you are being very constructive and thinking things through. In fact it all tends to spiral downwards.

TH: Can you say a bit more? How does it spiral downwards?

NA: Your thinking process sort of nose-dives. For example if you think I am going to buy a house, then you think about the houses you have seen and you have to get a mortgage. Then you think you are not going to get a mortgage because there are too many repairs. Therefore you cannot get a mortgage and therefore you'll never be able to move. Every step takes you down instead of along.

Some patients report a fairly idiosyncratic prodrome. Like the eliciting of mania prodromes, it is important to anchor them in a meaningful personal context. Patients suffering from manic depression can exhibit frightening psychotic symptoms earlier on and as the depression deepens, the psychotic experience becomes more and more bizarre.

TH: We talked about how everything becomes grey, you take yourself to bed more, your thinking becomes more negative. What else?

NA: If I am shopping, I see other people and think they are someone else. You then call and you realise they are not the person. It is frightening. If it happens I know it is a significant problem.

TH: You mean when you are well, you don't do that?

NA: No, never when I am well. It happened to me six or seven times now. And allied to that it is faces on the wall. The faces happens later.

TH: These are the faces on the wall at your hairdressers. Tell me about them again.

NA: My hairdressers, for reasons best known to themselves, have these three-dimensional faces plastered onto the wall. They are hideous at the best of time but if I am ill they are evil and alive. You have to keep watching them just in case they move.

TH: You mean they actually moved in front of your eyes?

NA: No I don't think so but you have to keep watching them just in case they move. It is very unsettling and last time I had to walk out because I could not hack it. You are scared and wearied all the time.

TH: What else?

NA: Dogs. My mother has this lovely pair of dogs, one of which, Pete, is a totally reasonable and lovely dog, except when I am ill. It looks evil when I am ill. It just looks at you, I interpret it as being a malevolent, evil sort of look and I can't be in the same room with him, poor creature. Oh, and cars. There is something about people in cars spying on you.

Similar to manic prodromes, it is important to anchor the symptoms into a meaningful interpersonal context. This has the advantage of working out how the significant people around the patient are sensitive to the patient's early mood changes. Furthermore, therapists can also get a sense of whether the patient can rely on and work with people around them for emotional and practical support.

TH: Now these are mostly subjective experiences, you wake up earlier full of negative thoughts, you sleep more during the day, misidentifying people, thinking that these three-dimensional faces may move and people in cars spy on you. What about people around you, do you pick up any clues from them?

NA: In what sense?

TH: In the sense that they spotted that you are not well and their responses to you sometimes are useful in gauging where you are at.

NA: Yes, the early signs nobody notices. When it gets later, I think people do notice, saying are you all right? I also asked a close colleague I trust and he said I just changed in three days.

TH: In what way?

NA: He said that he thought I was cross.

TH: What about people outside work? Would they comment?

NA: Yes, my Mum would. She asks if I am all right. If she notices I am avoiding Pete, she would know. Then she would suggest I go and see someone, a psychiatrist or my GP. It doesn't always get to that very late stage when I lie in bed 24 hours a day, not moving or eating much if I catch it early.

The therapist then asked Natalie to sort her prodromes into three piles as described above. They are:

Stage 1. Early stage of depression prodrome: (one week)

- sleep more than usual (more than 3 hours during the weekend or go straight to bed after work);
- people at work think I am cross;
- things change to grey and negative;
- slow down at work.

Stage 2: Middle stage of depression prodrome (about two weeks)

- misidentifying people when shopping;
- waking up at 4 a.m.;
- Pete (mother's dog) becomes evil and Mum notices me avoiding him;
- uneasy about driving because I find people on the road unfriendly.

Stage 3: Late stage of depression prodrome (about two weeks)

- early morning waking with nose-dive negative thoughts;
- misidentifying people at work;
- 3-D faces at hairdressers move;
- people in cars spying.

Natalie has a long depression prodromal stage. She has about one week before she moves from the very early stage to the middle stage, and about two weeks before she moves from the middle stage to the late stage of prodromal stage.

Coping with Depression Prodromes

Similar to the coping with mania prodromes, the patient and the therapist work collaboratively to develop a systemic plan of coping. Again the cognitive model of emotional disorder is used. The cognitive–behavioural techniques of routine, prioritising, pleasurable and mastery activities and challenging of negative thoughts have an important part in coping with depression prodromes. During the depression prodromal stage, activating the patient's social network for support is important for most patients. Like coping with mania prodromes, early medical consultation and self-medication with prior agreement from the prescribing doctor are seen as good coping. The therapist and the patient discuss every possible way of stopping the prodromal stage developing into a full-blown depressive episode, which can persist a long time and can be very resistant to treatment.

Coping with the early stage of depression prodromes

TH: I am pleased to hear that if you catch your depression early, you can somehow stop it from spiralling down. However, what I suggest is that we spend some time to explore how you may systematically cope with your early warnings at different stages. From our previous discussion, I remember you said routine was very important. You also said that when you were at university, there was no one and you were allowed to lie in bed. You became disorganised. Work is very important because it is an essential part of your routine. Two people you said were helpful: your Mum and Peter with whom you shared an office (your social network).

NA: I like that. Even though I sometimes manage to stop myself becoming depressed, I agree that there is a point in looking at how I cope systematically.

TH: At the early stage, what can you do to tackle the early stages of depression? One thing I heard was that routine business. Over the weekend, there isn't the routine and you said that you could easily have stayed in bed for three or four hours. How do you normally feel after you have done that?

NA: I feel distinctly cross with myself for having done so and I am usually pretty miserable at the same time because I haven't done things I should have done. I am usually more sluggish and slower for the rest of the day.

TH: It doesn't sound like you were refreshed after four hours in bed and you were cross with yourself for wasting time. Have you tried to tackle it in a different way? Sometimes with depressed patients, the more they do, the less tired they are. That's my experience of working with depressed patients. And it also links in with the idea that routine is very important for you. You might not kick yourself for wasting time if you do not stay in bed for hours.

NA: Yes, I agree.

TH: So what are we saying?

NA: It is difficult because when you are depressed, all you want is to curl up in bed. At that stage it is difficult to convince yourself what you actually want to do is to leap out of bed and mow the garden. But I can try it.

TH: What have you got to lose? I guess what we are talking about is trying to do things in different ways. Knowing how important it is to get things done, I guess it wouldn't help you to feel good about yourself if you just stayed in bed. You also don't get refreshed anyway. Are you with me?

NA: Yes I am. I can play the saxophone.

TH: What about routine, are there things you don't do when you are at that stage?

NA: Lots of things, cleaning, tidying, and especially weeding.

TH: I am again linking it back to your university days when you did not have a routine and you usually slid down. So I was wondering if there is anything you can do to help you structure the day.

NA: Yes it will be helpful to make a list. I am a very 'listy' sort of person. And lists are very good when you are running out of motivation and impetus. Have a list you can tick off. It gives a childish pleasure of ticking off. And so a list is good.

TH: What about using the activity schedule? Perhaps you can try using it to schedule your days so that you do not go from one extreme to the other. Maybe you can also schedule in pleasure activity too so that there is a balance of pleasure-orientated and achievement-orientated activities.

NA: Yes, I can walk Sam (her own dog) and play the saxophone.

Coping with the Middle Stage of Depression Prodromes:

TH: What about the middle stage of early warnings? Can we think of a way of coping with it that may stop you from going further down the depression road?

NA: I can do all we have discussed plus making sure that I take on less at work. I am in the habit of taking on more when I am slightly depressed. I think that I am not functioning very well and in order to avoid colleagues noticing it, I just put on a front and take on more. It becomes counter-productive. I usually end up regretting it.

TH: Good. What else?

NA. If I go shopping and thought I know someone (when I do not), I can stop myself from going up to the person I misidentify and greeting the person. It is better to wait for the person to come to me if it is indeed someone I know. I had gone as far as going up to speak to the person I misidentified a couple of times. I became very distressed and embarrassed when that happened. I definitely will take an extra pill, sulparide. It does not stop me from misidentifying people but I do not get too distressed.

In addition to using the patient's own resources in coping with the prodromal stage, social support can be very important in the coping with prodromes of depression. Most patients need some form of social support during this stage. However, the social support must be acceptable to the patient. Family and close friends may just be over-concerned and too worried for the patient when they pick up early prodromes. In these circumstances, patients may find them unhelpful. Generally it is a good idea to work out a plan of social support as illustrated in this case example.

TH: What else can you do about having some structure when you are more depressed?

NA: I will take on less at work and schedule in more pleasurable activities. But the weekend is difficult. There is not the normal 9 to 5 structure.

TH: What about social support over the weekend?

NA: I will need to go away at that stage. But I do not want people to panic and fuss about me.

TH: Who might these people be?

NA: I can stay with my friends in Dorset. But my mother would panic and start pestering me to go and see a doctor. In the past, my doctor in turn got panicky.

Making good use of hospital and professional help is part of the patient's coping strategy. In the case of Peter, he already has an agreement with his psychiatrist to take some extra medication if he is going high. It is very important for patients to have a mutually respectful and trusting relationship with their psychiatrists. Professional people can be drawn in at any stage. In the case of Natalie, who is very independent and headstrong, it is particularly important for her to have a good relationship with her psychiatrist and discuss what her needs are at the different stages of her illness.

Coping with the Late Stage of Depression Prodromes

TH: What about the very late stages?

NA: I would have to stop work. I simply cannot function at work and colleagues become very alarmed if I go in. I just become so slow and sometimes I give the impression that I am incoherent.

TH: What can you do about routine if you stop working altogether?

NA: By this stage of thinking people in cars are spying on me, I am very scared. I would be better off to be in hospital.

TH: I understand you had been very reluctant to go into a hospital and sometimes people had to threaten to bring you in under the Mental Health Act.

NA: Yes. I found going into hospital very difficult. The best thing is to have something in between, somewhere outside the hospital where I can feel safe.

TH: We do not have a day hospital in the community. What about going to the ward as a day patient?

NA: Yes, but it still has the connotation of going to a hospital. Besides, at that stage, I need a psychiatrist who does not panic.

TH: Having worked with you in therapy, I do think you would benefit from having a psychiatrist with whom you can form a mutually trusting and respecting relationship.

NA: Yes but where do you find them? Advertise that a shrink is wanted?

TH: I can hear your sentiment. But one doctor–patient relationship is very different from another.

NA: Yes, there are some good ones. I did find one or two good psychiatrists. But I had to change consultants because of changing jobs due to training in the past.

TH: Perhaps the best time to find a good psychiatrist is when you are relatively well.

NA: Yes, I think I would cope a lot better if I can find a good psychiatrist who does not panic and listens to me even when I am not too well. It would also be easier to accept help from someone I know and respect, particularly when I am not well.

The patient then agreed to start looking around for a psychiatrist she can trust. Figure 10.2 shows the completed Coping with Depression Prodromes Form by Natalie.

Problems in Identifying and Coping with Prodromes

As mentioned above, some bipolar patients find it hard to detect depression prodromes. This may be due to the insidious onset of bipolar depression. Some prodromes of depression are qualitatively the same as depressive symptoms but of a milder degree and some bipolar patients never recover completely from a depressive episode. Under these circumstances, it will make detection of depression prodromes particularly difficult. Other reasons for difficulties in detecting depression prodromes include attitudes to emotions and avoidance. Some patients were brought up to believe one should not dwell on bad emotions and patients who are very perfectionistic may find negative emotions unacceptable and try to dismiss how they feel. Patients whose coping strategies have been avoidance may be very skilful in avoiding/suppressing depression prodromes as a matter of habit.

In terms of coping, seeking social support may be a difficult coping strategy for some patients who feel very stigmatised about having the illness and hence find disclosing and asking for support difficult. Patients who are perfectionistic may fear rejection if they show signs of 'weakness' in asking for support. On the other hand, dependent patients may exhaust the good will of their network. Working out when is the appropriate time for social support is important for these patients. Moreover, finding a sympathetic psychiatrist may also be difficult. There should be a lot more about educating the medical profession about collaborative relationships in working with patients suffering from long-term illnesses and not being afraid to let patients take more responsibility when it is appropriate. This is important for general practitioner's training. A significant proportion of

Name: Natalie X

Stage 1: My very early warnings of depression are (one week)

1. Sleep more than usual (more than three hours during the weekend or go straight to bed after work)
2. People at work think I am cross
3. Things change to grey and negative
4. Slow down at work.

Action:

1. Taking tablets
2. Avoid going to bed
3. Prioritise and make list of chores and tick them off
4. Structure pleasurable activities, e.g. going away, walk my dog and play the saxophone.

Stage 2: My middle stage of early warnings of depression are (2 weeks)

1. Misidentifying people when shopping
2. Waking up at 4 a.m.
3. Pete (mother's dog) becomes evil and Mum notices me avoiding him uneasy about driving because I find people on the road unfriendly.

Action

1. Take extra pills
2. Take on less at work
3. Stay with friends for the weekend
4. Make sure I do pleasurable activities.

Stage 3: My late stage of early warnings of depression are (2 weeks)

1. Early morning waking with nose-dive negative thoughts
2. Misidentifying people at work
3. 3-D faces at hairdressers move
4. People in cars spying.

Action:

1. Stop work.
2. See a psychiatrist.
3. Attend a day hospital or get admitted.

Figure 10.2   Coping with early warnings of depression form

manic-depressive patients get their medication from their general practitioners. Like many aspects of therapy, detecting and coping with prodromes needs practice. Patients should be asked and helped to continually practise and update their repertoire. In many instances, the initial coping strategies may not be practicable, in which case therapists and patients need to work on new coping strategies together. Finally therapists need to be encouraging and understanding. Some patients are very scared of taking control themselves. In these circumstances, patience and good clinical judgement comes into play. Patients can be encouraged to take increasing responsibility for their illness.

Summary

The pattern of prodromes are different for different patients. An interview approach is advocated here as it accesses patients' recall of the most prominent prodromes for them. To maximise the detection of prodromes for individual patients, it is best to construct their own idiosyncratic prodromes and anchor them within the patients' social environment. A card-sorting technique is described in this chapter as a useful tool to help patients to map out systematically their prodromal stages into three phases: early, middle and late stages. Once this is done, patients and therapists work out together to identify coping strategies for the three phases, using cognitive–behavioural principles. The approach is very much a collaborative one. Both the resources within the individual and social supports are used to combat the prodromal signs and symptoms.

OTHER AREAS OF SELF-MANAGEMENT

In this section, only the general principles of self-management are discussed below under the various areas of self-management as the relevant cognitive and behavioural techniques have been described in the previous two chapters.

Forming a Good Routine

Clinicians have long noticed that a chaotic lifestyle can lead to more manic-depressive episodes. Regular sleep routine is also crucial. Clinically it has also been observed that patients can develop a hypomanic state from long-distance travelling or jet lag. Lack of sleep is a common precedent to developing early prodromes of hypomanic states. Hence therapists should help patients suffering from manic depression to form a good routine. Having a structured routine, regular eating and exercise can help to regulate sleeping patterns. The activity schedule can be a useful tool to help patients to monitor and structure their routine.

Maintaining structure and routine is particularly important during an episode. When patients are depressed, a graded approach is important. It is also important to teach patients to let themselves off the heat by having self-compassion and not blaming themselves for functioning at a low level. When patients are slightly high, they should do less and avoid further stimulation. In both cases, patients need to learn to prioritise in their routine. It may sound dull to have a regular routine and avoid stimulation. During a high period, patients need to rein themselves in when the temptation is to succumb to behaviour that seeks sensation. However, the general idea is that what seems like a good idea when slightly manic may not be such a good idea after all when the patient's mood is more stable. If the idea is still good a couple of weeks later, it is then a genuinely good idea. Regulating behaviour and avoiding the temptation of enjoying the experience of going high after months of depression is particularly hard. However, good self-management does not mean leading a life without any sparkle. It is a matter of finding a fine balance between excitement and over-stimulation that may lead to a relapse. When it works well, it means a balanced life style of work, rest and leisure.

Monitoring Mood

Many manic-depressive patients are anxious about any normal mood swings, thinking that they may be swinging into a depressive or manic episode. Hence teaching them how to discriminate prodromal stages from normal mood swing is important (+10 to –10 rating). However, mood is only one of the prodromal symptoms. As discussed below, in working out the individual's prodromes, patients need to look at a pattern of symptoms. Furthermore, relating normal mood swings to external events is a useful way of helping patients to make sense of their moods. Patients can be taught to use their activity schedules to relate events to their mood swings and to understand them. A patient very sensibly said that coming back from a skiing holiday and feeling happy for a couple of days is fine. However, if his mood keeps going up for the rest of the week without any obvious reason, this may mean he is slipping into a manic phase.

Learn from one's Past Experience to Eliminate or Cope with Stress

Patients can learn what kind of stress may have led to previous episodes. Stress happens to all of us and sometimes it may not be possible to eliminate or avoid it. However, patients should learn from experience the best way to cope with it. For example, one patient learned that going abroad is often a form of overstimulation for her. Besides she also finds travelling long distances involving losing sleep particularly difficult. She now has cut down the number of trips abroad and she only travels abroad for business meetings. However, she takes sleeping pills to ensure adequate rest and sleep abroad.

Set up a Good Professional Support Network

Professional help is seen as a resource that the patient can use. In order to be active in managing the illness, patients need to learn as much as possible about their illness. They are then empowered to have intelligent discussions with their psychiatrists or general practitioners and take an active role in making informed decisions. It may also mean having prior agreement with their prescribing doctors to self-medicate at an early stage of an episode. Patients can also actively decide the use of various professional services, including attending a day hospital or getting admission into the hospital to contain any acute crisis so that they do not have to face the often embarrassing or sometimes destructive behaviour during an acute relapse. If prior agreement can be made in the context of a trusting relationship, hospitalisation is often easier to accept when the patient becomes acutely ill. Hence, the relationship between the patient and the professional is one of mutual trust and mutual respect. Patients are encouraged to find a doctor to form such a relationship as in the case of Natalie described above. This aspect of self-management may sound daunting for some patients who are different in their willingness and ability to take control of their illness. Furthermore, patients' eagerness to take control may change from time to time in the context of a long-term illness. Clinicians need to be sensitive to this. However, the general principle is to work collaboratively as much as possible with the patients.

Build on a Good Social Network and Repair any Damage

When patients are well and stable, they should be encouraged to work on their close interpersonal relationships. Often their relationships with their spouses and partners suffer during an acute phase. Sometimes, they can be too friendly with people they are attracted to or even may go as far as having an affair. When they are well, they should be encouraged to repair or build up on their intimate relationships. Similarly, with non-intimate relationships, when patients are more of their 'usual' self, they should build up a supportive network.

Working on Countering the Long-term Vulnerability

Some patients invest heavily in one domain in their life and have their self-esteem coming exclusively from one aspect of their life. For example, some patients invest almost exclusively in their work or other achievement-orientated domains at the expense of their relationships with their spouse, family or friends. In some extreme cases, there may be very few pleasurable activities. Apart from being an unbalanced life style, it can be a problem when they need to engage more in pleasurable activities during the pro-dromal stage of depression. Another common temptation is for patients to make up for lost time because of previous episodes that may have inter-rupted their career, studies or other commitments. Some manic-depressive patients can be very driven and get into a vicious circle of having repeated episodes and working very hard when they are well. The self-imposed pressure can then become a potential trigger for subsequent episodes. Hence patients should be encouraged not to 'put all their eggs in one bas-ket'. For the achievement-orientated patients, they should be encouraged to cultivate other domains in their life, such as relationships or pleasurable activities, so that they do not invest so much in achieving at the expense of relationships or personal interests.

Take Positive Action to Minimise Further Stress when Recovering from an Episode

When patients have recovered from an acute episode, often there are steps to be taken to avoid stress which resulted from the acute episode mount-ing up. For example, extravagant and unnecessary items may be taken back to the shops or sold to alleviate financial problems. Likewise, a frank discussion with the bank manager to sort out a bank loan is often helpful so that debts do not get out of hand. Friends can be contacted again after a depressed episodes and hobbies can be recultivated too.

Summary

The general principles of self-management involve the patient finding out generally about the illness: how the illness has affected the patient; what sort of stress may serve as a trigger for an episode for the individual; having a good sleep routine; having a healthy life style including forming a good informal social network; and curbing excessive dysfunctional behaviour. Taking control and responsibility over the illness also means using the professional network intelligently. Forming a mutually trusting and respecting relationship with the prescribing doctor can be very help-ful. Every treatment step can then be discussed and in some cases self-medication may be a useful skill to acquire. All these tasks described above involve an element of self-monitoring and regulating. The cognitive–behavioural techniques described in the previous two chapters can be used to help patients to achieve some of the goals of good self-management.

Chapter 11

LONG-TERM ISSUES; MANIC DEPRESSION AND THE SELF

Anyone who has given an introductory lecture on the techniques of cognitive therapy more than once or twice has probably encountered the common question: 'What if the patient's negative thoughts are really true?' In other words, suppose that the patient's automatic thought is that he is not very good at his job and is going to be sacked, or that his wife is tired of him and wants to leave him, and this turns out to be, in fact, true. Of course cognitive-behavioural therapy has a great deal to offer patients in such situations. However, it remains the case that very often we must help our patients cope with their traumas and losses, rather than being able to remediate them. Our consumer society puts a tremendous emphasis on competition and success; those who 'fail' in competition, whether it be for honours, riches or a partner, may well feel that their lives are devalued in ways that those who are part of other, supposedly less 'developed' societies, do not. By the same token, it is common for those who are successful to wish to blame or devalue those who are not, thus compounding their problems (Lerner & Miller, 1978). For this reason, strategies for dealing with such long-term losses form a necessary part of the CBT approach to any form of serious mental illness, and to many other serious life problems as well (e.g. Moorey, 1996).

These issues are highlighted in the case of manic depression. It is a long-term, relapsing disorder, and nothing in the armamentarium of either medical or psychological treatment can offer a 'cure'. The sufferer will, almost of necessity, be set apart, to a greater or lesser extent, from others in ways that he or she may or may not be able to acknowledge. Thus questions of identity, and of the self, will probably be paramount in considering the sufferer's long-term adjustment to manic-depressive illness. This chapter will focus on some of these long-term issues. After first discussing the sense of self in general, we will consider five specific sets of issues. The issue of *stigma* results from the undoubted fact that anyone who acknowledges the diagnosis of any major mental illness is bound to encounter a certain amount of misunderstanding and prejudice, and may well meet with a variety of occupational and social barriers. The issue of *guilt and shame* focuses on the sufferer's own responsibility for events in the past and occasions when he or she has not managed the illness successfully. The issue of *loss* centres around the undoubted losses, of success, status, and relationship, and even of the sense of personal wholeness, that many sufferers have had to endure. Finally, *anger* and *avoidance* may represent responses to these three other emotions. These five reactions are of course interrelated, and all offer difficult therapeutic problems. We will offer some suggestions as to how to deal with them, but it would be presumptuous for anyone who has not had to undergo such experiences to suggest that he or she can offer easy solutions. As Shakespeare observed in Macbeth, 'In that the patient/Must minister to herself.'

THE SELF: DESCARTES IS ALIVE AND WELL

Some readers may have seen the recent film *The Madness of King George*. Nigel Hawthorne, playing the King, offered a brilliant portrayal of the sufferings of someone suffering from mental illness. It was interesting, therefore, to hear him explain in a radio interview that 'the King wasn't really mentally ill'. Hawthorne based this remark on the view, expressed in the film, that the King's symptoms were caused by porphyria: presumably anything with a 'physical' cause isn't really a 'mental' illness. This sounds like a modern version of Cartesian dualism: mind and body are two different things, and the mind is linked to an immaterial soul and can make free choices and accept moral responsibility. Presumably Descartes was just summarising the common opinion of his time, and of our time too. It is for this reason that mental illness is so threatening. Sufferers from a variety of mental illnesses often say, 'I wish I suffered from a physical illness; then people would understand.' By the same token, sufferers often report a change in sense of self: who is the 'real me', the badly behaved manic, the pessimistic and negative depressive, or the consumer of long-term medication, plagued by emotional flatness and side effects. Such thoughts may contribute to the fragile sense of self-esteem which we have often observed in manic-depressive patients. It is often observed that self-esteem is especially impaired during periods of depression, but it is our impression that self-esteem is often fragile in euthymic and manic states as well. Bentall and co-workers (French et al., 1996; Lyon et al., submitted for publication) offer interesting evidence that even in manic states, indirect tests of attributions and emotional functioning often resemble those of depressives rather than those of euthymic normals, giving some credence to the concept of 'manic defence,' which suggests that mania can be conceptualised as a defence against depressive thoughts.

There are perhaps three common ways by which bipolar sufferers may define themselves, all of which have their disadvantages. One is to deny the presence of illness. Especially in a manic state, the sufferer can simply describe that he or she is superior to others, possessed of special powers, and highly creative. It is also worth noting that, at times, the hypomanic state is characterised by a high level of creativity (Goodwin & Jamison, 1990, Chapter 14, Jamison, 1993). One of our team visited a colleague, who herself suffered from mood swings, to discuss a student's research proposal. As he sat in her office, he was amazed with the series of creative ideas that she generated: within 15 minutes she described a series of related studies that could easily have been the basis for a ten-year research project. All of these ideas were both highly original and eminently practical. The unfortunate follow-up to this interview was that when the project was completed, she was not able to act as a discussant because she was too depressed. But it must be acknowledged that in some elevated states patients do experience a variety of successes which they may be loath to part with. This may be especially true of artistic and literary creativity; Jamison (1993) offers extensive evidence for an association between bipolar disorder and a superior level of creative ability as a widely observed pattern.

A second approach may be to attribute one's problems to some external factor. For example, some patients find it easier to attribute their illness to alcohol or drug abuse, or even to the effects of their prescribed medication. Trauma or stress may also provide what are seen as more socially acceptable explanations. At times it may be helpful to accept the patient's preferred explanation and try to work within it, since it may play a useful role in defending self-esteem. However, this must be done with care, to avoid colluding with unhelpful explanatory models.

Janine was an intelligent woman with a university degree, but was plagued by the sense that her parents did not consider her to be as high an achiever as her brothers. After graduation she obtained a good job in her chosen profession, but lost it following a manic episode. She acknowledged that she had an illness, but focused on her belief that the health authority that had treated her at that time had mishandled her care, and that until she was able to prove this she would not be able to get 'justice' or to move on. Many of her therapy sessions were devoted to trying to deal with her anger over this poor treatment: unfortunately, this proved in the end to be an insuperable barrier to therapy, as she felt that any attempt at progress was a ploy to prevent her from gaining the vindication she deserved.

Finally, a wholehearted acceptance of a simplistic medical model may also have its disadvantages. On the one hand, it may be used as an explanation for bad or dysfunctional behaviours and an excuse for not taking responsibility. On the other hand, it may lead to excessive pessimism about one's possible accomplishments, or to the placing of excessive limits on the self, leading to depression and social isolation. Such a model could also be disempowering, since it could be interpreted as an exclusive emphasis on medication, with no role for changes in the individual's behaviour. In line with the concept of the 'normalising rationale' (Kingdon & Turkington, 1994), we would urge the eschewing of such black and white models of illness, and greater emphasis of the continuum between illness and so called 'normal' behaviour. We also might speculate about the benefits of such routines as emphasis on diet, regular exercise and healthy lifestyle. They may or may not help to control episodes or mania or depression, but we feel that they can play a valuable role in improving self-esteem and quality of life, at least in part because they help the sufferer to feel that there is something he or she can do about his or her illness, aside from simply following 'doctor's orders.'

STIGMA

As we have discussed in another context, there is considerable evidence that members of the general public have views of the mentally ill that can be described as 'stigmatising' (Hayward & Bright, 1997), and research has demonstrated that being labelled as mentally ill can lead to real problems in areas such as employment and housing (e.g. Farina & Felner, 1973; Page, 1977). Attempts to attack stigma on the societal level, for example through education, have had some successes (e.g. Wolff et al., 1996), but have also registered some spectacular failures, as in the famous study by Cumming and Cumming (1957), in which the population of a small Canadian town was so averse to receiving educational messages about mental illness that the researchers were forced to leave town. More relevant to our subject, there is evidence that the 'feeling' of being stigmatised can lead to depression and poorer functioning. An often cited study by Link (1987) found a correlation between greater belief in social stigma, increased demoralisation and poorer employment. Link inferred that feelings of stigmatisation lead to the other consequences, a point that can be debated. However, it would seem likely that awareness of social stigma should be demoralising in two ways. First, stigmatising beliefs on the part of others can interfere in the sufferer's life: for example, if one is applying for a job, should one inform the employer, who may be wary of employing someone who is 'disabled,' or should one keep it secret and risk being found out in a lie?

Confronted with such dilemmas, it would not be surprising if the sufferer became depressed. There is also the possibility of a more insidious effect: faced by prejudices and false beliefs, the sufferer may internalise the idea that he or she is defective, a person of less worth than others. Such responses would seem to be especially likely in an illness like manic depression, where sufferers often have a high degree of insight, and where periods of depression are likely to intensify self-doubt and self-criticism.

Monica is a woman in her late 30s. Her mother was a manic depressive and spent most of her later life in a long-stay mental hospital. She was raised in a series of foster homes and suffered both physical and sexual abuse. However, she did well in school, earning advanced secretarial and information processing qualifications. Earlier in her life, before being stabilised on lithium, she had several admissions to hospital, but she was very wary of revealing this to potential employers. When receiving psychological treatment for her illness, she insisted on receiving it late in the day, so that she could minimise her time off work, thus concealing her appointments from her employers.

Link et al. (1991) describe three possible strategies for dealing with stigma. These are secrecy (concealing the fact that one is a sufferer), withdrawal (avoiding situations in which the illness might be revealed) and education (explaining one's illness forthrightly to others). They devise a questionnaire to measure these 'stigma coping orientations', but argue that their results suggest all three strategies to be ineffective. Their conclusion, 'that labelling and stigma are "social problems", not "individual troubles" (p. 302), would seem to suggest that only a reform of social attitudes offers any hope for the sufferer, a belief that would seem to engender a sense of therapeutic nihilism. While admitting that the problem exists in a social context, it is our task as therapists to minimise the effects of stigma as best we can. We offer the following suggestions, referring the reader to Hayward and Bright (1997) for a somewhat fuller discussion of the whole issue of stigma:

(1) Certainly the existence of stigma should not be denied. We suggest a problem-solving approach: given the existence of stigma, what steps can be taken to minimize its effects in the life of the individual sufferer? The patient for whom this is a problem should be asked to offer specific examples of the effect of stigma in his or her life, for which specific approaches can be devised.

(2) In light of the above, a first step would be to assess each patient's specific stigmatising (and therefore self-denigrating) beliefs, using a

cognitive–behavioural approach to combating them. Issues to be addressed might include maladaptive views of cause, dangerousness, prognosis, or the degree to which an individual's efforts can ameliorate the effects of his or her illness. Behavioural tasks (see Chapter 9) should focus on challenging dysfunctional beliefs about manic depression. Such beliefs would presumably take the form of statements such as, 'I can't cope with ... because of my illness.' Graded task assignments could be used to increase positive interactions and improve social functioning. Such an approach, of course, targets feelings of stigmatisation rather than stigma itself. However, Desforges et al. (1991) suggests that steps promoting positive interactions between the sufferer and others should reduce both the sense of stigma and stigma itself.

(3)   We believe that the model of manic depression proposed in this book should be helpful in reducing stigma. A holistic conception of mental illness, incorporating both psychosocial and biological models, should offer patients a greater sense that there are steps that they can take to reduce the effects of illness, and also the effects of stigma. The development of self-management skills, and the building of a healthy lifestyle, with a focus on structuring the day and setting realistic priorities and goals, should help to build a sense of self-efficacy and personal worth (see Chapters 7 and 10).

(4)   This model avoids the idea of sharp demarcations between health and illness, emphasizing that they lie on a continuum. Eschewing sharp diagnostic divisions and thinking in terms of specific behaviours might be helpful, as it would undermine the notion of the mentally ill as a different group. Emphasis here would not be on applying a diagnostic label but on management of a particular set of problems —to engender a sense of self-efficacy and control, in line with newly developing models of mental health care (Kingdon & Turkington, 1994). If possible, goal setting should focus on behaviours that seem incompatible with a stigmatising conception of mental illness. Use can also be made of the 'continuum technique', in which patients are encouraged to see qualities as lying on a continuum rather than being represented by polar opposites (see Padesky, 1994; Greenberger & Padesky, 1995); this would entail thinking about 'degrees' of illness.

Melanie had a long history of both manic and depressive episodes; during her depressions she felt as if she was uniquely responsible for the misfortunes of others, such as members of her family. When she was relatively well she was still troubled by the sense that she would not be able to work and participate normally in society: thus, she felt like a burden on others. The use of the continuum technique (see above) was very helpful to her, as it helped her to see her illness as part of a continuum of functioning with many other sufferers, rather than seeing herself as a uniquely stigmatised person. She was also able to train as a welfare advisor, and in fact was able to work for a period of time for a disabled rights organisation, in a post reserved for people with disabilities. Unfortunately, recurrences of her illness prevented her from keeping her job, and her sense of herself as a burden on society remains an ongoing issue:

ME: It is so difficult, accepting the idea of having a mental illness.

TH: Why?

ME: For one thing, I feel so different from everyone else. And I feel that they also see me as different, as someone who could 'go off' at any time.

TH: How do you mean?

ME: They must see me as someone who can't be relied on. I feel that they're all watching me, waiting for me to do something bizarre.

TH: Why do you think they might feel that way?

ME: I've been in hospital twice. And both times it seemed to come out of the blue. They must think I'm completely unpredictable, that I can change completely from one day to the next.

TH: Has anyone said this to you?

ME: Well, no.

TH: Has anyone you know said anything about the onset of your illness, or the degree to which they can rely on you?

ME: Well, my sister did say that before I got ill last time, she felt that I had been under some strain.

TH: Has anyone complained about the fact that they can't rely on you?

ME: No. But I know that they can't.

TH: So on a scale of zero to 100, how reliable are you (he draws a continuum line)?

ME: Very low—5.

TH: So you only do what you say you will do 5 times out of 100?

ME: Well no. When I'm well I'm very reliable. But I certainly might get ill at any time.

TH: So, including both your well and ill periods, what percent of the time that you promise to do something do you actually do it?

ME: I suppose about 70% of the time.

Melanie was also asked to relate the reliability of many of her friends, and to look at the various problems and quirks that made them less than perfectly reliable. The issue of the degree to which her illness set her apart from others recurred throughout her therapy, as will be seen below.

Will (See Chapter 6) was 27 and worked in construction. He noted that during manic episodes he became very gregarious, while at other times he was shy and rather withdrawn, a feeling which he equated with feeling that he was different from others because of his diagnosis. He felt especially inhibited around his bosses. He was given the behavioural task of being more chatty to them on the job, and reported that this worked well and made him feel more confident.

Feelings of stigmatisation can also complicate problems of compliance with treatment. To agree to take medication, for example, is to accept that one is a member of a stigmatised group, that one is 'different' from others, that one must take extra steps in order to 'stay well', and patients may have similar feelings about the advice to abstain from certain recreational drugs. Patients may argue that their particular problems don't fit with the general diagnosis of manic depression, and, given the diversity of presentation of affective disorders, they may have some justification for this belief. The 'normalising rationale', combined with emphasis on the degree to which all individuals are vulnerable to stress, and reconstruing the use of medication as providing an extra 'protective layer' against stress, may be helpful. There is evidence that a package of cognitive-behavioural techniques can help in improving medication compliance (see Kemp et al. 1996a,b, 1998). The key point to emphasise here is that the patient does not have to accept any particular diagnosis, but only to decide, through trial and error if necessary, that continued use of medication promotes superior functioning. In line with this approach, the autonomy of the sufferer is supported.

Raisa, a 25 year old university student, told her therapist that she felt as if she was forced to take medication, since if she decided to stop it, her psychiatrist would be displeased and would not allow her to do so. Her therapist set her the task of discussing this with her psychiatrist, and he was in fact very willing to discuss the possibility, saying that he would of course advise her as to what he felt was best, but that the decision was hers. She described this to her therapist as a very liberating experience.

In addition to dealing with the issue of stigma as it relates to society as a whole, the issue may arise in terms of the sufferer's partner or family:

Will (see above) had been in the same relationship for two years. He noted that he and his girlfriend had different interests, and that at times he felt estranged from her. He also noted that whenever he did anything slightly unusual, perhaps being slightly more cheerful and chatty than usual, his girlfriend would say to him: 'Have you been taking your pills?' His perception of his girlfriend's question was that it was mainly motivated by the desire to avoid trouble rather than by genuine love and concern, and it is not surprising that during the course of the therapy he ended the relationship and entered into a new one with a woman whom he perceived to be more supportive.

In Will's case the outcome seems to have been benign. However, the problem might have been more difficult to resolve if the relationship had been more longstanding, or if he and his girlfriend had had children. In such cases the therapist may need to work on the client's perception of the partner or family; in some cases a session including the partner or family may be useful, but this should be considered carefully, since if the outcome is unhelpful, it may make the situation worse (see Chapter 12).

GUILT AND SHAME

Excessive and irrational guilt and shame are characteristic of a number of psychiatric conditions. It is, of course, often observed in depression: the moderately depressed patient may often be obsessed with seemingly minor faults or pieces of supposedly bad behaviour, while patients with psychotic depression may feel guilty because they feel responsible for events which are in fact completely outside their control, such as genocide or global warming. Those who have suffered trauma, such as transportation disasters or childhood abuse, often feel a sense of guilt and responsibility: perhaps they feel guilty for surviving when others did not, so called 'survivor guilt,' or perhaps they believe that they could have prevented the traumatic event. Shame is also very important in cases of abuse or sexual violation: the victim may not feel to blame, but may still feel tarnished and unworthy (see Gilbert, 1997). It is our belief that guilt and shame often play a part in the experience of manic depression.

Guilt is of course most common during the depressive phase of bipolar illness. Such guilt may commonly be focused on actions that took place in the manic state. It may be helpful to think of guilt and responsibility, in terms of a continuum: each of us may feel varying degrees of guilt and responsibility, depending or our state of mind. Thus, for example, all of us, at one time or another, may have littered in a public place or hurried past when a beggar has asked for money. In a depressed state the sense of guilt and responsibility are exaggerated: the depressed person may remember the time, years ago, when he threw away a candy wrapper, seeing in it a sign of his own deep selfishness and lack of civic feeling. In a manic state, this same sufferer might feel a blessed relief from such guilty feelings: 'I am so charming, clever and important that I am above such trivial worries. Besides, the council pays people to clean the street, and I am giving them work.' It is worth bearing in mind that each of us, at some time, may have felt something like the above. In this, as in so many other areas, the manic and depressive states represent exaggerations of normal thinking processes: pointing this out is part of what Kingdon and Turkington call the 'normalising rationale' (1994).

Excessive guilt may be attacked on two fronts. First, the standard cognitive challenge called the 'friend technique' can be employed (Gilbert, 1992). The sufferer can be asked how they would feel if someone else had performed the action in question. The depressed patient may then see that she is condemning herself for the action in question much more strongly than she would condemn another. The second challenge is a related one: the patient is asked about the utility of guilt. Socratic questioning is then used to suggest that a moderate amount of guilt, which discourages bad actions and promotes reparation when possible, is good, while excessive or disabling guilt is of no special social utility. Both excessive guilt and grandiose lack of remorse can be related to views of the self: the guilty depressive may feel less worthy or deserving than others, the grandiose patient more worthy or deserving. It can be suggested that a moderate amount of guilt is related to a model of self and others as equal members of society, while deferring to others can be attacked as putting someone (i.e. oneself) in a subordinate role. One discussion of this issue will of course not be sufficient to remove all excessive guilty beliefs: continual practice at challenging guilty thoughts, as well as behavioural experiments in assertiveness, will, in most cases, be necessary.

Shame and guilt may overlap, but they may also manifest themselves in different ways. Cognitions related to shame focus on being disgraced in the eyes of the other, either in the sense that others may know of one's actions, or that others would be repelled if they knew. A sense of shame grows out of feelings of stigmatisation: the patient can see the diagnosis of manic depression as a guilty secret, which must be hidden from the incomprehension and bigotry of 'normals'. Often sufferers will feel that their illness, as well as the episodes of difficult behaviour which it produces, are 'my own fault'.

Janine, mentioned above, was so angry at the health services in part because of a sense that she was responsible for her first breakdown. This breakdown occurred in the context of a relationship in which she had allowed herself to be exploited and of which she felt very ashamed; had she not been drawn into the relationship, the breakdown might have been avoided. Discussion of her feelings about this relationship proved to be somewhat helpful, but unfortunately did not defuse the anger described above.

Sandra presented a rather atypical case of manic depression, in that her first episode seems to have occurred in her late fifties. She had worked for many years as a clerical worker for a hospital, and believed that her illness had been precipitated by her own inflated opinion of her abilities and consequent tendency to overwork. When the therapist tried to explore the opposite possibility, that the overwork was due to the onset of illness, Sandra was very resistant. This might be conceptualised as a desire to assume blame because the other possibility, that she was not in control of her own behaviour, was unacceptable to her. Sandra found it difficult to work within the cognitive model because of a tendency to think in 'moral' terms: for example, she would often not do homeworks, having previously agreed them, because she said she felt 'rebellious'. She admitted that this had roots in her own childhood, in that her mother was very organised and strict, while her father was messy and self-indulgent. She enjoyed discussing these issues, but unfortunately these discussions did not seem to help her gain control of her illness.

During a depressive phase of her illness, Melanie (see above) stated that she believed that she was completely responsible for her illness, and therefore was to blame for all of its effects. A pie chart technique (see case example below) was used first to examine possible causes for other patients' illnesses, and a model involving genes, early experiences and current environmental factors was agreed. The therapist subsequently explored the extent to which this model could be applied to Melanie herself. Over several sessions this technique helped Melanie to see her illness as something explicable through natural causes, rather than something for which she was entirely to blame.

A difficult problem is presented by the situation in which the guilt has been generated by an action, generally performed in a manic state, which are, in fact, socially damaging or reprehensible. In some cases, the guilt may be about actions that have damaged the self.

Raymond (see Chapter 6) is in his late 40s. For many years his bipolar illness was well controlled by lithium, but he had to be taken off lithium following some kidney problems. He was put on carbamazepine, but in the months that followed he went high and ran up large debts on his credit cards, mostly for things like holidays and restaurant meals. He also borrowed a large sum of money from his sister. Now again well controlled on lithium, he feels guilty and embarrassed by his behaviour. He has been able to make steady progress in paying off all his debts, but this has forced him to live a restricted lifestyle. He has also cancelled all his credit cards, and written to the credit card companies saying that he does not want any further cards to be sent to him.

In dealing with guilt, the degree of damage to both self and others must be carefully assessed. Some actions, like Raymond's abuse of his credit cards, are only damaging to the self. Various actions which take place in a manic state are 'victimless crimes', only damaging to the sufferer. Examples of such acts might include excessive gambling, promiscuity, and drug abuse. In other cases, however, others, such as family or friends, may be damaged. Often family issues are of particular importance:

Gemma is a housewife who works part time in her GP's surgery as a receptionist. She had been dissatisfied with her marriage for a long time, finding her husband self-preoccupied and emotionally unresponsive, but had remained faithful to him. During a manic episode she had an affair with a neighbour which left her with a great sense of guilt. The therapist employed the 'pie chart' technique to address the degree to which she was responsible for what happened.

TH: (Draws a circle) Now, let's draw a pie chart representing the total responsibility for what happened. How much of this responsibility belongs to you?

GE: All of it.

TH: And Allen (the other man)? Does any of the responsibility belong to him?

GE: I don't think it does. It wouldn't have happened without me.

TH: Who first suggested that you should sleep together?

GE: Well, he did. But I had made it clear that I was willing.

TH: I see. Do you feel that he was also willing or that you compelled him in some way?

GE: (Pause) I didn't force him, I suppose. But I think I led him on.

TH: So you feel the responsibility was more yours than his

GE: Yes.

(Patient and Therapist negotiate and finally agree to allot 1/3 of the responsibility to Allen.)

GE: Does your husband have any of the responsibility?

(The husband's behaviour is discussed, and Gemma finally agrees that 1/6 of the responsibility belongs to him. The role of genetic factors leading to illness, stresses caused by others such as Gemma's mother-in-law, and poor management by the GP are also discussed and responsibility is allotted accordingly.)

In using this technique, the aim is not to totally exonerate the patient; Gemma was left with a portion of the responsibility, and discussion focused on why her actions might represent a poor choice under the circumstances and what she could learn from what happened. Discussion can also focus on the rights and wrongs of the particular action: why is it wrong, who is harmed by it, to what degree have they been harmed, is some form of restitution possible, and how does it compare in culpability with other wrong actions? Guilt is reframed as learning to recognise one's mistakes so as not to repeat them. These techniques, like the continuum, helps to challenge black-and-white thinking. Guilt that has not been discussed in this way is allowed to loom large, a vague, amorphous sense that one is totally in the wrong; discussions of degrees of guilt help to normalise it and put it in a context of many life choices, some of which have undoubtedly been wrong. The function of guilt can also be discussed: like a wise teacher, a guilty conscience is meant to guide us to better behaviour in the future without causing us so much suffering as to ruin the rest of our lives.

The example of Gemma also illustrates the role of shame in therapy. The therapist had a sense that there was something she was not telling him for several sessions before she finally revealed the truth. The therapist's calm and sympathetic acceptance of this admission helped to invalidate Gemma's feeling that what she had done was deeply shameful, as well as wrong. The basic role of the therapist as a warm, empathic listener was of course a key part of the therapy in this instance.

LOSS

As mentioned above, manic-depressive illness can result in a huge variety of losses. The loss of a job or limitations on one's possible employment are common, but there may be other losses: loss of a partner, the loss of contact with family or friends, or the loss of possible futures or attainments that are made very difficult or ruled out entirely by illness. As noted at the beginning of this chapter, no therapeutic approach can undo all these losses: rather, our goal must be to help patients adjust to their changed circumstances, rather in the way a bereaved person might adjust to the loss of a loved one (see Murray-Parkes, 1972).

Employment may provide a good example. The work that a person does has always been an important factor in determining his or her lifestyle and place in the world. It has been argued that the high level of stress for those in work, combined with unemployment and the low status of those out of work, promotes relapse of serious mental illness in our so called 'developed' world, with the result that the mentally ill in 'underdeveloped' countries may have a better prognosis (Warner, 1997). Certainly, suffering with bipolar illness puts one at risk of unemployment, not only because of stigma (see for example Farina and Felner, 1973), but also because the work environment may be too stressful and destabilising for some sufferers:

Monica (see above) was unwilling to come to sessions during working hours, but still lost her job due to conflicts at work. These were often related to angry outbursts on her part, which may or may not have been related to irritability brought on by her illness. Melanie was unable to keep her job because she found she did not have the energy to work full time. Raymond (see above) was relatively content in his driving job, especially since he noted that he had always enjoyed driving. He did note that his job was somewhat lower than others for which he was qualified, and also that he had been offered promotion more than once. He had decided, however, that the safest course was to remain in his current job rather than risk exacerbating his illness.

We have more than once seen patients for whom the loss of occupational opportunity followed the onset of manic-depressive illness. In some cases a standard CBT approach can be used, with the aim of combating negative cognitions regarding employability, combined with behavioural work on finding and securing suitable jobs.

Damon was a recently trained social worker who lost his first job following the onset of bipolar illness. Extensive cognitive work was necessary before he was willing to apply for another job. Following this, his therapist offered her advice and rehearsed coping strategies to use during his job interview. He was, in fact, able to obtain this job and return to work.

In some cases, however, this may not be an appropriate model, in that the ideal of returning to previous, possibly highly stressful, employment may not be practical. In such cases a model based on 'emotional processing' or 'guided mourning' may be more appropriate (see Murray-Parkes, 1972; Rachman, 1980; Pennebaker, 1993). Part of successful therapy may involve appropriate acknowledgement of the loss suffered by some patients, with the hope of promoting adjustment to their new situation (Moorey, 1996).

After a number of hospital admissions, Melanie (see above) was hired as an advice worker in an agency for the disabled. The job was part time, but she found it very difficult keep up with its demands. Ultimately she relapsed and was admitted to hospital. The job had been on a temporary contract, and her employers decided to readvertise it as a full-time post, a position which Melanie did not feel she would be able to hold down successfully. As a result, she again found herself unemployed:

ME: It's all so upsetting. I was so glad to be back at work; it made me feel like a real person, somebody valuable.

TH: And how do you feel now?

ME: Like a nobody. I just hate being back on Benefit. When I had to fill out those forms again, my heart just sank.

TH: Can you tell me why?

ME: When I got on the bus in the morning, I thought, 'I'm going to work! I've got a job!' It made me feel that I had a right to exist, that I was a real person.

TH: And now?

ME: Now I'm just a drain on other people.

TH: How do you feel about other people on Benefit?

ME: I know that they have a perfect right to the help; I helped lots of people with mental health problems to get their benefits. But I feel differently about myself. I'm so tired of being identified as a mental patient, of living in the mental health system. Then, for a little while, I had a real job, helping other people, but now I'm back where I started from.

TH: We talked before about you doing some volunteer work. What do you think about that?

ME: It just doesn't feel the same. When you're a volunteer, you're not really earning your keep.

In fact, the therapist did not feel that he could challenge Melanie's feelings of loss. Instead, the session proceeded to examine other possible courses which she could follow. She decided to seek other, part-time, work, but was also able to consider doing volunteer work as a stopgap, as well as taking a writing course. It seemed important at this point to validate Melanie's feelings of loss. This strategy is not always successful: in the case of Janine, discussed above, repeated discussions of her sense of loss regarding her job did little to help her to think about alternatives; many of the alternatives suggested to her were seen as 'not good enough' and not providing adequate replacements for her lost employment.

As these cases highlight, alternative, less taxing employment, perhaps affiliated to the mental health services, may be helpful to some patients but not be acceptable to others. Care must be taken in suggesting such employment, as some patients may find it demeaning.

The sufferer may experience losses in other areas of life besides employment. A long-term relationship may not survive the onset of illness, or a sufferer may become alienated from a friend or rejected by a group in which he or she used to be involved. Relationships entered into during the manic phase of the illness may in retrospect appear idealised, especially if the patient is still somewhat high.

Joanna is an unemployed woman in her mid 30s. She identifies herself as a poet: she was involved in writing groups and other projects, although her work had not been published commercially. She described to her therapist a man who was her 'ideal love' and with whom she had a 'spiritual relationship' based on the attunement of their auras; objectively, it appeared to the therapist that the man considered Joanna to be only an acquaintance. Fortunately in Joanna's case this preoccupation dissipated as her mood stabilised. Karla reported a powerful attachment to a previous therapist; she had ultimately pursued the therapist so avidly that she was banned from visiting the agency for which she worked. Subsequently Karla reported that she felt that this therapist was still in contact with her and was reaching out to her in some psychic way. She was very clear that a large part of her attachment to the therapist was her belief that they were in love with one another, and that this love would enable Karla to sort out her life problems. These ideas did not prove amenable to cognitive interventions, and the therapist contacted Karla's psychiatrist and suggested a possible increase in her medication.

From a larger perspective, in may be worth commenting that problems of loss become more difficult in a society that emphasises individual fulfilment as the primary goal of life. In other societies, with more emphasis on the family or group or on spiritual attainments, the sufferer may be able to focus on goals that lie outside the self. But the thought, 'You only get one chance in life and mine has turned out badly', may be a very difficult one to address in therapy.

ANGER

We have already mentioned issues of anger. Anger is an emotion which can sometimes, as in the case of Janine, cited above, constitute a serious block to progress in therapy. It can often be triggered by the feeling that one has been treated unjustly, perhaps by fate, but more often by specific people or social institutions. Janine felt that she had been deprived of a job she loved by poor medical treatment, a belief which, on the face of it, was certainly possible. In our experience, the first step to tackling such problems lies in securing the client's agreement that his or her anger is a problem which can be an appropriate focus for treatment.

Derrick had trained as an architect but never attained professional success. He had various plans of a somewhat grandiose nature, none of which had come to fruition. He had also been cautioned following an altercation he had with a female landlord: he felt that this woman had treated him badly, taken advantage of him, and stolen his possessions, some of which were necessary for the completion of his projects. He and his therapist agreed on a number of sessions for 'emotional processing' work (see Rachman, 1980; Pennebaker, 1993, 1997). During these sessions he went through his version of the altercation, explaining why he felt he was in the right. The therapist explored with him what had happened at each step and what lessons might be learned from what happened, as well as exploring what steps might be taken to remediate the situation. Derrick reported that he found this helpful: he felt more able to focus on future projects, and did not feel so inclined to brood about past events.

The reader is referred to Pennebaker's work for a helpful discussion of how to facilitate useful emotional processing. In a nutshell, it can be seen as similar to guided mourning or imaginal exposure work with PTSD patients (Richards & Rose, 1991; Foa et al., 1991). As with issues of loss, simply expressing negative emotions may not be enough to facilitate progress: the patient in some sense must take the decision to try to move on from hurtful past events. The therapist's role is to provide an empathic ear and to help the patient make sense of his or her own feelings. The references cited above support the efficacy of such an approach to a variety of examples of loss, with their associated forms of self-blame and anger. It is our experience that such an approach can be helpful in some cases: much depends on the willingness of the patient to 'step back from' the immediate experience and think about it.

The case of Monica, cited above, raises a second issue related to anger, the irritability often seen in manic states and the consequent clashes that may occur with friends, colleagues and loved ones. The reader is referred to Chapter 13 for a fuller discussion of this issue, as well as to Novaco's well-known work on anger management (Novaco, 1976). Novaco advocates use of CBT techniques to explore the roots of anger in particular situations, with the use of cue-controlled relaxation as a coping strategy. In our experience, this technique can be successful, but many angry patients can be unwilling to even enter into discussions about whether or not their anger is maladaptive.

AVOIDANCE

In our experience, avoidance, like anger, can often block progress in therapy. Such avoidance can often be a factor in maintaining maladaptive states. Janine's anger seems to have been fuelled partly by the fear that she would never be able to succeed to the same level as her brother. By remaining angry, she avoided having to test herself and her abilities, but the price she paid was to remain blocked and unable to move toward her goals. Avoidance may also play a role in depression: lowered motivation can help to maintain avoidance as well as providing a convenient rationale for failing to confront frightening situations. A variety of states can be maintained by avoidance.

Quentin was 55, and had worked for many years as a manager in the health service. His work was highly stressful, and a period of overwork seems to have triggered a manic episode. During this episode he chose to take early retirement. While in hospital he was very resistant to taking medication, as well as being very vocal in his complaints about the hospital and stirring up other patients to complain also. His therapist hypothesised that much of his resistance to 'coming down' was motivated by fear: having structured so much of his life around his job, he was very afraid that he would not be able to cope with retirement. This was in fact put to him at a ward round, and he admitted the truth of it. He finally agreed to take medication, and the treatment team agreed to offer him a package of support aimed at helping him to make the adjustment to his new lifestyle.

Cognitive behavioural therapy has well-established techniques for dealing with avoidance. A collaborative approach and the setting of reasonable goals are of course essential. Unfortunately, if avoidance is strong enough, and especially if it takes the form of dependence on alcohol or recreational drugs, it often presents a very difficult therapeutic problem.

CONCLUSIONS

Some of the case examples presented in this chapter are clearly less positive in their outcome than those described in other chapters. In large measure, this is because the clinical problems presented by long-term manic-depressive illness are complex. The illness can be a devastating one, and no therapy, no matter how skilful, can 'cure' all the problems it poses. In a larger sense, this is true of cognitive-behavioural therapy in general: if it is successful, the patient may cope much better with his or her problems, but a quick and permanent cure is seldom on offer. We also note that the case examples given could often be considered under more than one heading: feelings of stigma, loss and guilt often go together, and both anger and avoidance may be common responses to a variety of stressors. We hope that we have also pointed out the complex interactions between illness, treatment, and the social milieu in which both of them occur, and that we have offered some approaches which may prove helpful. Perhaps in the future effective treatments, both psychological and pharmacological, combined with educational work through the media and other means of mass communication, will help to modify negative social attitudes towards all types of psychological and psychiatric illness.

Chapter 12

FAMILY AND SOCIAL ASPECTS

INTRODUCTION

People exist in a wide social context. The person and the social environment constantly influence each other. Hence manic depression affects not just the patient but also people around them. Conversely people, particularly those close to the patient, can also influence how the illness may develop and how the patient may fare. There is evidence to support that the patient's social environment is important. The quality of relationships with key relatives as reflected in the ratings of expressed emotion (Miklowitz et al., 1988; Priebe et al., 1989) and affective style (Miklowitz, 1988) have been shown to predict the course of manic depression. A high expressed emotion family denotes critical, rejecting or over-involved attitudes or behaviour of relatives. A negative affective style connotes a critical, demanding or intrusive style of communication towards the patient. Patients from high expressed emotion families or families with a negative affective style tended to relapse significantly more frequently. Furthermore, the ratings of affective style (based on the occurrence and frequency of supportive statements, critical statements, guilt-inducing statements and neutral-intrusive statements) during a family discussion of two issues of conflicts also predicted the patient's social adjustment at follow up over 9 months (Miklowitz et al., 1988) and a year (O'Connell et al., 1991).

Expressed emotion is generally regarded as reflecting carers' best ability to cope (Lam, 1991). Relatives who are rated as high on expressed emotion tend to cope less well. Given that a good social environment has implication for the course of the illness, it is important to help the family to cope with the patient's illness in a more adaptive way. In order to help the patient's family to adjust to the illness effectively, it is important to have a good understanding of the family's stress and burden as a result of the illness. These include loss of income, hope and aspiration for the family. There are also illness-related behaviours that the family find difficult to deal with. The family may be confused about the patient's switching from one emotional state to the other and wonder who the real person is.

Moreover family members may also believe that patients have control over their mood and behaviour based on their mildly depressed or elated experience. Furthermore, the illness also shapes and alters the family's development. The effect on the patient's parenting ability and how children with a parent suffering from manic depression may be affected are often discussed in therapy. This chapter will cover the general burden on families and spouses, the effect of the illness on marriage, childcare, issues of independence and social support. The clinical implications of these issues will also be discussed.

GENERAL FAMILY BURDEN

Burden is defined as problems, difficulties or adverse events explicitly attributed to the illness (Gibbons et al., 1984). Bipolar illness may create burdens of a special nature due to its extreme swing of moods at both the manic and depressive end with periods of relative normality during which the sufferer's mood is relatively stable. Burden can be present during the acute phases and between episodes in bipolar illness. Manic phases are more public, and the expansive mood, increased goal-directed activities, increased pursuit of pleasurable activities, sexual over-arousal, irritability and grandiose ideas are more noticeable and have immediate and long-term consequences. Family, friends and colleagues may be offended due to the patient's impulsivity, apparent extravagance, grandiose ideas and irritability. During the depressed phase, patients can be withdrawn, indecisive, hopeless and suicidal. Recurrent severe depression may also hinder the sufferer's social functioning including work, intimate relationships and child care. The long-term burden associated with financial difficulties, child neglect, marital problems, infidelity, loss of status and fear of recurrence of the illness can be understood as a result of the impaired social functioning due to the acute phases and the recurrent nature of the illness. Furthermore 15% of first-degree relatives are at risk of developing manic depression compared with 2% to 3% of the general population. This is an added burden of families worrying about offspring inheriting the tendency to develop the illness.

Understanding the family's perspective of problematic symptoms or behaviour is critical to helping families cope more effectively with their sick relatives' illness. Yet the body of literature on empirical work on burdens and stress in bipolar patients' families is very small. Often the studies are of mixed diagnostic groups and the samples are small. For example, Fadden et al. (1987) reported significant burdens including restrictions in social and leisure activities, a fall in family income and a strain on marital relationships in spouses of chronically depressed patients. However, the sample consisted of only 24 subjects and only 8 subjects were bipolar patients. Mueser et al. (1996) compared the perceptions of relatives' report of burden with professionals' perception of family burden of schizophrenia and bipolar disorders. They asked professionals and relatives of schizophrenic and bipolar patients to rate 20 vignettes on 5-point Likert scales of how frequently the problem occurred and how much distress it caused. The authors reported that relatives of bipolar patients rated manic symptoms such as irritability, labile mood, overactivity, blaming others etc. as more distressing than relatives of schizophrenic patients. However, relatives of bipolar patients also found most positive symptoms (such as delusion, talking to self, noncompliance and strange behaviour) and negative symptoms (such as inactivity, avoiding people, poor social skills and poor follow through) equally burdensome compared to relatives of schizophrenic patients. Interestingly professionals made the false assumption that relatives of bipolar patients find manic symptoms more burdensome and relatives of schizophrenic patients find both positive and negative symptoms more burdensome. This study showed that professionals may not understand the true nature of burden in families of bipolar patients. Families may not just find the manic behaviour difficult to handle. Some of the negative symptoms that are characteristic of chronic depression and positive symptoms such as delusions and hallucinations during the acute bipolar episodes have an equal impact on relatives of bipolar patients.

It is important to bear in mind that families of manic-depressive patients are under a lot of stress and burden. They need emotional and practical support from time to time. Emotional support serves the function of making the individual feel valued and cared for. Practical support is often needed during times of difficulties when families may be overwhelmed by many practical problems. However, social support is possible only if relatives feel that they can disclose their problems to others. People who feel that they are looked down upon due to their problems do not disclose, hence preventing support from others around them who may be willing to help if they know about the problems. This is one of the reasons why a sense of general stigma and shame in the family needs to be tackled. From time to time, relatives may also need some form of support from professionals. Apart from emotional and practical support, informational support about the illness and affirmation by professionals that the family is doing their best to cope is often invaluable. There are also support groups run by the Manic Depressive Fellowship. Some families find knowing they are not the only people who are distressed and burdened helpful. Brainstorming and sharing solutions to similar problems may also be useful. Most relatives and patients have found these groups helpful. However, we have also come across those who are dissatisfied with these groups and find them upsetting. For those who find the groups overwhelming and unhelpful, support from the professional will have to be offered. Some relatives' level of distress and depression may reach a clinical level. In these circumstances, they should be referred for help in their own right. All these options should be available to families in a well-run service. Furthermore, in view of the high level of stress and burden in families, professionals should not take it for granted that families can necessarily be enlisted without feeling further burdened. Much sensitivity is needed when enlisting the family's help. Finally from the research findings of the importance of family environment such as expressed emotion, it is also a good idea to watch out for criticism from key relatives. Therapists may specifically target these symptoms so that there is less burden and criticism around, making the social environment more conducive to a good outcome.

EFFECT ON MARRIAGE AND COUPLE RELATIONSHIPS

The effect of manic depression on spouses' marital satisfaction is relatively unknown. During the two extreme mood states, different problems in the couple's relationship may emerge. For example during the manic phase, spouses may feel more tense and anxious and find patients' increased sexual drive hard to deal with. Likewise during the manic phase, spouses may find it hard to appreciate patients' sense of humour. They may feel that there is more disloyalty and less give and take from the patient. The impulsivity, intrusiveness and apparently unreasonable behaviour may lead to anger, criticism and eventual rejection. During the depressed phase, spouses may find it hard to please their partner. Spouses may feel the patient is more critical of them and they may find some of the vegetative symptoms difficult to understand. Hooley et al. (1987) found that spouses of schizophrenic and affective disordered patients who exhibited mainly negative symptoms (social isolation, depression, lack of emotion and impairment of routine or leisure time) reported lower levels of marital satisfaction, compared to patients who exhibited mainly positive symptoms. The authors speculated that the spouses' attributions of the patients' behaviour may be important. Negative symptoms (behavioural deficits) may easily be attributed to an unwillingness of the patient to engage in appropriate behaviour, whereas florid symptoms, by nature, are more easily construed as illness related or unintentional. However, in a study of 15 bipolar patients and their spouses, Janowsky et al. (1970) reported that spouses often believed that the manic phase was a wilful, spiteful act, while patients felt they were victims of the illness which was beyond their control. Some behaviour during the manic phase can be seen as arising out of maliciousness, selfishness and lack of consideration. This is particularly the case if manic patients have periods of apparent reasonableness when calm. Logical discussion can take place, promises are made and plans for working out problems are developed. Shortly afterwards, the patient may distort or ignore all plans and the spouse may feel betrayed and angry. Some patients then may attempt to out-talk the spouse and conflicts may ensue. Both studies illustrated the importance of the spouses' attribution of difficult behaviour. Overtly florid symptoms are by and large short-lived and easier to understand as a manifestation of the illness. However, certain negative symptoms and episodic hypomanic swings are more easily seen as under the patient's own volition and control.

John was a 40-year-old accountant. He had been married for 18 years and the illness started soon after the marriage. Since then he had had six episodes of mania/hypomania and three episodes of depression despite prophylactic medication. The manic/hypomanic episodes tended to last less than 2 weeks but the depressive episodes could be very lengthy, lasting up to 9 months. John managed to keep his illness to himself for 7 years and his wife, Jane, just did not understand these mood swings of 'highs and lows' until she listened to a radio programme about manic depression and realised the description applied very much to her husband. Jane found the depressed phases easier to handle. During his depression, John lost all his confidence and was very scared of failures. Jane handled these lengthy depressions well. She recognised John was a completely different person when he was depressed. She encouraged him and was able to talk to John about the unrealistic consequence of his 'apparent' mistakes at work or at home. She said that 'You just want to wrap him up and protect him. He is so vulnerable and needs nurturing.' However, Jane found John's hypomanic episodes very difficult: 'He is worse and becomes aggressive, selfish and interfering.' During a therapy session with Jane alone, she criticised how John was interfering with her routine and criticising her and their children over trivial things. What bothered her most was that there was no consistent effort from John to help look after the children. There were often discussions about how the child care should be shared out, particularly now that Jane had returned to work as a nurse. John agreed with Jane and pledged that he would do his best. However, later on, during the hypomanic phase, John could not keep to his side of the bargain. He was often unreliable in picking the children up from school or looking after them. When challenged, John always had other more important things in mind and became very defensive. Jane did not see his unreliability as due to John's subclinical mood swings and criticised him for being selfish and inconsiderate.

Therapists often have to deal with interpersonal issues including spouses' burden and distress. The perception about the marriage may be very different between the patient and the spouse. In a study of 19 bipolar patients and their healthy spouse by Targum et al. (1981), 53% of healthy spouses compared to 5% of bipolar patients indicated that they would not have married if they had known about bipolar illness before their marriage. Interestingly only 11% of the patients thought that their spouse would not marry them if they had known about the illness prior to marriage. Similarly, 43% of healthy spouses compared to 5% of patients indicated that they would not have children if they had known more about manic depression; 89% of patients compared with 47% of their spouses thought that mania should not deter people from having children.

Clinically we often observed hyper vigilance of the patient's mood swings by both the patient and the spouse. Sometimes, spouses may be very controlling because they are afraid of the patient's 'losing control' and becoming impulsive, leading to social and financial damage. Living with a spouse with bipolar illness also demands regular adjustment by the healthy spouse. There may be a role shift during an episode. During an episode, the healthy spouse may have to take on more household responsibility. Running a home means more than keeping the house clean and making sure meals are provided. Bills have to be paid and insurance policies have to be renewed on time. There are also day-to-day and major decisions that need to be made. The couple may be able to achieve more had it not been for a sick spouse. In both manic and depressed states, spouses may feel lonely even when the patient is around.

It may be necessary to have a couple of sessions with the spouse and the patient. It is important to make the purposes of these sessions clear for both the patient and the spouse. Prior consent from the patient is necessary and if sensitive or tricky issues are going to be raised, the patient's prior permission is essential. In any case, it may be polite to get the patient's view about what issues are to be disclosed. Therapists should not take it for granted that patients necessarily have no reservations about full disclosure. The purpose of these sessions is to enlist the spouse to help the patient to cope with the illness. The goals can be: educating the spouse about the illness, discussing how the couples may cope with the illness, facilitating the couple to agree or compromise on tricky issues such as hyper-vigilance. Sometimes the spouse can also help in refining the list the prodromes and the couple can agree what the spouse's role is in helping to identify early warnings and dealing with the prodromal stages. Some patients reported spontaneously that one of their ways of coping with the illness was to enlist their spouses' support. However, support from spouses may not always be welcomed or accepted. Some manic-depressive patients may find that the suggestion of going to see a doctor when slightly high offends their sense of autonomy. Our experience is that couples often work out accepted ways to signal that the partner suffering from manic depression may be relapsing and need extra help such as seeking an early medical appointment. Before working out the individual acceptable styles of communicating possible relapse, the patient needs to agree that such help is a good idea. Sometimes it takes several discussions before the patient agrees to it. Often in the end, the patient understands that the motive of the spouse is to help and to strive towards some common goals for the family. However, as mentioned above, manic episodes can be very damaging for the couple or the family relationship. The sessions suggested here should not be truncated couple therapy. If there are fundamental difficulties with the relationship, the couple should be referred to couple therapy.

Steve was a 36-year-old man and had been suffering from manic depression for the last ten years. Prior to the illness, he was working as a teacher and met his wife, Sally, when both of them were at college. Steve was older and he used to be the more dominant one in the couple's relationship. They had plans to spend a couple of years in London after they got married and then they would move out to the country and start a family. They got married after they finished their studies. However, Steve's illness started a year afterwards. He could not cope with the pressure at work and became manic. He had to give up his job. Since then there was another attempt at going back to work as a part-time supply teacher. However, he found the job too stimulating and could not resist taking on more and more tasks. He went back full-time by the end of the week and became manic. During these two manic episodes Steve also ran up quite a lot of credit card debts. The couple were disappointed. They had lost their plans and aspirations about the future. Sally was very scared about the manic episodes. She perceived Steve as being argumentative and over-active as sure signs of the manic episode happening again. She constantly watched out for any early signs of Steve being argumentative and doing too much. If there was any hint of disagreement or Steve doing too much, Sally nagged Steve to take extra medication and to get an early appointment to see his GP or psychiatrist. Steve resented this and often there were arguments about Sally's hyper-vigilance and over-controlling behaviour. Steve felt Sally used his illness to control him. The couple was seen over several sessions to help them to come to some compromise. Initially Sally was extremely angry with both Steve and the therapist for not understanding her point of view and threatened to storm out of the session. However, gradually the couple could communicate their disappointments and fears. Sally's anxiety was allayed somewhat by the couple going through the list of prodromes together and agreeing at what stage Sally could ask Steve whether they need to watch out, take extra medication or seek a doctor's appointment.

CHANGES IN LIBIDO

Sexual feelings and behaviour are among the most personal of experiences, and are often hard to discuss in a calm, value-free way. At the same time, both level of libido and sexual behaviour often change radically during episodes of both mania and depression, and can be used as diagnostic signs in both cases. Many of the same behavioural and cognitive techniques discussed in other chapters can be applied to dealing with changes in sexuality: for example, impulsiveness in sexual relations can be seen as similar to impulsiveness in the areas of spending or other forms of risk taking, while depressive guilt about lack of libido in a relationship might be seen as similar to guilt about other effects of depression. In these cases, the cognitive and behavioural techniques discussed in Chapters 8 and 9 can be applied. However, sexuality has an interpersonal dimension that is much more marked than with many other sorts of behaviour, which can raise some complex additional issues.

In a manic or hypomanic state libido can increase; in some cases this can be seen as desirable, especially if it lends additional pleasure to an established relationship. In fact, some research suggests that this is one aspect of the hypomanic or manic state that many patients value, and that it can be seen as beneficial to the marital relationship (Demers & Davis, 1971; Jamison et al., 1979). Problems are most likely to arise when increased libido leads the patient to engage in promiscuous and risky behaviour. As noted above, such incidents should be examined and their benefits and risks weighed, possibly leading to a discussion of some of the 'delay strategies' discussed in Chapter 8. A problem-solving approach which addresses the patient's perceptions of risk and risky behaviour may also be useful.

Delilah, an art student in her 20s, had an initial manic episode while doing her foundation course. This episode led to some increase in libido, which manifested itself in a student romance. However, the more marked effect was a great increase in confidence, including a belief that she was well able to calculate risks and protect herself. Following a conversation in a pub about art and music with three men, she accompanied them back to their flat. She was clear that she did not want to have a sexual encounter, but was persuaded to stay later and later and ultimately to stay the night. One of the men manipulated her into a situation in which it was very difficult for her to refuse to have sex with him, an experience which she found very disagreeable and which subsequently made her very angry, especially since the incident led to the breakup of her romantic involvement.

This incident raised a number of possible areas for intervention. First of all, it led to some discussion of Delilah's perceptions of risk; when in a hypomanic state, she tended to think of herself as strong and invulnerable, which led her to some unwise behaviours (e.g. walking around alone late at night in 'risky' areas of London). A second issue concerned her boyfriend, and whether or not she should talk to him about her illness; in the end she decided that she did not want to do this. The issue of her anger at the man who seduced her was also very important; it was suggested that she draft a letter to him, a procedure she found to be helpful, although she did not, in the end, send it. This also led to discussion of the 'injustice' of the limits placed on women's mobility and safety by sexual inequality, leading Delilah to consider taking a self-defence course.

When the patient is not in an established relationship, an increase in libido, leading, perhaps, to an increased number of casual sexual encounters, can still cause problems. Sometimes an impulsive sexual encounter or romantic adventure may also give rise to various interpersonal complications, particularly if the other party involved is still in the patient's social network. These complications may need to be addressed in therapy.

While in a manic state, Damon tended to become strongly attracted to particular women and seek to enter into relationships with them. When his mood dropped, he would often feel that he had made a mistake. If the woman in question had rejected him, he would feel that he was 'pathetic' and that he had made a fool of himself. Some cognitive work was done in this area. A normalising technique was used: it was pointed out that Damon's behaviour represented an intensification of the behaviour of 'falling in and out of love'. Damon felt particularly guilty regarding one woman, who lived on his housing estate. He had felt a powerful attraction for her when in a hypomanic state, but when he became depressed he underwent a violent reversal of feelings, so that he now felt embarrassed that he had ever been involved with her. She clearly liked him and was hurt and disappointed when he began to avoid her. Various strategies, such as continuing to avoid her without giving an explanation or writing her a letter, were discussed, but it was finally agreed that he should offer to meet with her and talk about his feelings. Through role play he and the therapist explored what he would say to her. In the end, they did meet, and Damon was pleased with how the interaction went. In fact, they were able to become friends, an outcome which Damon felt very good about.

In a committed relationship, increased libido can at times be positive for both partners. Problems arise, however, if the increased libido is directed, not at one's partner, but at a third party. As illustrated in the case of Delilah, above, a sexual indiscretion can disrupt any relationship. A partner might be more accepting of infidelity if he or she attributed it to illness rather than choice (e.g. see Janowsky et al., 1970; Hooley et al., 1987), but even the most understanding partner is likely to feel a sense of betrayal. This may be exacerbated by the thought of the many difficulties that often come with being in a relationship with a sufferer, including possibly periods of little sexual activity during depressions: the partner may feel, 'I've had to put up with all this, and now, he/she is unfaithful to me!' Such issues are bound to complicate therapy, and may provide a stimulus for joint sessions. If the partner does not know about the infidelity, this may pose a dilemma for the therapist. The decision of whether to confess infidelity to the patient's spouse or partner is always a tricky one. Here, therapists can only help the patient to make a well-thought-out decision. At no point should the therapist impose his or her own values onto the matter.

We have already discussed Gemma's guilt over an extramarital affair (See Chapter 11). Even though she had remained faithful to her husband prior to that affair, she had felt for a long time that he was self-absorbed and made no effort to understand or support her. Their sexual relations were infrequent and unsatisfying to her. Her husband was unaware of her infidelity, and at times she felt guilty about this, feeling that she owed it to him to tell him, but being afraid of the complications that would follow. The therapist explored the pros and cons of different options, including suggesting that her affair as conveying a message about the state of her marriage as unsatisfactory and that something needed to be done about it. The therapist explored the possibility of marital or sexual therapy for the couple, but Gemma rejected this, saying that things had been too bad for too long, and that she did not think she could ever come to find her husband to be desirable. She felt some guilt about this, which provided a focus for a cognitive intervention. In the end, she and the therapist formulated the idea of her marriage as a 'working partnership'; she would choose to stay with her husband and be faithful to him, and problem-solving methods would be used to help them get along better. A couple of joint therapy sessions were used to explore ways of making the relationship less conflictual and of finding joint activities that they might enjoy. Although neither husband nor wife was really satisfied with the marital relationship, they agreed that the intervention of the therapist had been somewhat helpful. Gemma in the end chose not to tell her husband of her affair.

We report these case examples to illustrate the complexity of the sort of problems that changes in libido can produce. As with the marital issues discussed above, the decision to involve partners in therapy should be considered with care, and will be indicated in some cases and not others. In some cases, the patient may not perceive such behaviour as problematic, and the therapist may need to think in terms of harm minimisation, in the form of practical strategies to decrease the risk of sexually transmitted diseases or criminal victimisation.

CARING FOR CHILDREN

The raising of children is one of the most complex tasks that any human being can undertake, so it is not surprising that episodes of mania, hypomania and depression can also disrupt child care. Goodwin and Jamison (1990) review a number of studies that illustrate this point, although it is interesting to note that one study found unipolar depression to be more disruptive than bipolar disorder (Anderson & Hammen, 1993). Some studies suggest that the presence of another parent can have an important role in mitigating these effects (Radke-Yarrow et al., 1985). It is interesting that one small study of a group of children with manic-depressive mothers found that more than 50% of the manic patients were married to sufferers from unipolar depression (Zahn-Waxler et al., 1988); presumably some assortative mating was operating, although this might also reflect the strains of living with a manic-depressive partner.

Thus, the effects of bipolar illness on child raising are likely to be diverse. In some cases, where the illness is well controlled, there may be little apparent effect, while in other cases involving extremes of mania and depression, the children may be put at risk. In the therapeutic setting one is not likely to have to deal with either of these extremes: in the former cases because there are few problems which need addressing, and in the latter because the patient will be too ill to attend. Instead, we would like to consider some possible intermediate cases and offer suggestions about their management.

In the case of relatively mild mood changes, the effects of parent–child interaction may be small and relatively benign. In some cases, the high spirits and creativity which can appear in a mildly hypomanic state may lead to interesting and beneficial interactions, such as an interesting family outing or the creation of a creative pastime. In states of mild depression, the parent may still be fully capable of fulfilling his or her role, though with reduced pleasure. In somewhat more extreme cases, it may be suitable to apply the problem-solving or anti-impulsiveness techniques described in Chapter 8. The hypomanic parent may need to stop, consider, and perhaps check with someone else before instituting that new, creative, child-raising idea. In both hypomania and depression, irritability may also be a problem: anger-control strategies, perhaps involving the use of relaxation, may be appropriate. If a parent is troubled with excessive guilt, cognitive challenges may be used: obviously there is no perfect parent, and it might be argued that the ability of children to learn about and accept their parent's imperfections is a necessary part of maturation. In such cases, it may also be worth exploring what age-appropriate explanation can be given to the child for Mummy's or Daddy's periods of out-of-character behaviour.

Naomi was the mother of two children, aged 10 and 3. During a hypomanic episode she suddenly decided to take both of them to the zoo. This involved a long journey by train and underground, which Naomi did not plan with sufficient care. In the end, she ran out of money, and was not able to pay for the journey home. As a result, her children had a wait at the zoo before their father could come to bring the family home, leading to misbehaviour on the part of the children, an angry outburst by Naomi, and a row between her and her husband. Naomi subsequently became depressed and spent considerable time brooding about this incident, feeling that it showed her to be a bad and inconsiderate mother. At the same time, she was angry at her husband, whom she felt to be unempathic and critical. This incident was the focus of considerable work in therapy. In the first instance, the therapist helped her to reattribute her behaviour to illness: her impulsive outing and irritable behaviour were discussed as prodromal signs of elevated mood, and the incident was discussed as a learning experience. Naomi agreed to discuss any future unusual family activities with her husband, who was invited to a session which focused on his attitude towards Naomi's illness, and which both partners described as helpful. Naomi was also advised to discuss the incident with the older child, who was told that Mummy hadn't been feeling well, and so had been absent minded. This child was also given the task of reminding her mother about key things to bring on an outing (e.g. keys, money, credit cards); this made the child feel more mature and helpful, and was seen as a useful learning experience.

With somewhat older children, and especially in the case of a long history with many episodes and considerable disability, it is not unusual for one child to fall into the role of substitute parent or carer, with responsibility for the parent and/or younger siblings. If this child is old enough, he (or, in our experience, more usually she) may be able to take part in a family session, bringing up his or her own issues. In such cases, the parent may feel considerable guilt, feeling that the child has been deprived of a childhood. A problem-solving approach may be useful here: feeling guilty may be less useful than finding ways of supporting this 'parentified' child and allowing her more time to live her own life. As with spouses, the attribution that the parent is choosing to be difficult and changeable will produce a different reaction to the feeling that the parent is ill and cannot help his or her behaviour: this point may provide a useful focus for family work.

In more severe cases, thought needs to be given to support when a parent is not coping. Family, friends, or, in some cases, the social services, may be enlisted and made aware of likely prodromes, and occasions when additional or alternative care may be needed. This may represent a parent's worst nightmare: a mother, for example, may believe that she must not admit to any illness because 'the social worker' is waiting in the wings to snatch her child. Liaison with social services and a care plan which specifies, not only when the child may need care, but also when that care can be terminated, can be reassuring.

Corinne was a woman of 27 with a small baby. During an episode of depression her husband had great difficulties in organising child care, because he was afraid that taking too much time off work would jeopardise his job. Subsequently, Corinne was haunted by the fear that she might 'lose her child', and that this would show her to be a bad mother. It emerged that her fears regarding her parenting skills were of long standing, but that in fact she was performing much better in the role than she thought she was. She was given a homework assignment to discuss these matters with her husband, and subsequently also with her mother. Her mother agreed to help out in future emergencies, and she and her husband discussed options for organising their daughter's care. Corinne later reported that this matter of fact discussion of parenting problems had helped her to get a better perspective on her own role as a parent.

A final possibility must be mentioned: there are certainly cases in which bipolar illness has led to the complete estrangement of parent and child. In the last chapter we discussed the issue of loss, and what loss could be more severe than the loss of a child? In extreme cases, the parent may have harmed the child in the course of an episode of illness, or the child may have been taken into care or adopted because of prolonged incapacity on the part of the parent. At times this may turn to anger: we have known of a case of a mother who attempted to murder an estranged child, perhaps feeling slighted by that child's behaviour. The alternative may be a sense of profound and irremediable loss: as noted in the previous chapter, there are some loses which it would be presumptuous for any therapist to feel that he or she could 'put right'. In such cases, a sympathetic and informed understanding of the feelings of the patient is all the therapist can offer.

Bella was a woman in her 40s who had suffered a long period of uncontrolled bipolar illness and been homeless for a considerable period of time. More recently she had been living in a hostel and had a more regular life with the help of lithium. However, she still had periods of heavy drinking, during which she was tempted to harm herself. She revealed that her level of functioning had declined fifteen years ago, because she had been persuaded to put her child up for adoption. She had been managing to make a home for her child and herself, but a social worker suggested to her that her child could have a better and more successful life if she was adopted by well off, stable parents. After much hesitation she decided to do this for her child's sake, but she subsequently felt both depressed and guilty. When seen in therapy she stated that she was waiting for her child's 18th birthday, and that if her child did not attempt to contact her within a reasonable period of time after that, she would probably kill herself. She discussed all these issues with her therapist and told him that this discussion had been helpful, but that her child was so important to her that she felt she would not be able to carry on in the long run without some kind of contact.

ISSUES RELATED TO TRANSITION INTO ADULTHOOD

So far we have discussed the ways in which bipolar illness can disrupt the marital relationship and interfere with the sufferer's performance as a parent. But it can also interfere with normal family processes during late adolescence and early adulthood. The first onset of bipolar illness often occurs in the late teens and early 20s (Goodwin & Jamison, 1990); Weissman et al. (1988) found a median age of onset for bipolar I disorder of 18, an age critical to one's assertion of autonomy and independence. During the transitional years between childhood and adulthood, the adolescent is expected to show gradually increasing independence, to pick up, one by one, the various tasks and roles of adulthood, including job, independent living, mature sexual relationships, etc. Bipolar illness can prolong or, in some cases, prevent this transition. This can lead to an enmeshed family system, in which the child remains in a childish role well into adulthood, as well as to critical comments and family pressure. Our experience with bipolar patients is that they often manage to leave their parental home. Hence our approach does not emphasise family work. However, some patients may not have full independence from their parents even though they are not living at home. In these cases, family issues relating to separation and independence often need to be addressed in sessions. Some parents may be critical and hostile, blaming the patient for becoming ill or being personally offended by behaviour that occurred during episodes of elated mood. Other parents may be overprotective, involving themselves in every aspect of the patient's life, so that he or she is prevented from becoming fully adult.

June always remembered her parents as very protective of her; when she was young, for example, they never put any pressure on her to achieve at school, and would always write sick notes for her if she wanted to take a day off. Her first manic episode occurred at 16, when she was away at college, and she was forced to come home. A period of depression followed, and she had another manic episode at 18. When she entered therapy at the age of 21 she was living away from home in London and working. Her parents were living in the country, but she felt that both of them, and especially her father, continued to exercise a great deal of control over her and did not treat her like an adult. Her father would telephone her twice a week and insist on discussing all her major life decisions with her; she believed that this was because her parents considered her to be 'delicate' and did not feel that she was capable of functioning as an adult.

With the help of her therapist, who discussed with her what she wanted to say to her parents and rehearsed it with her using role play, June was able to talk about these issues with her parents during a visit home. Her mother admitted to her that it was very difficult to stop trying to look after her because she had been so ill just when she was leaving home, while her father continued to maintain that she needed to be protected from stress and responsibility. However, her parents did agree that they would limit their calls to once a week, with June making the calls on alternative weeks. Her parents also said that they would try not to intrude into her life, and that June had the right to speak up if she felt that they were intruding. This compromise seemed to please both June and her parents, with June subsequently reporting that her relationship with her parents had improved as a result.

SOCIAL SUPPORT

We have explored some of the complex family burdens and family dynamics that can arise as a result of bipolar illness. We believe that helping families to cope with such burdens and dynamics can have important implications for management and relapse prevention, and that they need to be explored in therapy. Furthermore, families can also provide social support for patients. It has been found generally that people with greater social support are of better mental health and are at a lower risk of psychological problems. Social support serves the important function of enabling patients to believe that they are cared for and loved; esteemed and valued. It also provides the social context in which the patient belongs to a network of mutual respect and obligation. Living in a family where practical and emotional support are readily available may also reduce the likelihood of adversity. In the context of chronic illness such as manic depression, motivational support is important to maintain hope and to sustain a belief in a chosen course of action such as a regulated but not restricted lifestyle and taking long-term prophylactic medication.

There are a variety of ways social support can be utilised for manic-depressive patients. Support during a depressive phase is important as family members and friends can help to provide social company, structure and routine. Emotional support can mean offering a sympathetic ear and injecting some reality into the patient's negative and pessimistic world. During the manic phase, social support can mean gently encouraging the patient to cut out stimulation, engaging in calming activities with the patient and helping the patient to be realistic and to prioritise. On a more practical level, the patient may make prior arrangement to surrender their credit cards and cheque books to their trusted one in order to minimise future financial hardship. Powers of attorney with the patient's prior consent have been discussed amongst some manic-depressive patients and their trusted ones.

The causal link between social support and better psychological health is not clear (Alloway & Bebbington, 1987). There are two competing hypotheses about the beneficial effects of social support. The first hypothesis is that social support itself leads to direct, independent positive effects on psychological well-being: people with better social support simply enjoy better psychological well-being. Another hypothesis is the buffering hypothesis which proposes that social support acts as a buffer during a stressful life event: social support does not lead to better psychological health but moderates or mitigates the effect of adversity and hence prevents psychological ill health. However, the distinction between a buffering hypothesis or a direct positive effect on psychological health is artificial. In any case, social support is only available if social relationships are established and maintained. However, the illness itself can lead to a dwindling social group. As discussed above, both manic and depressive symptoms can be detrimental to social relationships in different ways. Hence it is important to encourage patients to re-establish good relationships when they are relatively stable. When patients are out of an acute episode, they should be encouraged to 'mend' their relationship if there are problems due to emotional expansiveness, indiscretion or social withdrawal. Any marital issues such as flirting with the opposite sex or extramarital affairs should be addressed. Extra efforts should be put in to make sure the relationship is strong during periods of relatively stable mood.

The family is only part of the important social network for the patient. For a long-term illness, the other important aspect is the formal network including the therapist, the patient's GP and psychiatrist, the psychiatric team and social services. It is to that topic that we now turn. Some manic-depressive patients tend to have little contact with the psychiatric team when they are stable. Their prophylactic medication is often from their own GP, who is often the first person they contact if they are relapsing. Early intervention may mean a variety of strategies of coping which include self-medication with the prior consent of their prescribing physician. Within a trusting relationship with mutual respect, it is often easier for professionals to manage an acute phase. Often, suggestions to manic patients made by someone they trust are accepted by the patient who previously rejected similar suggestions from someone they did not know or trust. Similarly, other than forming a good relationship with the patient's GP, psychiatrist or health professionals, a demonstration of good and responsible track records in managing one's own finances is important. If the patient has overdrawn from the bank or accumulated large credit card debts, a visit to the bank manager to transfer the debts into a bank loan may be a painful but preferred option. Similarly at work, striving for a steady and reliable track record at work and forming a good relationship with colleagues are to be encouraged. The general principle of forming a good and supportive network applies to both informal network (that is the patient's family and friends) and formal network (health professionals, social services and financial personnel). This aspect of work is very much in keeping with a 'responsible and healthy' life style.

Chapter 13

INTERPERSONAL ISSUES IN THERAPY AND ISSUES RELATED TO SERVICES

INTRODUCTION

So far we have tried to offer the reader an outline of the rationale for our therapy package and a description of the techniques employed. Our experience suggests, however, that the way in which therapy, and other psychiatric services, are offered to this group of patients may make the difference between successful management and failure. In this chapter we look at some of the issues regarding interpersonal issues and service provision for this group.

INTERPERSONAL RELATIONSHIPS

It has long been argued that the personal relationship between client and therapist is a key element in the therapeutic process (Rogers, 1957; Strupp & Hadley, 1979; Torrey, 1986). More recently, empirical research has validated the importance of the therapeutic alliance in cognitive behavioural therapy (Krupnick et al.,1996; Safran & Siegal, 1996; Raue et al., 1997). Luborsky et al. (1985) found that the most significant variable that distinguishes successful from unsuccessful therapists was the ability to form a good therapeutic alliance with the patient. Patients with manic depression may put particular strains on the therapeutic alliance, and at the same time, as with other more serious psychiatric conditions, it may play a key therapeutic role with some patients. Goodwin and Jamison (1990) note that therapists who work with manic-depressive patients are frustrated both by the inconsistencies that patients show during different mood states in their behaviour and attitudes towards self, therapist and medication, as well as the fluctuating levels of intimacy and trust within the therapeutic relationship. We would like to offer a brief review of some interpersonal factors and their importance with this client group.

Trust

Cognitive therapy has the explicit expectation that trust, respect and rapport are necessary but not sufficient conditions for change in therapy. Beck et al. (1979) distinguish three different levels of trust observed in patients, basic trust, pseudo-trust and basic distrust. Patients with basic trust will readily form a good working relationship with the therapist and those with apparent but not 'real' trust and basic distrust must have these issues dealt with before any productive work will be possible. The therapist's implicit and sometimes explicit messages should be that he or she cares about and values the patient, is confident they can work together and is not overwhelmed by the patient's problems. Techniques such as frequent summarising as well as checking the patient's perception at the end of each session are ways of demonstrating respect for and collaboration with the patient (J. S. Beck, 1995).

Trust implies a two-way interaction between patient and therapist. Patients will only trust a therapist if they know that the therapist can be relied on to endeavour to understand their perspective, regardless of their mood state. It is neither necessary nor desirable to agree with the patient's views, but the therapist must convince the patient that he or she is making every effort to understand that point of view. The patient also needs to feel that the therapist believes he /she is acting in the patient's best interest, even if they disagree on the required action. It is also very important that the therapist is reliable, that he or she will be there when they say they will be and will live up to any promises or agreements that have been made. Patients come to rely on the certainty that therapists will not overstep their professional boundaries and behave like a friend or relative. Bipolar patients can show great interpersonal charm which can be very engaging: during highs they can exhibit warmth, charm and ebullience, while when depressed they may inspire compassion and concern. Naive or inexperienced therapists can be encouraged to act like a friend. This will backfire as this will only confuse the patient, leading to an eventual lack of trust.

Judith had been in hospital for several weeks suffering from a manic episode, which had occurred after the break-up of her marriage and her move to a new district to take up a new job. Prior to this and after discharge she had found her relationship with her therapist a considerable comfort and support as she was missing her social support network. Her therapist became very concerned about Judith and suggested that Judith visit the therapist at her at home. Instead of being pleased Judith became very anxious about the relationship, feeling uncertain of herself within it, and stopped going to therapy, so losing a valuable source of support at a time when she needed it most.

A trusting relationship is particularly salient when patients are becoming high: the frequency of contact needs to be stepped up and case management issues arise. At such times a patient's level of trust in the therapist may make the difference between being able to consider 'holding strategies', 'delaying tactics', or an increase in medication and disengagement from services. Therapeutic techniques in the context of a trusting therapeutic alliance may not always be able to stave off a full-blown manic episode, but as time goes on and the alliance strengthens, the management strategies developed can be put into practice in a hypomanic episode and may prove to be sufficient to prevent a further full-blown episode.

Patients suffering from manic states are difficult because they often appear immature and behave in childlike ways, as if to test the therapist's commitment to them. The patient may appear to 'blackmail' the therapist, suggesting that in order to be empathic, the therapist must also give permission for the patient's manic state. Empathising with a manic mood can be a task that requires the therapist to draw on memories of their own experiences, in order to have some sense of the excitement and 'devil may care' aspect of it, where caution is thrown to the winds and the voice of reason is deliberately ignored. Feeling high can be a seductive and unusual state for most people. Jamison in her book *An Unquiet Mind* describes it as such: 'Shyness goes, the right words and gestures are suddenly there, the power to captivate a felt certainty' (Jamison, 1995, p. 67). She goes on, 'Sensuality is pervasive and the desire to seduce and be seduced irresistible.' Who can deny that to feel like that would be extremely attractive, and who would willingly give it up?

The corresponding emotions this presentation elicits in therapists may be irritation at the extreme nature of the behaviour, anxiety that the patient is getting ill, and feelings of gloom because of the fear that all the previous work in therapy has been for nothing. The patient still gets high. Anger and frustration can also be engendered when the patient rejects an effective treatment (Goodwin & Jamison, 1990). Therapists have to very aware of their emotional responses, have insight into their aetiology, and the knowledge to control, dissipate or use them to some therapeutic advantage. It may be useful for a hypomanic patient to be aware of these anxieties in the therapist, particularly if the trust in the relationship is strong. The patient may be forced to consider why the therapist is so concerned about them. Boundaries need to be clear, and the relationship must always be a therapeutic one encompassing respect for the patient, regardless of how inappropriate his or her behaviour may be.

For a patient the onset of an elated mood may signal an upturn in creative output, in terms of both ideas and actions, and some previous endeavours in this state may have reaped rewards for the patient. Unfortunately this state often rapidly escalates to mania, with thoughts and behaviour becoming out of control. However, patients often feel thwarted and irritable when the therapist does not share their joy. Also they are often very sensitive to any criticism and can easily feel rejected and misunderstood. In terms of conducting therapy in a way that will encourage trust, a balance needs to be struck between allowing the patient to talk, plan and take some control of the therapy and keeping a structure to sessions. It is important that the therapy remain goal-directed and that limits be set, but this must be done in a way that is not too restrictive and containing.

During a hypomanic period, Joanna formed a strong conviction that she had found a fulfilling love relationship, as discussed in Chapter 11. This presented a problem for her therapist: Joanna clearly wanted support and approval, and was somewhat annoyed when her therapist appeared to be sceptical regarding the relationship. Rather than confronting this annoyance directly, the therapist encouraged Joanna to talk about the feelings she was experiencing, also asking her about whether or not she had felt them before. Joanna admitted that she had similar infatuations before, at the same time pointing out that she was sure this relationship would be different. The therapist replied that she hoped this was so, while also suggesting that Joanna would still need to manage her mood states whatever the outcome. At the same time, Joanna wrote a considerable amount of poetry, of which she was very proud, some of which she read to the therapist. Here again the therapist had to strive to listen sympathetically and validate Joanna's pleasure in her creativity, while at the same time encouraging her to adjust her medication and moderate her lifestyle. When Joanna's mood moderated, the therapist had to help her to gain perspective on these events, as well as empathising with her understandable unhappiness about what she perceived as a loss of creative energy. One useful strategy here was to encourage her to revise some of the poems she had written in her hypomanic state: this is a process often seen in creative artists who suffer from bipolar disorder. (Jamison, 1993)

Rapport

Rapport is an aspect of the therapeutic alliance that merits a mention. Beck et al. (1979) describe rapport as a harmonious accord between people. Once achieved a good rapport will mean that the patient feels comfortable with the therapist, accepted and understood by him/her but not necessarily always agreed with. Good rapport enables a disagreement to occur between patient and therapist without the patient feeling judged, enabling the patient to correct the therapist when there has been a misunderstanding. Strategies such as attentive listening, regular summarising and a clear attempt to understand the patient's perspective will go a long way to build good rapport and trust between patient and therapist.

When Quentin (see Chapter 11) was in a manic state, he tended to talk about religious and mystical ideas. At these times he would say that his religious views were supremely important to him, giving life meaning and making it impossible for him to consider using medication. In this case the therapist emphasised his understanding of this feeling, while at the same time pointing out that there might be a terrible cost to allowing an unchecked manic state to continue. One point that was useful was that during depressive states Quentin experienced terrible religious doubts, a kind of 'dark night of the soul'. At times Quentin would say that even this would be worth while, because at least he would be able to enjoy his continued state of spiritual exaltation in the present. By empathising with this state, while at the same time making clear his own practical concerns, the therapist was able to maintain the relationship. Quentin was subsequently detained in hospital and forcibly medicated, a very distressing experience for him. However, the therapist's empathic response while Quentin was high enabled the two of them to continue working together.

Grandiose Ideas

Grandiose ideas are best described as ideas that encompass a concept of the self that is significantly positive and includes beliefs about abilities, physical and mental attributes and status that are obviously irrational in a positive direction. This is accompanied by an increase in self-confidence and sense of well-being often involving a raft of new ideas and elaborate plans. Patients often overestimate their abilities and underestimate the consequences of their behaviour. Some patients develop ideas about having special powers in a selective area. For example a patient may think they have the power to seduce anyone they choose. At such times the patient tends to select environmental cues that appear to substantiate their ideas and ignore any that disconfirm them. Considering that many patients are often frequently lacking in self-esteem most of the time it is not surprising that these grandiose thoughts driven by hypomania are very enticing to the patient. The ability of the patient to realise that they are unhelpful is difficult and needs considerable prior discussion. Discussions of the advantages and disadvantages of taking certain courses of action are discussed, as are behavioural as well as cognitive 'holding' strategies. However, patients can become irritable and resentful towards their therapist, feeling that he is trying to thwart their chance for 'real success' or 'genuine happiness'. Therapists can often minimise these feelings by acknowledging them and pointing out that they are a response to the

therapist's obvious concern. Grandiose ideas can reach psychotic propor-
tions and as such are no longer amenable to psychological interventions.
Psychological interventions are more likely to be effective before delusional thinking begins—that is, when patients are able to reason through
their ideas, to look at them objectively and evaluate their thought
processes (Basco & Rush, 1996).

Although patients who have had prior experiences of mania are often desperately keen to avert another episode, this is not always the case. Some
patients are quite addicted to their manic states and almost encourage
them, even though they are also aware that they can be destructive.
Patients like this have an ambivalent relationship with their elated moods
and need more work to enable them to reframe their experiences and optimistic thoughts as symptoms. This task is best done as a retrospective exercise. Some people feel their manic states are part of their personality and
define them as a person in some way. These patients are understandably
loath to contain them. At the same time, most patients who form a commitment to therapy do so because part of them recognises a need to contain the extremes of their emotions to enable them to lead more productive
lives. It is this desire, which may be hidden in hypomania, that is the therapist's strongest ally.

Quentin had always been a consistent refuser of medication was also very
driven with perfectionistic tendencies and had held down a professional job for
many years using psychological techniques with some success. However, after
a particularly painful admission where he had been admitted under a Mental
Health Act section he gradually and finally began to present his difficulties in
therapy with the aim of 'giving up his mania'. He related how he believed he
had always needed his manic episodes as he had seen them as a spiritual journey which he needed from time to time to help him gain a sense of who he was.
Giving them up by accepting either medication or implementing psychological
strategies would mean involving himself in considerations about his concept of
self and his place in the world. He said he would need to reconsider who he
was. This prospect was frightening to him: 'better the devil you know than the
one you don't know.'

However, in therapy he was able to examine past and present consistencies in
his beliefs and desires in order to begin to devise a consistent image of himself
and discovered that he was someone who always needed to be 'looking after
or taking responsibility for people less able than himself '. For example, after
discharge from the ward he acknowledged that he had been scared to leave
hospital with no job to go to as he worried he would not know who he was.
However, he rapidly became involved in organising a magazine for the users of
the hospital service. He also realised he was someone who pushed himself to

the limits, needing to 'give it his all' regardless of what it was he was involved in.

Patients are only likely to be amenable to cognitive interventions in the early stages of hypomania and therefore as soon as a suspicion of hypomania appears it is important to intervene straight away. Step up the frequency of the sessions to at least twice a week, if necessary to interpose sessions with telephone contact.

Patients with manic depression may well have been admitted to hospital under a Mental Health Act Section and have many understandable residual resentments because of this experience. One patient to whom this happened became very anti-psychiatry and on discharge wanted the therapist to agree with her that her hostility towards the ward staff and consultant psychiatrist had good cause. In these cases the approach can only be one of empathic concern whilst retaining and putting forward an objective stance on the issues of medical treatment of mania. This requires a very sensitive approach. On discharge the patient was still somewhat irritable and wanted an agreement by the therapist that medication was used primarily to 'control patients, in order to keep them quiet' and was not usually in the patients' best interests. It is an understandable but flawed perspective. The task here, using collaboration and showing respect for the patient's perspective, is to place the problem in context saying something like, 'given your experience it is understandable that you feel and think like this' and then to be relatively direct about the fact that therapists make observations, consider the evidence and attempt to arrive at a balanced view. The stance is one of being supportive and understanding whilst not necessarily agreeing with a patient.

Patients with manic depression are often very creative and may have lost confidence as well as jobs because of their illness; it is important to recognise this and respect patients for their achievements, abilities and insight. As noted above, there is considerable evidence of an association between bipolar disorder and artistic creativity of a very high level (Jamison, 1993). Some creative patients (e.g. Joanna, see above) may feel that professionals label the creative work they have done as 'just mental illness'. Therapists must guard against this idea: it is worth bearing in mind that professional qualifications in psychology and psychiatry do not grant one superior artistic, literary or musical insight. A safer course in this area is to encourage the creative bipolar patient to seek support, encouragement and validation from fellow artists, who can help the patient to preserve what is best in what they have produced while pruning what is 'excessive'.

IRRITABILITY WHEN HIGH

Irritability and Criticism of Others

Patients in the early stages of a manic episode often present as irritable. Irritability can seriously interfere with a therapeutic relationship. Patients can be disinclined to want to listen, compelled to talk continuously, convinced that their point of view is right and even openly hostile. This is often present in therapy and may manifest itself as criticism of both the therapy and of the therapist. Comments about the therapy being not conducted properly, not being helpful, the therapist not being skilled enough or showing enough interest in the patient can often be difficult to deal with. The temptation to defend oneself comes in and interferes with the therapeutic endeavour. Therapists need to stand back from their own feelings about being criticised and deal with the comments therapeutically. Irritability is often a sign that the patient does not feel understood. A stance of calm listening, with a demeanour of taking the patient seriously whilst not obviously agreeing with him, often defuses the situation and allows the patient to calm down sufficiently to consider things with some objectivity. The therapist should say, in effect: 'I am prepared to listen to your criticisms, to try to be as objective as I can, and to accept those that I feel I can agree with. I will be happy to modify the way I work with you, in line with your criticisms, as long as I do not feel that my fundamental therapeutic approach is being altered.' Even if the patient chooses to end therapy, the therapist should make it clear that it can be resumed in the future if the patient wishes: this point will be discussed below.

Some patients may even say they think therapy is a waste of time and they do not intend to continue with it. In any case what must be avoided is any semblance of argument with the patient. The aim is to create a therapeutic ambience of support, careful listening and an obvious commitment to ironing out the problems if at all possible. The approach of concerned collaboration rather than out and out combat will help defuse the patient's hostile demeanour.

May is a jeweller who has been making a good living at her trade. She tends to have low self-esteem as a rule, believing that she is not really a person of much importance. However, when hypomanic she becomes resentful and somewhat hostile because she thinks people are not paying her sufficient attention. She demonstrated this in therapy by failing to complete homeworks and coming to therapy each week with a different problem, summarily dismissing all attempts by the therapist to stick to a particular set of issues. She finally accused the therapist of not being structured enough and failing to stick to the agenda.

MA: You just put my file away when I leave this office and only open it when I arrive. You don't consider my problems at all when I'm not here. I don't think you have any real interest in me.

TH: Can you help me to understand why you feel that way?

MA: Because you always expect me to come up with things to talk about. And you never seem to get through everything in the session. There's no real structure to the sessions. I think you just can't be bothered.

TH: I am sorry you think that. It is clearly important that we have a look at these things in detail. Which is the aspect of therapy that you are most concerned about? Perhaps we could start with that.

The therapist conceded that it had been difficult for them to be structured and suggested that they put their heads together to work out in detail what the difficulties were in order to come up with strategies to overcome them. The collaborative nature of the response cemented a very good therapeutic relationship and therapy was able to proceed more productively. It transpired that the patient had a core assumption that if she disagreed with people she would push them away and the therapist's response to her irritability was an experience for her where this assumption had not been borne out. She said that in the past when she had been irritable she had upset people and this had added substance to this core assumption, which had been borne out of early life experiences of parental disapproval for stating her mind, leaving her with a feeling of rejection.

The thought that 'therapy is useless and not doing any good' can be dealt with in systematic CBT method, looking back over previous sessions and using therapy notes to identify gains and evidence of progress. A focus on sessions where the patient has expressed the thought that something was particularly helpful is important. A list can be drawn up and offset against a similar list of the patient's complaints. An attempt to directly force the patient to agree to return to therapy may well be met with resistance and therefore should be avoided. The best approach is often to curtail the immediate session as hypomania can quickly be enhanced with stimulation; this gives the patient a little time within the next few days to review the situation. If they say they will not attend it is important for them to know that the session is available to them if they need it. They often do return.

Shorter sessions and a behavioural approach are often useful in dealing with irritability. Homework tasks for calming down can include unplugging the telephone, no loud music, calming baths, solitary walks in parks and use of anxiolitic medication if appropriate. In some cases a part of a session may be devoted to preparing a relaxation tape tailored to the individual patient. Each patient will have their own coping strategies, and it is important that these should be derived, elaborated on and made explicit at an early stage in therapy. Monitoring the success of these strategies ensures that the most useful strategies are the ones retained and elaborated. It is often unproductive to attempt in-depth challenges to beliefs when patients are irritable as it can sometimes inflame their irritability, although this will depend upon the patient. It is also a good idea to step up the contact with patients when they are irritable to ensure that they are using calming strategies and that the irritability is not escalating.

Occasionally, in the context of a hypomanic episode, a patient develops romantic ideas about their therapist. A patient may make inappropriate suggestions such as asking the therapist to accompany them on a social outing, or demonstrate inappropriate behaviours in a therapy session, such as trying to make physical contact with the therapist. This issue can be addressed in therapy using standard cognitive therapy techniques such as employing Socratic questioning to guide patient to the understanding that the therapeutic relationship is different from other relationships and it is in the patient's best interest to sustain it rather than to try to change it into a relationship that cannot be.

MEDICATION COMPLIANCE

Compliance with medication is often a problem for several reasons. Some patients actively decide they are now 'better' and no longer in need of medication. Patients who are disorganised can forget to take it frequently enough for the lithium levels to remain at a therapeutic level. Other patients have genuine mixed feelings about taking medication and sometimes are able to overcome their reservations and at other times are not. Reservations about taking or refusal to take medication may stem from several sources. Some patients have a resistance to taking medication in general, believing they are basically foreign substances to their body and will eventually do them some harm, whereas others are unable to accept the chronic nature of their illness and see it as a series of discrete illnesses which only need treating when symptoms arise. Others have great difficulty with side effects. Goodwin and Jamison (1990, Ch. 25) review the many barriers to long-term compliance and the variety of side effects observed; they note that subtle cognitive effects are often a major barrier to compliance, and Jamison (1995) offers a personal account of the cognitive impairment that lithium can often induce. Given these problems, the temptation not to comply must obviously be a strong one.

Another group are unhappy with the idea of taking medication as a preventative measure in the context of a chronic illness or vulnerability. Often the issue is really about the patient's difficulties in coming to terms with the idea that they have a chronic illness (see also Chapter 11).

Discussions about the probable outcomes of taking or not taking medication to prevent relapse often helps. Also a controlled trial can be suggested where the patient agrees to take medication on a trial basis over a certain length of time whilst monitoring their mood state and other symptoms as such as sleep disturbance on a daily basis. One key issue in the medication debate is the patient's ability to feel able to raise the question with their doctor in order to express their opinion with the expectation that it will be heard.

It is sometimes the case that patients are unable to take medication for medical reasons. One patient was unable to tolerate lithium or carbamazepine because of a raised heart rate. In this case the patient was given melleril to use when she felt she was becoming agitated and was finding the agitation difficult to control by psychological means. This patient was unable to tolerate any medication to alleviate her symptoms of depression also: as a result, much work was needed to highlight early warning signs of depression. However, patients like this are the exception. We believe that, in general, a combination of medication and CBT provides the optimum package for this patient group.

Some patients may feel that, because they are receiving cognitive therapy, they no longer need medication, feeling perhaps that therapy is sufficient. This may happen especially when therapy is going well and giving patients more sense of control over their illness. The pros and cons of this step will need to be discussed carefully. If a patient is adamant that this is a step he or she wishes to take, we suggest working towards a compromise, an agreed period of stability, preferably several months long, before the patient takes the next step. The patient can then be encouraged to discuss medication with the prescribing psychiatrist. It is worth pointing out to the patient that it is not wise to stop medication abruptly, since a gradual tapering of medication has been shown to reduce the rate of relapse (Faedda et al., 1993).

The general message which we feel that the reader should take away from this discussion is that the best approach to compliance is through a discussion predicated on the patient's freedom to determine his or her own medication regime. Rational consideration of the pros and cons of maintenance medication should help patients to realise that it is in their interest, in spite of side effects and other problems. We feel that this conclusion is reinforced by a trial of psychological treatment aimed at improving compliance in patients with serious mental illness with which one of our authors was involved. An approach known as 'compliance therapy' was employed, using discussion of pros and cons and a gentle, non-confrontational approach. Such an approach resulted in improved compliance compared to a control group (Hayward et al., 1995; Kemp et al., 1996b, 1998). Readers consulting our discussions of how the therapy was carried out will note many similarities to the present approach (Kemp et al., 1996a; Kemp et al., 1997), such as review of medication history and use of a problem-solving approach. Another important element in these approaches is that medication compliance is presented as a freely chosen strategy to take control of one's illness. Such an approach emphasises the importance of patient autonomy, a subject to which we now turn.

AUTONOMY AND CHOICE

Cognitive therapy by its very nature is a collaborative venture, giving patients choices and skills to help them solve their problems and make their own life decisions. The issue of medication compliance, which we have just discussed, highlights this issue, but it is certainly not the only example. Patients when in a hypomanic or manic state may make a variety of life choices which we might feel to be inappropriate. These might include accepting new responsibilities, changing job or conditions of employment, entering into or leaving relationships, changing home, taking up new interests or hobbies etc. Seemingly minor life choices may also be seen as problematic: for example, a patient may clearly be getting too little sleep but yet fail to take steps to correct this situation and instead continue to work or socialise to an excessive degree. The problem may also occur during a depressive episode, though in this case the pattern is more often one of withdrawal; examples here might include quitting a suitable job or avoiding social situations.

As clinicians we may be aware that a particular patient is making a life choice which we see as inappropriate, but we must accept that it is not our place to intervene directly in such situations. Coercion is inappropriate, because the feeling of autonomy is an important one for most patients (Hatfield & Lefley, 1993). A straightforward direct approach to patients, treating them as autonomous beings, is best, but it should be done in such a way that the patient is aware of your concerns and views even though they may not coincide with theirs. Each patient needs to feel that they will not be abandoned or 'punished' in some other way if they make a choice a therapist does not agree with. As with medication compliance, the idea of a continuum of change is useful in this case: patients may need to make such choices, and we are not granted the wisdom to 'know' how they will turn out. At the same time, if they turn out badly, the patient needs to know that he or she can learn from a mistake and that the therapeutic relationship will continue. Such views are common in the substance abuse field, where a relapse can be seen as part of a process of attitude change rather than as a therapist failure (Prochaska & DiClemente, 1986; Prochaska et al., 1992). It is our feeling that in such situations, the therapist must make his or her concerns clear, while giving the patient the ultimate freedom, a freedom which, obviously, they have in any case. The cognitive techniques described in Chapter 8 can be employed, but one must accept that they may not always work. If they do not, then the therapist must try to seek whatever common ground can be found.

Will (see Chapter 11) left his critical girlfriend to enter into a new relationship. At this time he was very happy, and the therapist was worried that he in fact might be getting high. However, he did not show the usual prodromal signs of relapse. He then decided to leave therapy and discontinue his medication: this was done with a show of gratitude towards the therapist, and he stated that therapy had helped him but he no longer needed it. The therapist was able to persuade him to have a few further sessions but could not persuade him to continue his medication. The only alternative was to accept that perhaps a trial of how he managed without medication might be necessary for Will. The therapist reviewed Will's common relapse signature and made sure that he had medication, that he would remain in contact with his psychiatrist, and that his girlfriend also knew what signs of relapse to watch out for. Having done everything possible to prepare Will for a possible relapse, the therapist was forced to step back and wait to see what would happen. He did, however, make it clear to Will that he was free to resume therapy in the future if he wished to do so.

SERVICE PROVISION ISSUES

Patients with manic depression often have more than one professional involved with their care. For example most have a doctor, often a psychiatrist or a GP, to prescribe and monitor medication and in some cases the patient is in therapy with a psychologist as well as attending day services and occupational therapy programmes. When patients are attending a doctor's outpatients appointments and therapy sessions conflicts do sometimes arise. If the patient views taking medication with suspicion it can lead patients to try to entice the psychologist to side with them against the psychiatrist. Also patients who are key worked by a community psychiatric nurse who also delivers medication can turn up for psychology sessions and avoid seeing their key worker. This can create difficulties between members of a team caring for these patients. It needs to be made explicit to the patient that the professionals are all subscribing to the same perspective in terms of what is the most appropriate care package for the patient. Frequent meetings between the professionals involved, including ones where the patient is present, are essential to prevent tensions arising. Clear lines of communication need to drawn which should include the patient's GP if he or she is taking a role in the care and ongoing monitoring of the patient's mental health state.

Of course relationships between the therapist and other members of the treating team may be more or less close: on the one hand the therapist may be a fully integrated member of the treatment team, while on the other hand a private therapist might never meet the patient's psychiatrist or GP and only exchange a few letters with them. In any case, the therapist must be sensitive to the views of other professionals: if the therapist is not careful he or she may seem like an interloper who comes late on the scene and tells everyone else how things ought to be done. It is also important to remember that the doctor may have a much longer-term relationship with the patient than the therapist does, and might have to manage the patient for many years after the therapy is over. That being said, the therapist should use whatever influence he or she has to make sure that the treating team provides the best care for the patient. Ideally such care should be integrated and flexible. Thus, there should be continuity of care if the patient is hospitalised, flexibility in prescribing which is sensitive to changes in the patient's mental state, and the availability of increased support at times when there is an increased risk of relapse. A therapist who is well integrated into the treating team may also be able to provide supervision and support to other professionals, making sure what has been learned in therapy informs the patient's subsequent care. Finally, support for fellow professionals may also be important: manic-depressive patients can be difficult and frustrating, and a consultative role within the team may help other professionals to be more effective.

Appendices

SCHEDULE FOR ASSESSING THE THREE COMPONENTS OF INSIGHT (David et al., 1992)

1a. Does patient accept treatment * (includes passive acceptance)?

  2 = Often   (may rarely question need for treatment)
  1 = Sometimes   (may occasionally question need for treatment)
  0 = Never   (ask why)

  *medication and/or hospitalization and/or other physical and psychological therapies

  If 1 or 2 proceed to Question 1b.

1b. Does patient ask for treatment unprompted?

  2 = Often   (excludes inappropriate requests for medication etc.)
  1 = Sometimes   (rate here if forgetfulness/disorganization leads to occasional requests only)
  0 = Never   (accepts treatment after prompting)

2a. Ask patient: 'Do you think you have an illness?'

  Alternative: 'Do you think there is something wrong with you?' (mental or physical unspecified)

  2 = Often   (thought present most of the day, most days)
  1 = Sometimes   (thought present occasionally)
  0 = Never   (ask why doctors/other think he/she does)

2b. Ask patient: 'Do you think you have a mental/psychiatric illness?'

  2 = Often   (thought present most of the day, most days)
  1 = Sometimes   (thought present occasionally, minimum once per day)
  0 = Never

2c. Ask patient: 'How do you explain your illness?'

  2 = Reasonable account given based on plausible mechanisms
  (Appropriate given patient's social, cultural and education background, e.g. excess stress, chemical imbalance, family history etc.)
  1 = Confused account given, repetition of overheard explanation without adequate understanding or 'don't know'
  0 = Delusional explanation

3a. Ask patient: 'Do you think the belief that ... (insert specific delusion) is not really true or happening?'

  or 'Do you think the belief that ... (insert specific hallucination) is not really true or happening?'

  2 = Often   (thought present most of the day, most days)
  1 = Sometimes   (though present occasionally, minimum once per day)
  0 = Never

  If 1 or 2 proceed to Question 3b.

3b.   Ask patient: 'How do you explain these phenomena?
      (the belief that ... or hearing that voice/seeing that image etc.)'

      2 = Part of my illness
      1 = Reaction to outside event/s (e.g. 'tiredness', 'stress' etc.)
      0 = Attributed to outside forces (may be delusion)

                                                    Maximum Score = 14

Supplementary Question (Hypothetical Contradiction)

'How do you feel when people do not believe you?'
(when you talk about ... delusions or hallucinatory experience)

4 = That's when I know I'm sick
3 = I wonder whether something is wrong with me
2 = I'm confused and do not know what to think
1 = I'm still sure despite what others say
0 = They're lying

Reference: David, A. S., Buchanan, A., Reed, A. & Almeida, O. (1992). The assessment of insight in psychosis. *British Journal of Psychiatry*, **161**, 599–602. Reproduced by permission of the Royal College of Psychiatrists.

APPENDIX 5.2
THE DYSFUNCTIONAL ATTITUDES SCALE—24-ITEM VERSION (Power et al., 1994)

This scale lists different attitudes or beliefs which people sometimes hold. Please read each statement carefully and decide how much you agree or disagree with what it says.

For each of the attitudes, please indicate your answer by placing a tick (✓) under the column that *best describes how you think*. Be sure to choose only one answer for each attitude. But please note that because people are different, there is no right or wrong answer to these statements.

To decide whether a given answer is typical of your way of looking at things, simply keep in mind what you are like *most of the time*.

ATTITUDES	Totally agree	Agree very much	Agree slightly	Neutral	Disagree slightly	Disagree very much	Totally disagree
1. If I fail partly, it is as bad as being a complete failure							
2. If others dislike you, you cannot be happy							
3. I should be happy all the time							
4. People will probably think less of me if I make a mistake							
5. My happiness depends more on other people than it does on me							
6. I should always have complete control over my feelings							

ATTITUDES	Totally agree	Agree very much	Agree slightly	Neutral	Disagree slightly	Disagree very much	Totally disagree
7. My life is wasted unless I am a success.							
8. What other people think about me is very important							
9. I ought to be able to solve my problems quickly and without a great deal of effort							
10. If I don't set the highest standards for myself, I am likely to end up a second rate person							
11. I am nothing if a person I love doesn't love me							
12. A person should be able to control what happens to him							
13. If I am to be a worthwhile person, I must be truly outstanding in at least one major respect							
14. If you don't have other people to lean on, you are bound to be sad							
15. It is possible for a person to be scolded and not get upset							

ATTITUDES	Totally agree	Agree very much	Agree slightly	Neutral	Disagree slightly	Disagree very much	Totally disagree
16. I must be a useful, productive, creative person or life has no purpose							
17. I can find happiness without being loved by another person							
18. A person should do well at everything he undertakes							
19. If I do not do well all the time, people will not respect me							
20. I do not need the approval of other people in order to be happy							
21. If I try hard enough, I should be able to excel at anything I attempt							
22. People who have good ideas are more worthy than those who do not							
23. A person doesn't need to be well liked in order to be happy							
24. Whenever I take a chance or risk I am only looking for trouble							

Reference: Power, M. J., Katz, R., McGuffin, P., Duggan, C. F., Lam, D. & Beck, A.T. (1994). The Dysfunctional Attitude Scale (DAS): A comparison of forms A and B and proposal for a new sub-scaled version. *Journal of Research in Personality*, **28**, 263–276.

APPENDIX 5.3
VIEWS ON MANIC DEPRESSION QUESTIONNAIRE
(Hayward et al., unpublished manuscript)

Please rate how strongly you agree or disagree with each of the following statements by circling a number.

	Strongly agree				Strongly disagree	
1. Most people would willingly accept a manic depressive sufferer as a close friend.	1	2	3	4	5	6
2. Most people believe that a person who has been hospitalised with manic depression is just as intelligent as the average person.	1	2	3	4	5	6
3. Even though I have suffered from manic depression, I feel just as capable as the next person of getting and holding a job.	1	2	3	4	5	6
4. Most people believe that a manic depressive sufferer is just as trustworthy as the average citizen.	1	2	3	4	5	6
5. Most people believe that entering a mental hospital is a sign of personal failure.	1	2	3	4	5	6
6. I am able to do things as well as most other people.	1	2	3	4	5	6
7. Most employers will hire a former manic depressive sufferer if s/he is qualified for the job.	1	2	3	4	5	6
8. Even though I have suffered from manic depression it has not affected my ability to sustain close relationships.	1	2	3	4	5	6
9. Most people in my community would treat a former manic depressive sufferer just as they would treat anyone.	1	2	3	4	5	6
10. Most young women would be reluctant to date a man who has been hospitalized with manic depression	1	2	3	4	5	6
11. Once they know a person has been in a mental hospital, most people will take his or her opinions less seriously.	1	2	3	4	5	6
12. There have been many occasions when I have avoided social situations because of my manic depression.	1	2	3	4	5	6
13. Having a manic depressive illness makes it more difficult for me to make friends.	1	2	3	4	5	6
14. I feel that I am a person of worth, at least on an equal plane with others.	1	2	3	4	5	6

APPENDIX 5.4
THE SELF-CONTROL BEHAVIOUR SCHEDULE
(Rosenbaum, 1980)

NAME: DATE:

Please indicate how characteristic or descriptive each of the following statements is of you by using the code given below.

+3 very characteristic of me, extremely descriptive
+2 rather characteristic of me, quite descriptive
+1 somewhat characteristic of me, slightly descriptive
–1 somewhat uncharacteristic of me, slightly undescriptive
–2 rather uncharacteristic of me, quite undescriptive
–3 very uncharacteristic of me, extremely nondescriptive

Please circle one of the numbers underneath each question.

1. When I do a boring job, I think about the less boring parts of the job and the reward that I will receive once I am finished.

       +3   +2   +1   –1   –2   –3

2. When I have to do something that is anxiety arousing for me, I try to visualize how I will overcome my anxieties while doing it.

       +3   +2   +1   –1   –2   –3

3. Often by changing the way of thinking, I am able to change my feelings about almost everything.

       +3   +2   +1   –1   –2   –3

4. I often find it difficult to overcome my feelings of nervousness and tension without any outside help.

       +3   +2   +1   –1   –2   –3

5. When I am feeling depressed I try to think about pleasant events.

       +3   +2   +1   –1   –2   –3

6. I cannot avoid thinking about mistakes I have made in the past.

       +3   +2   +1   –1   –2   –3

7. When I am faced with a difficult problem, I try to approach its solution in a systematic way.

       +3   +2   +1   –1   –2   –3

8. I usually do my duties quicker when someone is pressuring me.

       +3   +2   +1   –1   –2   –3

9. When I am faced with a difficult decision, I prefer to postpone making a decision even if all the facts are at my disposal.

       +3   +2   +1   –1   –2   –3

10. When I find that I have difficulties in concentrating on my reading, I look for ways to increase my concentration.

    +3   +2   +1   −1   −2   −3

11. When I plan to work, I remove all things that are not relevant to my work.

    +3   +2   +1   −1   −2   −3

12. When I try to get rid of a bad habit, I try to find all the factors that maintain this habit.

    +3   +2   +1   −1   −2   −3

13. When an unpleasant thought is bothering me, I try to think about something pleasant.

    +3   +2   +1   −1   −2   −3

14. If I would smoke two packages of cigarettes a day, I probably would need outside help to stop smoking.

    +3   +2   +1   −1   −2   −3

15. When I am in a low mood, I try to act cheerful so my mood will change.

    +3   +2   +1   −1   −2   −3

16. If I had the pills with me, I would take a tranquillizer whenever I felt tense and nervous.

    +3   +2   +1   −1   −2   −3

17. When I am depressed, I try to keep myself busy with things that I like.

    +3   +2   +1   −1   −2   −3

18. I tend to postpone unpleasant duties, even if I could perform them immediately.

    +3   +2   +1   −1   −2   −3

19. I need outside help to get rid of some of my bad habits.

    +3   +2   +1   −1   −2   −3

20. When I find it difficult to settle down and do a certain job, I look for ways to help me settle down.

    +3   +2   +1   −1   −2   −3

21. Although it makes me feel bad, I cannot avoid thinking about all kinds of possible catastrophes in the future.

    +3   +2   +1   −1   −2   −3

22. First of all I prefer to finish a job that I have to do and then start doing the things I really like.

    +3   +2   +1   −1   −2   −3

23. When I feel pain in a certain part of my body, I try not to think about it.

    +3   +2   +1   −1   −2   −3

24. My self-esteem increases once I am able to overcome a bad habit.

    +3   +2   +1   −1   −2   −3

25. In order to overcome bad feelings that accompany failure, I often tell myself that it is not so catastrophic and that I can do something about it.

    +3   +2   +1   −1   −2   −3

26. When I feel that I am too impulsive, I tell myself 'stop and think before you do anything'.

    +3   +2   +1   −1   −2   −3

27. Even when I am extremely angry at somebody, I consider my actions very carefully.

    +3   +2   +1   −1   −2   −3

28. Facing the need to make a decision, I usually find out all the possible alternatives instead of deciding quickly and spontaneously.

    +3   +2   +1   −1   −2   −3

29. Usually I do first the things I really like to do even if there are more urgent things to do.

    +3   +2   +1   −1   −2   −3

30. When I realize that I cannot help but be late for an important meeting, I tell myself to keep calm.

    +3   +2   +1   −1   −2   −3

31. When I feel pain in my body, I try to divert my thoughts from it.

    +3   +2   +1   −1   −2   −3

32. I usually plan my work when faced with a number of things to do.

    +3   +2   +1   −1   −2   −3

33. When I am short of money, I decide to record all my expenses in order to plan more carefully for the future.

    +3   +2   +1   −1   −2   −3

34. If I find it difficult to concentrate on a certain job, I divide the job into smaller segments.

    +3   +2   +1   −1   −2   −3

35. Quite often I cannot overcome unpleasant thoughts that bother me.

    +3   +2   +1   −1   −2   −3

36. Once I am hungry and unable to eat, I try to divert my thoughts away from my stomach or try to imagine that I am satisfied.

    +3   +2   +1   −1   −2   −3

Reference: Rosenbaum, M. (1980). A schedule for assessing self-control behaviors: Preliminary findings. *Behavior Therapy*, **11**, 109–121. Copyright 1980 by the Association for Advancement of Behaviour Therapy. Reprinted by permission of the publisher

APPENDIX 5.5
HAMILTON DEPRESSION SCALE—17-ITEM
(Hamilton, 1960)

1. Depressed Mood (Sad, hopeless, helpless, worthless)
    0 = Absent
    1 = Gloomy attitude, pessimism, hopelessness
    2 = Occasional weeping
    3 = Frequent weeping
    4 = Patient reports virtually only these feeling states in his/her spontaneous verbal and non-verbal communication

2. Feelings of Guilt
    0 = Absent
    1 = Self reproach, feels he/she has let people down
    2 = Ideas of guilt or rumination over past errors or sinful deeds
    3 = Present illness is punishment
    4 = Hears accusatory or denunciatory voices and/or experiences threatening visual hallucinations. Delusions of guilt

3. Suicide
    0 = Absent
    1 = Feels life is not worth living
    2 = Wishes he/she were dead or any thoughts of possible death to self
    3 = Suicide, ideas or halfhearted attempt
    4 = Attempts at suicide (any serious attempt rates 4)

4. Insomnia Early
    0 = No difficulty falling asleep
    1 = Complains of occasional difficulty falling asleep, i.e. more than ½ hour
    2 = Complains of nightly difficulty falling asleep

5. Insomnia Middle
    0 = No difficulty
    1 = Patient complains of being restless and disturbed during the night
    2 = Waking during the night—any getting out of bed rates 2 (except for voiding)

6. Insomnia Late
    0 = No difficulty
    1 = Waking in early hours of the morning but goes back to sleep
    2 = Unable to fall asleep again if he/she gets out of bed

7. Work and Activities
    0 = No difficulty
    1 = Thoughts and feelings of incapacity related to activities, work and hobbies
    2 = Loss of interest in activity hobbies or work either directly reported by patient, or indirectly seen in listlessness, indecision and vacillation (feels he/she has to push self to work or activities)
    3 = Decrease in actual time spent in activities or decrease in productivity. In hospital, rate 3 if patient does not spend at least three hours a day in activities (hospital job or hobbies, exclusive of ward chores)

4 = Stopped working because of present illness. In hospital, rate 4 if patient engages in no activities except ward chores, or patient fails to perform ward chores unassisted

8. Retardation (Slowness of thought and speech, impaired ability to concentrate, decreased motor activity)
   0 = Normal speech and thought
   1 = Slight retardation at interview
   2 = Obvious retardation at interview
   3 = Interview difficult
   4 = Interview impossible

9. Agitation
   0 = None
   1 = Fidgetiness
   2 = Playing with hands, hair, obvious restlessness
   3 = Moving about, can't sit still
   4 = Hand wringing, nail biting, hair pulling, biting of lips, patient is on the run

10. Anxiety Psychic (Demonstrated by:
    — Subjective tension and irritability, loss of concentration
    — Worrying about minor matters
    — Apprehension
    — Fears expressed without questioning
    — Feelings of panic
    — Feeling jumpy)
    0 = Absent
    1 = Mild
    2 = Moderate
    3 = Severe
    4 = Incapacitating

11. Anxiety Somatic (Physiological concomitants of anxiety, such as:
    — Gastro-intestinal: dry mouth, wind, indigestion, diarrhoea, cramps, belching
    — Cardio-vascular: palpitations, headaches
    — Respiratory: hyperventilation, sighing
    — Urinary frequency
    — Sweating
    — Giddiness, blurred vision
    — Tinnitus)
    0 = Absent
    1 = Mild
    2 = Moderate
    3 = Severe
    4 = Incapacitating

12. Somatic Symptoms: Gastrointestinal
    0 = None
    1 = Loss of appetite but eating without staff encouragement
    2 = Difficulty eating without staff urging

    (Requests or requires laxatives or medication for G.I. symptoms)

13. Somatic Symptoms: General
    0 = None
    1 = Heaviness in limbs, back or head, backaches, headaches, muscle aches, loss of energy, fatiguability
    2 = Any clear-cut symptom rates 2

14. Genital Symptoms (Symptoms such as: Loss of libido/menstrual disturbances)
    0 = Absent
    1 = Mild
    2 = Severe

15. Hypochondriasis
    0 = Not present
    1 = Self absorption (bodily)
    2 = Pre-occupation with health
    3 = Strong conviction of some bodily illness
    4 = Hypochondriacal delusions

16. Loss of Weight
    0 = No weight loss
    1 = Probable weight loss associated with present illness
    2 = Definite (according to patient) weight loss

17. Insight
    0 = Acknowledges being depressed and ill
    1 = Acknowledges illness but attributes cause to bad food, overwork, virus, need for rest, etc.
    2 = Denies being ill at all

Reference: Hamilton M. (1960). A rating scale for depression. *Journal of Neurology and Psychiatry*, **23**, 56–62. Reproduced with permission from the BMJ Publishing Group.

MANIA RATING SCALE (Bech et al., 1978)

1   Activity: Motor
0.   Not unusual
1.   Slight or doubtfully increased motor activity (e.g. lively facial expression).
2.   Moderately increased motor activity (e.g. lively gestures).
3.   Clearly excessive motor activity, on the move most of the time, rises once or several times during interview.
4.   Constantly active, restlessly energetic. Even if urges, the patient cannot sit still.

2   Activity: Verbal
0.   Not unusual
1.   Somewhat talkative
2.   Very talkative, no spontaneous intervals in the conversation.
3.   Difficult to interrupt.
4.   Impossible to interrupt, completely dominates the conversation.

3   Flight of Thoughts
0.   Not present
1.   Somewhat lively descriptions, explanations and elaborations without losing the connection with the topic of the conversation. The thoughts are thus still cohesive.
2.   Again it is occasionally difficult for the patient to stick to the topic, he is distracted by random associations (often rhymes, clangs, puns, pieces of verse or music).
3.   The line of thought is regularly disrupted by diversionary associations.
4.   It is difficult or impossible to follow the patient's line of thought, as he constantly jumps from one topic to another.

4   Voice/Noise Level
0.   Not unusual
1.   Speaks somewhat loudly without being noisy
2.   Voice discernible at a distance, and somewhat noisy.
3.   Vociferous, voice discernible at a long distance, is noisy, singing.
4.   Shouting, screaming; or using other sources of noise due to hoarseness.

5   Hostility/Destructiveness
0.   No signs of impatience or hostility.
1.   Somewhat impatient or irritable, but control is maintained.
2.   Markedly impatient or irritable. Provocation badly tolerated.
3.   Provocative, makes threats, but can be calmed down.
4.   Overt physical violence; physically destructive.

6   Mood Level (Feeling of Well-Being)
0.   Not unusual
1.   Slightly or doubtfully elevated mood, optimistic, but still adapted to situation.
2.   Moderately elevated mood, joking, laughing.
3.   Markedly elevated mood, exuberant both in manner and speech.
4.   Extremely elevated mood, quite irrelevant to situation.

7   Self-Esteem
0.   Not unusual
1.   Slightly or doubtfully increased self-esteem, for example occasionally over-estimates his own habitual capacities
2.   Moderately increased self-esteem, for example, overestimates more constantly his own habitual capacities or hints at unusual abilities.
3.   Markedly unrealistic ideas, for example, that he has extraordinary abilities, powers or knowledge (scientific, religious, etc.), but can briefly be corrected.
4.   Grandiose ideas which cannot be corrected.

8   Contact (Intrusiveness)
0.   Not unusual
1.   Slightly doubtfully meddling, for example, interrupting or slightly intrusive.
2.   Moderately meddling and arguing or intrusive.
3.   Dominating, arranging, directing, but still in context with the setting.
4.   Extremely dominating and manipulating, not in context with the setting.

9   Sleep (Average of past 3 nights)
0.   Habitual duration of sleep.
1.   Duration of sleep reduced by 25%
2.   Duration of sleep reduced by 50%
3.   Duration of sleep reduced by 75%
4.   No sleep

10   Sexual Interest
0.   Habitual sexual interest and activity.
1.   Slight or doubtful increase in sexual interest and activity, for example, slightly flirtatious.
2.   Moderate increase in sexual interest and activity, for example, clearly flirtatious.
3.   Marked increase in sexual interest and activity; excessively flirtatious; dress provocative.
4.   Completely and inadequately occupied by sexuality.

11   Decreased Work Ability

A   At First Rating
0.   Not present
1.   Slightly or doubtfully increased drive, but work quality is slightly down as motivation is changing, and the patient somewhat distractible.
2.   Increased drive, but motivation clearly fluctuating. The patient has difficulties in judging own work quality and the quality is indeed lowered. Frequent quarrels at work.
3.   Work capacity clearly reduced; the patient occasionally loses control. He must stop work and be written off sick. If hospitalized, he can participate for some hours per day in ward activities.
4.   The patient is (or ought to be) hospitalized and is unable to participate in ward activities.

B   At Weekly Ratings
0.   (a) The patient has resumed work at his normal activity level.
(b) The patient would have no trouble in working, but the effort is somewhat reduced due to changeable motivation

1.   (a) The patient is working, but the effort is somewhat reduced due to changeable motivation
     (b) It is doubtful whether the patient can resume normal work on a full scale due to distractibility and changeable motivation.
2.   (a) The patient is working, but at a clearly reduced level, for example, due to episodes of non-attendance
     (b) The patient is still hospitalized or written off sick. He is able to resume work only if special precautions are taken: close supervision and/or reduced working hours.
3.   The patient is still hospitalized or written off sick and is unable to resume work. In hospital he participates for some hours per day in ward activities.
4.   The patient is still fully hospitalized and generally unable to participate in ward activities.

Reference: Bech, P., Rafaelson, O. J., Kramp, P. & Bolwig, T. G. (1978). The Mania Rating Scale: Scale construction and inter-observer agreement. *Neuropharmacology*, **17**, 430–431. Copyright 1978. Reprinted with permission from Elsevier Science.

THE INTERNAL STATE SCALE (Bauer et al., 1991)

For each of the following statements, please mark an 'X' at the point on the line that best describes the way you have felt over *the past 24 hours*. While there may have been some change during that time, try to give a single summary rating for each item.

	Not at all Rarely	Very much so much of the time

1. Today my mood is changeable
2. Today I feel irritable
3. Today I feel like a capable person
4. Today I feel like people are out to get me
5. Today I actually feel great inside
6. Today I feel impulsive
7. Today I feel depressed
8. Today my thoughts are going fast
9. Today it seems like nothing will ever work out for me
10. Today I feel overactive
11. Today I feel as if the world is against me
12. Today I feel 'sped up' inside
13. Today I feel restless
14. Today I feel argumentative
15. Today I feel energized
16. Today I feel   Depressed/ Down   Normal   Manic/ High

Reference: Reconstructed from Bauer S., Crits-Christoph, P., Ball, W. A., Dewees, E. et al. (1991). Independent assessment of manic and depressive symptoms by self-rating: Scale characteristics and implications for the study of mania. *Archives of General Psychiatry,* **48**, 807–812.

Note: Please note that each visual analogue item above should be 100 mm.

SOCIAL PERFORMANCE SCHEDULE (Hurry et al., 1983)

	Day	Month	Year
Interviewer's initials	☐☐☐	☐☐	☐☐ ☐☐

1. Household Management (HM)

(EXAMPLES OF SERIOUS PROBLEMS: Shopping has to be done by someone else. Meals are not provided, or are inedible. House is filthy unless cleaned by someone else. Clothes have to be sent to the laundry by someone else. Do not include moderate forgetfulness in shopping, or inefficiency in housework, or lack of expertise in cooking.)

* Have you carried out your normal household duties in the past month?
(What are you normally expected to do?)   Yes   No

IF NO SIGNIFICANT CONTRIBUTION IS MADE OR EXPECTED.

*Why not?

SPECIFY REASON (e.g. wife does it)

IF SUBJECT IS NOT DISABLED, BUT NOT EXPECTED TO
DO HOUSEHOLD MANAGEMENT, SPECIFY WHO DOES _____

CUT-OFF (1) : RATE (9) ON 1.1 AND PROCEED TO SECTION 2

IF THERE IS SOME SIGNIFICANT CONTRIBUTION:

*How well have you managed with the housework,
shopping and so on, during the past month?   _____

*What about cooking, cleaning and laundry?   _____

CUT-OFF (2) : IF NO PROBLEMS, RATE (0) ON 1.1, PROCEED TO SECTION 2

SECTION 1 CUT-OFF

1.   HOUSEHOLD MANAGEMENT : BELOW CUT-OFF

IF THERE ARE ANY PROBLEMS, OR NO SIGNIFICANT CONTRIBUTION IS MADE:

What sort of problem has there been with   a) shopping?
                                               b) cooking?
                                               c) cleaning?
                                               d) laundry?
                                               e) danger?

SPECIFY: _____

_____

How long has it been going on?
(When did you last manage reasonably well?)

SPECIFY ONSET: _____

_____

How satisfied are you with this state of affairs?   _____

Does it bother you or distress you?   Yes   No

Have you tried to do anything about it?   Yes   No

If YES, what have you done about it?   _____

What do you think the problem is due to?
GIVE EXAMPLES OF REACTION, AND THE POSTULATED CAUSE:

_____

_____

1.1 RATE HOUSEHOLD MANAGEMENT DURING PAST MONTH

          0 Fair to good : cut-off (2)
          1 Serious problem(s) on occasions but can sometimes manage quite well
          2 Serious problems most of the time
          3 Virtually no contribution to household management
        9 Cut-off (1)

INTERVIEWER'S COMMENTS ON THE STATE OF THE HOUSE

_____

_____

_____

SOCIAL PERFORMANCE SCHEDULE

2.   EMPLOYMENT (EM)

(EXAMPLES OF SERIOUS PROBLEMS: Subject is constantly late for work, frequently takes time off, is extremely slow or turns out poor quality work, has frequent quarrels with others. In other words, subject is in danger of losing job. If in sheltered employment, e.g. Remploy, and functioning reasonably well, rate (2); if functioning poorly in Remploy, or if in day centre, etc., rate (3).)

Have you been doing any paid work during the month?   Yes   No
(include students on grants as employed)

IF NO WORK: Why aren't you working?

SPECIFY: _____

IF DISABILITY IS NOT THE CAUSE OF UNEMPLOYMENT, SPECIFY CAUSE:
(Independent income, retired, housewife, between jobs, factory closure etc.)

CUT-OFF (1) : RATE (9) ON 2.1 AND PROCEED TO SECTION 3

IF SUBJECT HAS BEEN WORKING DURING THE MONTH

What sort of work do you do?   SPECIFY: _____

*Have you had any problems with getting to work
on time or have you been taking days off?   Yes   No

Have there been any problems at work?   Yes   No

Can you work as quickly as they expect?   Yes   No

Have you made any mistakes?   Yes   No

Have you had problems in getting on   Yes   No
with colleagues and/or supervisors?

CUT-OFF (2) : IF NO PROBLEMS, RATE (0) ON 2.1, PROCEED TO SECTION 3

SECTION 2 CUT-OFF

2.   EMPLOYMENT : BELOW CUT-OFF

IF THERE ARE ANY WORK PROBLEMS OR SUBJECT IS UNEMPLOYED:

What sort of problem has there been with   a) timekeeping?
                                                  b) unauthorised absences?
                                                  c) output?
                                                  d) quality of work?
                                                  e) relations with mates?
                                                  f) supervisors?

SPECIFY: _____

How long has it been going on?
(When did you last manage reasonably well?)
SPECIFY ONSET: _____

Have there been previous occasions like this?   Yes   No

SPECIFY COURSE: _____

How satisfied are you with this state of affairs?   _____

Does it bother you or distress you?   Yes   No

Have you tried to do anything about it?   Yes   No

If YES, what have you done about it?   _____

What do you think the problem is due to?
GIVE EXAMPLES OF REACTION, AND THE POSTULATED CAUSE:

_____

2.1 RATE FUNCTIONING AT WORK DURING PAST MONTH

☐   0 Fair to good : cut-off (2)
           1 Serious problem(s) on occasions but can sometimes manage quite well
           2 Serious problems most of the time
           3 Unemployed throughout the month (due to some disability)
           9 Cut-off (1)

INTERVIEWER'S COMMENTS ON INFORMANT'S ACCOUNT

3.   MANAGEMENT OF MONEY (MM)

(EXAMPLES OF SERIOUS PROBLEMS: Subject spends very large sums on gambling, alcohol or unwise purchases, so that large debts are run up (or would be run up unless someone else handed out the money a little at a time)—rate (2).)

Have you any income of your own?   Yes   No

IF NONE OR VERY LITTLE: Why not?

SPECIFY: _____

IF *BY CHOICE* THE SUBJECT DOES NOT MANAGE HOUSEHOLD FINANCES
(and this is by choice not because of incapacity)

CUT-OFF (1) : RATE (9) ON 3.1 AND PROCEED TO SECTION 4

IF THE SUBJECT HAS ANY INCOME DURING THE MONTH (INCLUDE BENEFITS)

*How do you manage with (your own) money?   _____

(Has there been any unwise spending?)   _____

What about household bills, rent, hire purchase payments and so on?

_____

_____

CUT OFF (2) : IF NO PROBLEMS, RATE (0) ON 3.1, THEN PROCEED TO SECTION 4

SECTION 3 CUT-OFF

3. MANAGEMENT OF MONEY: BELOW CUT-OFF

IF THERE ARE ANY MONEY PROBLEMS OR NO SIGNIFICANT INCOME:

What sort of problem has there been with   a) housekeeping money?
b) paying hire purchase?
c) rent?
d) big debts?
e) unwise spending?
f) gambling?

SPECIFY: _____

How long has it been going on?
(When did you last manage reasonably well?)
SPECIFY ONSET: _____

Have there been previous occasions like this?   Yes   No

SPECIFY COURSE: _____

How satisfied are you with this state of affairs? _____

Does it bother you or distress you?   Yes   No

Have you tried to do anything about it?   Yes   No

If YES, what have you done about it? _____

What do you think the problem is due to?
GIVE EXAMPLES OF REACTION, AND THE POSTULATED CAUSE:

3.1 RATE MANAGEMENT OF MONEY DURING PAST MONTH

0 Fair to good : cut-off (2)
1 Serious problem(s) on occasions but can sometimes manage quite well
2 Serious problems most of the time
3 Income has to be completely managed for subject
9 Cut-off (1)

INTERVIEWER'S COMMENTS ON INFORMANT'S ACCOUNT

4.   CHILD CARE (CC)

(EXAMPLES OF SERIOUS PROBLEMS : Children are dirty, often miss meals, are poorly clothed and are not guarded against common dangers. Subject gives no affection, never plays with them and ill-treats them.)

Are there any children aged 15 or less in the house?   Yes   No

Are you responsible for any of their care?   Yes   No

IF NOT RESPONSIBLE FOR ANY CARE, SPECIFY RELATIONSHIP:

IF THE SUBJECT IS NOT RESPONSIBLE FOR THE CARE OF CHILDREN OR THERE ARE NO CHILDREN IN THE HOUSE

CUT-OFF (1) : RATE (9) ON 4.1 AND PROCEED TO SECTION 5

IF THE SUBJECT IS RESPONSIBLE FOR SOME OF THEIR CARE

How do you cope with the children?   SPECIFY: _____

(Have there been any problems with feeding,   SPECIFY: _____
keeping them clean and well-dressed, or keeping   _____
them out of danger?)   _____

(What about showing them affection, playing with them or disciplining them?)
SPECIFY: _____

CUT-OFF (2): IF NO PROBLEMS, RATE (0) ON 4.1, THEN PROCEED TO SECTION 5

SECTION 4 CUT-OFF

4.   CHILD CARE: BELOW CUT-OFF

IF THERE ARE ANY PROBLEMS:

What sort of problem has there been with   a) meals?   e) play?
                                            b) cleanliness?   f) discipline?
                                            c) clothes?   g) supervision?
                                            d) affection?   h) school?

SPECIFY: _____

How long has it been going on?
(When did you last manage reasonably well?)
SPECIFY ONSET: _____

Have there been previous occasions like this?   Yes   No

Have you tried to do anything about it?   Yes   No

If YES, what have you done about it?   _____

What do you think the problem is due to?
GIVE EXAMPLES OF REACTION, AND THE POSTULATED CAUSE:

4.1 RATE CHILD CARE DURING PAST MONTH

      0 Fair to good : cut-off (2)
☐   1 Serious problem(s) on occasions but can sometimes manage quite well
      2 Serious problems most of the time
      3 Not able to cope with child care at all
   9 Cut-off (1)

INTERVIEWER'S OBSERVATIONS ON CHILDREN

5.   INTIMATE RELATIONSHIP (IR)

Include relationships between subject and spouse (or cohabitee living in the same household). In other cases include a 'steady' relationship if a sexual component would be expected or would be likely to develop if the subject were not disabled. No introductory questions are listed since this is left for the interviewer's judgement.

(EXAMPLES OF SERIOUS PROBLEMS: Subject shows no affection, gives no companionship, seldom considers partner's needs, is hostile or violent, very suspicious or jealous, sexually inactive or only concerned with activities the partner reasonably finds obnoxious.)

For single subjects or others where there is no spouse/cohabitee in the household, select probe questions to determine presence of a steady relationship.

SPECIFY INTIMATE RELATIONSHIP:

CUT-OFF (1) : IF NO SUCH RELATIONSHIP EXISTS, RATE(9) ON 5.1 AND
PROCEED TO SECTION 6

How well do you get on together? _____

Are you able to show affection and companionship?	Yes	No
Are you considerate of your partner's feelings?	Yes	No
Can you give your partner good advice and support?	Yes	No
Have you lost interest in the sexual side of the relationship?	Yes	No

SPECIFY: _____

CUT-OFF (2) : IF NO PROBLEMS (PAST OR PRESENT), RATE (0) ON 5.1.
THEN PROCEED TO SECTION 6

SECTION 5 CUT-OFF

5.   INTIMATE RELATIONSHIP: BELOW CUT-OFF

IF THERE ARE ANY PROBLEMS IN CONTRIBUTING TO THE RELATIONSHIP:

What sort of problem has there been with

a) affection?	e) odd behaviour?
b) companionship?	f) jealousy?
c) support?	g) sexual relationships?
d) hostility?	

SPECIFY: _____

_____

How long have you been this way?
(Were you like this before?)

SPECIFY ONSET: _____

_____

Has it always been like this?   Yes   No

SPECIFY COURSE: _____

How satisfied are you with this state of affairs?   _____

Does it bother you or distress you?   Yes   No

Have you tried to do anything about it?   Yes   No

If YES, what have you done about it?   _____

What do you think the problem is due to?
GIVE EXAMPLES OF REACTION, AND THE POSTULATED CAUSE:

_____

_____

5.1 RATE SUBJECT'S CONTRIBUTION TO RELATIONSHIP IN THE PAST
      MONTH (OR DURING THE SUBJECT'S CURRENT EPISODE OF
      SYMPTOMS)

> 0 Fair to good : cut-off (2)
> 1 Serious problem(s) in contributing to the relationship
> 2 Serious problems most of the time
> 3 Virtually no contribution
>   9 Cut-off (1)

6. NON-INTIMATE RELATIONSHIP (NIR)

NB. Try to complete this section especially if Section 5 was not completed. Choose a person with whom the subject has most *regular adult contact/friendship*—if possible another adult living in the same household (e.g. parent, relative, friend) excluding an intimate relationship as described in Section 5.

Assess only the *subject's contribution/involvement* in the relationship.

Who is the friend or relative with whom you have most contact? _____
(excluding an intimate relationship as described in Section 5.)

(Is _____ the person with whom you have most contact?)

SPECIFY THE RELATIONSHIP: _____

(Most regular contact):

CUT-OFF (1): IF NO RELATIONSHIP MENTIONED OR ELICITED (PAST OR PRESENT), RATE (9) ON 6.1 AND PROCEED TO SECTION 7

IF ANY RELATIONSHIP MENTIONED:

How well do you get on together? _____

Are you considerate of 'Y's' feelings?	Yes	No
Are you able to give 'Y' good advice and emotional support?	Yes	No
Can 'Y' discuss his/her personal problems with you?	Yes	No

Have things always been this way?

SPECIFY: _____

CUT-OFF (2): IF FAIR TO GOOD INVOLVEMENT BY SUBJECT OR NO PROBLEMS (PAST OR PRESENT), RATE (0) ON 6.1. THEN PROCEED TO SECTION 7

SECTION 6 CUT-OFF

6. NON-INTIMATE RELATIONSHIP: BELOW CUT-OFF

IF THERE ARE ANY PROBLEMS IN CONTRIBUTING TO THE RELATIONSHIP:

What sort of problem has there been with

a) affection?	e) odd behaviour?
b) companionship?	f) jealousy?
c) support?	g) sexual relationships?
d) hostility?	

SPECIFY: _____

How long have you been this way?

(Were you like this before _____ ?)

SPECIFY ONSET: _____

How satisfied are you with this state of affairs? _____

Does it bother you or distress you?   Yes   No

Have you tried to do anything about it?   Yes   No

If YES, what have you done about it? _____

What do you think the problem is due to?
GIVE EXAMPLES OF REACTION, AND THE POSTULATED CAUSE:

_____

_____

6.1 RATE SUBJECT'S CONTRIBUTION TO RELATIONSHIP IN THE PAST
MONTH (OR DURING THE SUBJECT'S CURRENT EPISODE OF SYMPTOMS)

0 Fair to good : cut-off (2)
1 Serious problem(s) in contributing to the relationship
2 Serious problems most of the time
3 Virtually no contribution
9 Cut-off (1)

7. SOCIAL PRESENTATION (SP)

(EXAMPLES OF SERIOUS PROBLEMS: Subject disappears whenever there are visitors, never seeks company, is rude or aggressive towards others, has no regular companions, has no activities inside or ouside the household (except wandering, pacing), plays record player/radio very loudly for hours at a time many nights a week (far more than ordinary teenagers' lack of consideration), appears to other people as very withdrawn or odd or aggressive. Do not take appearance into account unless it is so grossly unusual that many people notice it. (Watching television for hours is NOT regarded as a serious problem in this context.)

NB. This section should be completed for everyone. It is intended to cover social roles other than those at work, or with a close relative or friend. It includes presentation of self in social situations, activities.

How do you get on with others in company? _____

Are you withdrawn, eager to get away, feel ill at ease?   Yes   No

How do you occupy yourself in your spare time? _____

Do you have any outside activities or hobbies?   _____

Have things always been this way?

SPECIFY: _____

CUT-OFF (1): IF NO PROBLEMS, RATE (0) ON 7.1. THEN PROCEED TO SECTION 8

SECTION 7 CUT-OFF

7.   SOCIAL PERFORMANCE : BELOW CUT-OFF

IF THERE ARE ANY PROBLEMS:

What sort of problem has there been with   a) friends?
                                             b) activities outside household?
                                             c) hobbies?
                                             d) avoidance of company?
                                             e) impression on others?

SPECIFY: _____

How long have you been like this?

(When did you last manage reasonably well?)

SPECIFY ONSET:

Have there been previous occasions like this?   Yes   No

SPECIFY COURSE: _____

How satisfied are you with this state of affairs? _____

Does it bother you or distress you?   Yes   No

Have you tried to do anything about it?   Yes   No

If YES, what have you done about it?   _____

What do you think the problem is due to?
GIVE EXAMPLES OF REACTION, AND THE POSTULATED CAUSE:

7.1   RATE SOCIAL PRESENTATION DURING THE PAST MONTH

☐   0 Fair to good : cut-off (2)
         1 Serious problem(s) in contributing to the relationship
         2 Serious problems most of the time
         3 Subject is virtually completely isolated and has no interest or activities

INTERVIEWER'S COMMENTS ON INFORMANT'S ACCOUNT (AND
IMPRESSION OF SUBJECT)

8. COPING WITH AN EMERGENCY (CE)

This section assesses how the subject would cope with a hypothetical crisis were it to occur now and were it to have occurred in the past—before the onset of present symptoms, if any.

* I am interested in how you might manage with some unexpected emergency. Imagine for example that some friend or relative were taken ill and you were asked to look after their two school-age children. How well do you think you could manage?
  (If the subject has his/her *own* family responsibilities, assume there is someone to help them in this respect).

SPECIFY:

_____

_____

_____

* Might you have managed better in the past? (Prior to your present symptoms/worries)
  (How well would you have managed then?)

SPECIFY:

_____

_____

_____

8.1 RATE ABILITY TO COPE WITH CRISIS AT PRESENT:

☐
0 Would have no problems coping
1 Some problem(s) coping but would manage
2 Serious problems coping
3 Could not cope at all

OVERALL RATINGS

1. Household management		5. Intimate relationship	
2. Employment		6. Non-intimate relationship	
3. Management of money		7. Social presentation	
4. Child care		8. Coping with an emergency	

REMIND INFORMANT OF PROBLEM AREAS: _____

	Day	Month	Year

Establish date of onset of disability

Establish course of disability:

_____

NB. If there has been a different onset or course in different areas, use the most serious problems to determine an overall pattern, e.g. overlapping episodes of different kinds of disablement should be treated as one episode.

9.1 LENGTH OF PRESENT EPISODE:

NB. Date the onset of present period of disablement irrespective of type of disablement.

Date of onset of present episode — Day Month Year

Date of interview — Day Month Year

Duration of episode prior to interview — Months

9.2 SOCIAL IMPAIRMENT

0 Not in episode (No current impairment)
1 Onset within past month
2 2–3 months before interview
3 4–6 months before interview
4 7–12 months before interview
5 13–24 months before interview
6 >25 months before interview

9.3 COURSE OF PRESENT EPISODE

0 Not in episode (No current impairment)
1 Performance improving
2 Performance getting worse
3 Much fluctuation in performance
4 Much the same level throughout the episode

9.4 OVERALL COURSE DURING ADULT LIFE

0 Never any episodes
1 Present episode is the first. During most of adult life, performance has been fair to good

Reference: Hurry, J., Sturt, E., Bebbington P. & Tennant C. (1983). Socio-demographic associations with social disablement in a community sample. *Social Psychiatry*, **18**, 113–121. Reproduced by permission of Steinkopff Verlag.

SIGNIFICANT OTHERS SCALE (Power et al., 1988)

INSTRUCTION : Please list up to 7 people who may be important in your life. Typical relationships include spouse, partner, father, mother, child, sibling, close friends, etc. For each person please circle a number from 1 to 7 to show how well he or she provides the type of help that is listed. The second part of each question asks you to rate how you would like things to be if they were exactly what you hoped for. As above, please put a circle around one number between 1 and 7 to show what the rating is.

Person 1

	never			some-times		always	
1a) Can you trust, talk to frankly and share your feelings with this person?	1	2	3	4	5	6	7
b) What rating would your ideal be?	1	2	3	4	5	6	7
2a) Can you lean on and turn to this person in times of difficulty?	1	2	3	4	5	6	7
b) What rating would your ideal be?	1	2	3	4	5	6	7
3a) Does he/she give you practical help?	1	2	3	4	5	6	7
b) What rating would your ideal be?	1	2	3	4	5	6	7
4a) Can you spend time with him/her socially?	1	2	3	4	5	6	7
b) What rating would your ideal be?	1	2	3	4	5	6	7

Person 2

	never			some-times		always	
1a) Can you trust, talk to frankly and share your feelings with this person?	1	2	3	4	5	6	7
b) What rating would your ideal be?	1	2	3	4	5	6	7
2a) Can you lean on and turn to this this person in times of difficulty?	1	2	3	4	5	6	7
b) What rating would your ideal be?	1	2	3	4	5	6	7
3a) Does he/she give you practical help?	1	2	3	4	5	6	7
b) What rating would your ideal be?	1	2	3	4	5	6	7
4a) Can you spend time with him/her socially?	1	2	3	4	5	6	7
b) What rating would your ideal be?	1	2	3	4	5	6	7

Person 3

	never			some-times		always	
1a) Can you trust, talk to frankly and share your feelings with this person?	1	2	3	4	5	6	7
b) What rating would your ideal be?	1	2	3	4	5	6	7

2a)	Can you lean on and turn to this person in times of difficulty?		1	2	3	4	5	6	7
b)	What rating would your ideal be?		1	2	3	4	5	6	7
3a)	Does he/she give you practical help?	1		2	3	4	5	6	7
b)	What rating would your ideal be?		1	2	3	4	5	6	7
4a)	Can you spend time with him/her socially?		1	2	3	4	5	6	7
b)	What rating would your ideal be?		1	2	3	4	5	6	7

Person 4

		never			some-times			always	
1a)	Can you trust, talk to frankly and share your feelings with this person?		1	2	3	4	5	6	7
b)	What rating would your ideal be?		1	2	3	4	5	6	7
2a)	Can you lean on and turn to this person in times of difficulty?		1	2	3	4	5	6	7
b)	What rating would your ideal be?		1	2	3	4	5	6	7
3a)	Does he/she give you practical help?	1		2	3	4	5	6	7
b)	What rating would your ideal be?		1	2	3	4	5	6	7
4a)	Can you spend time with him/her socially?		1	2	3	4	5	6	7
b)	What rating would your ideal be?		1	2	3	4	5	6	7

Person 5

		never			some-times			always	
1a)	Can you trust, talk to frankly and share your feelings with this person?		1	2	3	4	5	6	7
b)	What rating would your ideal be?		1	2	3	4	5	6	7
2a)	Can you lean on and turn to this this person in times of difficulty?		1	2	3	4	5	6	7
b)	What rating would your ideal be?		1	2	3	4	5	6	7
3a)	Does he/she give you practical help?	1		2	3	4	5	6	7
b)	What rating would your ideal be?		1	2	3	4	5	6	7
4a)	Can you spend time with him/her socially?		1	2	3	4	5	6	7
b)	What rating would your ideal be?		1	2	3	4	5	6	7

Person 6

		never			some-times			always	
1a)	Can you trust, talk to frankly and share your feelings with this person?		1	2	3	4	5	6	7
b)	What rating would your ideal be?		1	2	3	4	5	6	7
2a)	Can you lean on and turn to this person in times of difficulty?		1	2	3	4	5	6	7

b)	What rating would your ideal be?	1	2	3	4	5	6	7
3a)	Does he/she give you practical help?	1	2	3	4	5	6	7
b)	What rating would your ideal be?	1	2	3	4	5	6	7
4a)	Can you spend time with him/her socially?	1	2	3	4	5	6	7
b)	What rating would your ideal be?	1	2	3	4	5	6	7

Person 7

		never				some-times		always
1a)	Can you trust, talk to frankly and share your feelings with this person?	1	2	3	4	5	6	7
b)	What rating would your ideal be?	1	2	3	4	5	6	7
2a)	Can you lean on and turn to this person in times of difficulty?	1	2	3	4	5	6	7
b)	What rating would your ideal be?	1	2	3	4	5	6	7
3a)	Does he/she give you practical help?	1	2	3	4	5	6	7
b)	What rating would your ideal be?	1	2	3	4	5	6	7
4a)	Can you spend time with him/her socially?	1	2	3	4	5	6	7
b)	What rating would your ideal be?	1	2	3	4	5	6	7

Reference: Power, M. J., Champion, L. A. & Aris, S. J. (1988). The development of a measure of social support: The Significant Others (SOS) Scale. *British Journal of Clinical Psychology, 27*, 349–358. Reprinted with permission from the © The British Psychological Society

MANIC DEPRESSION—PATIENTS' EDUCATION PAMPHLET

1.0 Introduction

Manic depression magnifies common human emotional experiences of sadness and fatigue, happiness and energy, irritability and rage, creativity and sensuality.

When you are high, it is tremendous. Shyness goes, the right words and gestures are suddenly there, the power to seduce and captivate others a felt certainty. There are interests found in uninteresting people. Sensuality is pervasive and the desire to seduce and be seduced irresistible. Feelings of ease, intensity, power, well-being, financial omnipotence and euphoria now pervade one's marrow. But somewhere, this changes. The fast ideas are far too fast and there are far too many, overwhelming confusion replaced by fear and concern. You are irritable, angry, frightened, uncontrollable and enmeshed totally in the blackest caves of mind. ... It goes on and on and finally there are only others' recollections of your behaviour—your bizarre, frenetic, aimless behaviour ... —a patient's account published in Goodwin and Jamison (1990).

The same patient then talked about how all credit cards were revoked, cheques bounced, explanations due at work, apologies to make, intermittent memories of vague men, friendship gone or drained and a ruined marriage.

Manic depressive illness is a common illness. It is said that the chance of someone developing the illness is about 1 in 100 in a lifetime. The exact proportion of people affected by this illness depends on how tightly the illness is defined. There is a strong genetic component in manic depression. Often sufferers have a family history of either depression or manic depression. Yet the illness is often described as biological in origin and behavioural and psychological in expression. Furthermore, the illness and its recurrence are often triggered by environmental stress, particularly at the early stage of the illness. Hence both biological makeup and stress (diathesis–stress model) play a part in manic depression. There is some evidence that if manic depression is not treated, it would lead to more severe and frequent episodes later, often without a clearly identifiable environmental stress. Over the past thirty years, treatment has improved as a result of the discovery of lithium and antidepressants.

However, some patients believe that lithium medication

prevents my seductive but disastrous high, diminishes my depressions, clears out the wool and webbing from my disordered thinking, slows me down, gentles me out, keeps me from ruining my career and relationship, keeps me out of hospitals, alive and makes psychotherapy possible. But ineffably, psychotherapy heals. It makes some sense of the confusion, reins in the terrifying thoughts and feelings, returns some control and opens the possibility of learning from it all. ... No pills can help me deal with the problem of not wanting to take pills; likewise, no amount of analysis alone can prevent my manias and depressions. I need both. (Goodwin and Jamison, 1990).

For some less fortunate sufferers, they continue to have recurrence of mania or depression despite regular medication. In these cases, therapy may be able to help them to examine extra strategies that may help them to deal with their illness by monitoring, detecting and coping with early warnings; by establishing a routine in their lives of regular eating, exercise and sleep; by avoiding undue environmental stress and learning techniques to cope with stress; and by examining their 'rules of living'. Hence therapy can be seen as the stress side of the equation.

2.0 Cognitive therapy

Cognitive therapy is a form of psychotherapy that aims to empower patients by teaching them tools to deal with negative emotions and preventing future relapses. It is short-term and focuses on the here and now. The past is examined in order to understand and put the present problems into context. It is problem orientated. Patients and therapists work as a team to deal with some of the problems patients have. Therapists and patients often agree on certain tasks that patients carry out in-between sessions so that patients can practise what they learn in therapy and sometimes these tasks can serve the function of gathering information for therapy sessions. As therapy progresses, therapists and patients then work together to focus more on some of the 'rules' or 'assumptions' patients have in order to effect more long-term change. The following are some of the basic concepts of cognitive therapy.

2.1 Thought, Mood and Behaviour

Our thinking, behaviour and emotions can affect each other. Most of us have experienced occasions when we did not want to go out because we felt slightly low and could not be bothered. Yet when we actually went out, we enjoyed ourselves and felt better (behaviour affecting mood). On the other hand, most of us also have experienced the 'low' occasions when we decided against going out and sat at home 'like a lemon'. We did not feel any better and in fact felt more miserable. In clinically depressed patients these experiences also hold. Therapists often use behavioural techniques such as 'engaging in enjoyable activities, small goal-directed steps and keeping busy' to 'pull' these patients out of their depression somewhat. In a mildly high state (hypomanic state), therapists often persuade patients to act against their instinct of going out and seeking more stimulation. Instead, they are persuaded to do less and engage in calming activities to get out of a mildly 'high' state.

It is well known that when people are depressed, they have more negative thoughts. When people are euphoric, their thoughts can be unrealistic. In extreme emotional state, these thoughts can be unrealistically depressing or optimistic and they pop into the mind without any real effort (automatic thoughts). Furthermore, these thoughts can become very real despite objective evidence to the contrary. This in turn would make the emotional state even more extreme. For example when depressed, they may have accusatory thoughts that their depression is a result of being weak or useless. As a result of these negative thoughts, they become more depressed. When high, they may believe that they have unusual abilities and get very irritated when others do not understand or take a different view. They become more elated because of this belief of possessing unusual abilities and irritated with people they perceive as less able and who yet refuse to follow their ideas.

In cognitive therapy, patients are first taught to monitor thoughts and behaviour. They are taught to catch these automatic thoughts as they occur and write them down. They are also taught to monitor their behaviour or activities by filling in a record. Then later thoughts and behaviour are used to influence mood. Patients are taught how to deal with these automatic thoughts by techniques which enable them to step aside and examine the reality of these automatic thoughts. They are also taught to regulate their activity levels and to learn to use behaviour to influence their mood.

2.2 Early Warnings

Medication compliance and insight into the illness are important factors in determining how manic depressive patients fare. However, the patients who do really well are those who have learned to monitor their moods and to watch out for early warnings. Some patients learn to observe their moods in very sophisticated ways. One patient not only monitors his mood state, he also learnt to monitor the trend of his mood over several days. 'It is all right to be happy after a skiing holiday. But if my mood keeps going up for several days, then I know I have to be careful.' Early warnings are different for each patient. However, the common ones are lack of sleep, waking up early with the thought of 'it is wonderful to have three extra hours to sort things out before going to work' and tiredness. Another patient's early warning was if she started to read too much into 'Thought for the Day' on Radio 4. Because the early warnings are so idiosyncratic, a good way to find out what could be your early warnings for you is to go through previous episodes in detail with your therapist and to mark out any possible early warnings. Some patients can pinpoint the stressful antecedents or situations, such as a demanding period at work, that can lead to the identification of early warnings. Your previous ways of coping and their effects can also be elicited for therapeutic purposes.

2.3 A Routine for Daily Living

Clinically therapists notice that a chaotic lifestyle can lead to more manic depressive episodes. Hence many therapists suggest to patients suffering from manic depression that a structured routine is important. Furthermore regular sleep routine is also crucial. Lack of sleep or over-tiredness is a common precedent to developing early prodromal or hypomanic states. Patients can develop a hypomanic state from long-distance travelling or jet lag. Hence patients can be educated about the importance of sleep and routine. Having a structured routine, regular eating and exercise can help to regulate sleeping patterns. Hence part of therapy is also to establish a good self-management routine.

2.4 Coping with Maladaptive Rules or Assumptions

We all learn rules or assumptions from experience, particularly salient experiences from early childhood, in order to cope with the minefield of information thrown at us. Sometimes these rules or assumptions can be very rigid and hinder rather than help. For example, some manic depressive patients have this rule of having to be the 'top drawer' or else they are no good. Hence, achievement assumes a more profound significance to them. When they fail in certain tasks, they take on more and even bigger projects in order to make good. This 'upward spiral' can go on and on until they cannot cope and have a manic episode. Other patients have different rules or assumptions. Part of therapy is to examine these rules or assumptions and to learn ways to be more adaptive.

3.0 Conclusion

This pamphlet attempts to inform manic depressive patients briefly about their illness and what cognitive therapy is about. Some of the issues discussed above may or may not apply to you. You may want to share your own experience with your therapist and in doing so you may find it helpful to write comments on this copy and discuss any further thoughts or issues you may want to clarify with your therapist.

Self-help books

Copeland, M.E. & McKay, M. (1992). *The depression workbook—a guide for living with depression and manic depression.* New Harbinger Publications.

Jamison, K.R. (1995). *An unquiet mind: A memoir of moods and madness.* London: Picador. (Autobiography of a famous professor of clinical psychology and psychiatry.)

MANIC DEPRESSION AND MEDICATION

Four classes of medications might be used with manic depression. These are:

1. The *mood stabilisers*. These drugs are generally used when a patient is well, to prevent future episodes of mania or depression. They can also be administered when a patient is unwell, either alone or in combination with other drugs.
2. The *antidepressants*. These drugs are commonly used to treat depression; they have been proved to be effective with ordinary depression, but are less well tested in manic depression. With manic depression, there is a risk in some patients that they can trigger a manic episode.
3. The *anti-psychotics*, also known as the *major tranquillisers*. These drugs are often used to treat acute manic and hypo-manic episodes. There is some evidence that they can also be used, in reduced doses, to prevent relapse.
4. The *anti-Parkinsonian* drugs. These are prescribed with anti-psychotics, to alleviate some of the side effects of those medications.

We offer here a brief summary of the possible benefits and drawbacks of each of these types of medication. *All drugs used in psychiatry vary greatly in their effectiveness,* so that a highly effective dose for one patient may have no effect on another patient. Likewise, *all effective medications have side effects:* the only medications which have no undesirable effects are those which seem to have no effects at all. As with beneficial effects, side effects vary greatly from patient to patient. For the medications we discuss here, we offer lists of side effects: some of these commonly occur, but it would be very unusual for a patient to experience all of them. There are other, less common, side effects which we have not listed; *if you are in doubt, consult your doctor or pharmacist.*

There is no way to predict either how effective a drug will be for an individual patient or how bad its particular side effects will be. As a result, all psychiatric drugs have to be prescribed on an 'empirical', that is, a trial-and-error, basis. Some patients use the phrase, 'being treated like a guinea pig', because of this use of trial and error in setting drug dosages. All the drugs discussed below have been tested and have been shown to be reasonably safe, and to have been effective in at least some cases: if a patient is given any experimental or untested drug, they must be informed of the fact and give their written consent. However, unless a patient is very lucky and the best drug, at the best dosage, is initially prescribed, some adjustment of medication is practically inevitable.

It is important to note that the body's reactions to drugs may also vary over time. Factors such as stress, diet and level of exercise can change the way the body metabolises medications. This means that drug levels need to be periodically reviewed, and that for some drugs, repeated blood tests may be necessary to make sure that the level of drug in the body is safe and effective. It also means that maintaining a healthy lifestyle, with healthy diet and exercise and careful monitoring of stress levels, may be helpful in making sure that medications offer the maximum benefit. In addition, it is advisable that all patients know what medications they are on, understand their risks and benefits, and feel that they are in a position to collaborate with their doctors in making decisions about medication.

Various tests can be used to determine the blood level of some, but not all, medications. Any drug must be administered in a sufficient dose to reach its *therapeutic level*, the level at which it is effective. If the blood level of any drug is too low, it will not work. If the blood level of any drug is too high, it may reach a *toxic level*, a level at which it is harmful. For this reason, it is important to follow your doctor's advice when taking any medication.

One fact that confuses some patients about their medication is that most medications have more than one name. All drugs have a generic or chemical name (e.g. chlorpromazine), but they may also have names given by the company that manufactures them (e.g. Largactil). *Your doctor, pharmacist, C.P.N., or other keyworker should be able to answer any questions you may have: it is your right to be informed about your medication.*

Mood Stabilisers

Lithium

Lithium is a naturally occurring element, the lightest of the metals and commonly found in the form of a salt. An Australian doctor named Cade first discovered, by accident, that it might benefit those suffering from manic depression in 1949. Cade's results were ignored, and the benefits of lithium were not rediscovered until the 60s, but research done since that time shows that lithium can prevent relapse in a high percentage of those who have suffered from a manic episode, and that it also can have benefits in the treatment of depression. Its mode of action is not understood.

It comes in two forms, lithium carbonate and lithium citrate. Lithium is a very effective drug, but also a dangerous one, since its toxic level in the blood is not very far above its therapeutic level. For this reason regular blood tests are essential. It is also important to drink plenty of fluids every day, but alcohol, as well as coffee or strong tea, should be taken in moderation, as these drinks can increase urination and cause the body to lose water. Diuretic drugs, which increase urination, should be used with care; make sure to discuss this with your doctor if such drugs are prescribed.

Common Names: Priadel, Camcolit, Litrax.

Common Side Effects: Increased thirst and urination. Dry mouth. Trembling hands. Mild nausea. Acne.

More Serious Side Effects: Weight gain. Excessive urination.

Toxic Effects: Persistent diarrhoea. Intense thirst. Persistent nausea and vomiting. Confusion. Severe tremor. Blurred vision. *These symptoms could be a sign of excessive lithium in the blood. If this condition persists, it could result in kidney damage—* CONSULT YOUR DOCTOR.

Carbamazepine

This drug is generally prescribed for epilepsy, but it has mood-stabilising properties and can be used either instead of, or as a supplement to, lithium.

When it is prescribed, dosage is gradually increased; there are often initial side effects, but these commonly decrease after a few weeks. Regular blood tests are recommended when taking carbamazepine.

Common Name: Tegretol

Common Side Effects: Dry mouth. Nausea. Diarrhoea. Dizziness. Headache. Problems with walking. Tiredness. Rashes.

Antidepressants

Depression has been called 'the common cold of mental illness'; up to 10% of the population may suffer from depression during their lives. As a result the antidepressant drugs are now very widely prescribed. There are a number of different types of antidepressant drugs, but the two most common types are the tricyclic antidepressants (TCAs) and the serotonin reuptake inhibitors (SSRIs). The first type has been used for about 30 years, the second type for less than ten years. Both are about equally effective, and both take between two weeks and a month to actually relieve depression. Some patients stop taking their antidepressants before they have had a chance to work: *if you are prescribed anti-depressants, make sure to take them at the correct dose, and do not expect them to work right away!* The main difference between these two families of drugs is that they have different side effects. One of the new SSRIs, Prozac, earned a lot of media attention, but it is no more effective than any other antidepressant.

In manic depression, these drugs are used during depressive episodes. However, there is a risk, in some sufferers, that antidepressants can trigger an episode of mania. Patient and doctor should be aware of this and monitor the patient for early warning signs.

The Tricyclics: examples include Amitriptyline (Tryptizol), Dothiepin (Prothiaden) and Lofepramine (Gamanil).

Side Effects: These drugs have a wide variety of side effects, which are often worse during the first few weeks, before they begin to have any effect on depression. Common side effects include tiredness and excessive sedation, dry mouth, constipation, and difficulty in urinating. After the first few weeks, these side effects should decrease.

The SSRIs: examples include Fluoxetine (Prozac), Paroxetine (Seroxat) and Sertraline (Lustral).

Side Effects: As noted above, these drugs are said to have fewer side effects than the Tricyclics. However, they can have a number of varied side effects, including upset stomach, headaches, agitation and rashes. These can sometimes be alleviated by lowering the dose of medication.

There is one other class of antidepressants that is sometimes prescribed, the *MAO inhibitors*. These were the first antidepressants, but most of them cannot be mixed with certain foods, such as cheeses and yeast products, and for this reason are very seldom prescribed. A new type of MAO inhibitor, Moclobamide, does not require dietary restriction

Neuroleptics

These drugs are also referred to as the *antipsychotic* drugs or the *major tranquillisers*. Their principal use is in the treatment of psychosis, and they have been shown to reduce or eliminate many of the symptoms of psychosis, such as bizarre ideas (delusions) or the experience of hearing voices that others do not hear (hallucinations). In manic depression they are used during acute manic episodes to calm the patient, slow racing thoughts, reduce agitation and help the patient to sleep. They are generally not used as a long-term treatment in manic depression, although there can be exceptions to this.

Common Neuroleptics include: Chlorpromazine (Largactil), Haloperidol (Haldol), Droperidol (Droleptan), Thioridazine (Melleril) and Trifluoperazine (Stelazine), and there are also many others.

Side Effects: The neuroleptics have many side effects: these include sedation (sleepiness), dry mouth, constipation and sensitivity to sunlight. A common class of side effects, the so called extra-pyramidal or Parkinsonian side effects, include stiffness and restlessness—these can be treated with so called *anti-Parkinsonian* drugs (see below).

Anti-Parkinsonian Drugs

As noted above, these drugs are sometimes given with neuroleptic drugs to relieve side effects; they are also known as *anticholinergic drugs*. They are usually not prescribed initially, but only as a treatment for so-called *Parkinsonian* side effects, if they develop. The name refers to Parkinson's disease, a brain disease that can cause stiffness and rigidity of movement, restlessness, a tremor in the hands and a shuffling walk. Neuroleptics can cause these symptoms in some patients: they usually disappear when the drug dose is lowered or stopped, but they can also be treated with anti-Parkinsonian drugs.

Common anti-Parkinsonian Drugs include: Procyclidine (Kemadrin), Benztropine (Cogentin), Benzhexol (Artane).

Side Effects include: dry mouth, stomach upset, dizziness, blurred vision. Some of these drugs may also create a stimulating, mildly pleasurable effect.

REFERENCES

Abou-Saleh, M. T. (1983). Platelet MAO: Personality and response to lithium prophylaxis. *Journal of Affective Disorders*, **5**, 55–65.

Abraham, K. (1953). Notes on the psycho-analytical investigation and treatment of
manic depressive insanity and allied conditions. In *Selected papers of Karl
Abraham* (pp. 137–157). New York: Basic Books.

Akiskal, H. S., Khani, M. K. & Scott-Strauss, A. (1979). Cyclothymic temperamental
disorders. *Psychiatric Clinics of North America*, **2**, 527–554.

Alford, B. A. & Beck, A. T. (1997). *The integrative power of cognitive therapy*. New York:
Guilford.

Alloway, R. & Bebbington, P. (1987). The buffer theory of social support: A review
of the literature. *Psychological Medicine*, **17**, 91–108.

Altman, E. S., Rea, M. M., Mintz, J. et al. (1992). Prodromal symptoms and signs of
bipolar relapse: A report based on prospectively collected data. *Psychiatry
Research*, **41**, 1–8.

Ambelas, A. (1979). Psychologically stressful events in the precipitation of manic
episodes. *British Journal of Psychiatry*, **135**, 15–21.

Ambelas, A. (1987). Life events and mania: A special relationship? *British Journal of
Psychiatry*, **150**, 235–240.

American Psychiatric Association (1980). *Diagnostic and Statistical Manual of Mental
Disorders*. 3rd edn. Washington DC: The Association.

American Psychiatric Association (1987). *Diagnostic and Statistical Manual of Mental
Disorders*. 3rd edn revised. Washington DC: The Association.

American Psychiatric Association (1994a). *Diagnostic and Statistical Manual of Mental
Disorders*. 4th edn. Washington DC: The Association.

American Psychiatric Association (1994b). Practice guidelines for the treatment of
patients with bipolar disorder. *American Journal of Psychiatry*, December
Supplement, **151**, 1–36.

Anderson, C. A. & Hammen, C. L. (1993). Psychosocial outcomes of children of
unipolar depressed, bipolar, medically ill, and normal women: A longitudinal
study. *Journal of Consulting and Clinical Psychology*, **61**, 448–454.

Basco, M. R. & Rush, A. J. (1996). *Cognitive-behavioral therapy for bipolar disorder*. New
York: Guilford.

Bauer, M. S., Crits-Christoph, P., Ball, W. A. et al. (1991). Independent assessment of
manic and depressive symptoms by self-rating: Scale characteristics and implications for the study of mania. *Archives of General Psychiatry*, **48**, 807–812.

Bauer M. S., Whybrow, P. C. & Winokur, A. (1990). Rapid cycling bipolar affective disorder: I. Association with grade I hypothyroidism. *Archives of General Psychiatry,* **47**, 427–432.

Bauwens, F., Tracy, A., Pardoen, D., Vander Elst, M. & Mandlewicz, J. (1991). Social adjustment of remitted bipolar and unipolar out-patients: A comparison with age- and sex-matched controls. *British Journal of Psychiatry,* **159**, 239–244.

Baxter, L., Edell, W., Gerner, R. et al. (1984). Dexamathasone suppression test and axis I diagnoses of inpatients with DSM-III borderline personality disorder. *Journal of Clinical Psychiatry,* **45**, 150–153.

Bebbington, P. & Ramana, R. (1995). The epidemiology of bipolar affective disorder. *Social Psychiatry and Psychiatric Epidemiology,* **30**, 279–292.

Bebbington, P., Wilkins, S., Jones, P. B. et al. (1993). Life events and psychosis: Initial results from the Camberwell Collaborative Psychosis Study. *British Journal of Psychiatry,* **162**, 72–79.

Bech, P., Rafaelsen, O. J., Kramp, P. & Bolwig, T. G. (1978). The Mania Rating Scale: Scale construction and inter-observer agreement. *Neuropharmacology,* **17**, 430–431.

Beck, A. T. (1976). *Cognitive therapy and the emotional disorders.* New York: International Universities Press.

Beck, A. T. (1983). Cognitive therapy of depression: New perspectives. In P. J. Clayton and J. E. Barrett (eds) *Treatment of depression: Old controversies and new approaches.* New York: Raven Press.

Beck, A. T. (1986). Hopelessness as a predictor of eventual suicide. In J. J. Mann & M. Stanley (eds), *Psychobiology* (pp. 90–96). New York: Academy of Science.

Beck, A. T., Brown, G., Steer, R. A. & Weissman, A. N. (1991). Factor analysis of the Dysfunctional Attitude Scale in a clinical population. *Psychological Assessment,* **3**, 478–483.

Beck, A. T., Epstein, N., Harrison, R. P. & Emery, G. (1983). *Development of the sociotropy-autonomy scale: A measure of personality factors in depression.* University of Pennsylvania: Philadelphia.

Beck, A. T., Rush, A. J., Shaw, B., and Emery, G. (1979). *Cognitive therapy of depression.* New York: Guilford Press.

Beck, A. T. & Steer, R. A. (1987). *Beck Depression Inventory.* The Psychological Corporation: Harcourt Brace.

Beck, A. T. & Steer, R. A. (1988). *Beck Hopelessness Scale.* The Psychological Corporation: Harcourt Brace.

Beck, A. T. & Steer, R. A. (1991). *Beck Scale for Suicide Ideation.* The Psychological Corporation: Harcourt Brace.

Beck, A. T., Steer, R. A. & Brown G. K. (1996). *Beck Depression Inventory II.* The Psychological Corporation: Harcourt Brace.

Beck, A. T., Steer, R. A. & Garbin, M. G. (1988). Psychometric properties of the Beck Depression Inventory: Twenty-five years of evaluation. *Clinical Psychology Review.* **8**, 77–100.

Beck, A. T., Steer, R. A., Kovacs, M. & Garrison, B. (1985). Hopelessness and eventual suicide: A 10-year prospective study of patients hospitalized with suicidal ideation. *American Journal of Psychiatry,* **142**, 559–563.

Beck, A. T., Ward, C. H., Mendelson, M. et al. (1961). An inventory for measuring depression. *Archives of General Psychiatry,* **4**, 53–63.

Beck, A. T., Weissman, A., Lester, D. & Trexler, L. (1974). The measurement of pessimism: The Hopelessness Scale. *Journal of Consulting and Clinical Psychology*, 42, 861–865.

Beck, J. S. (1995). *Cognitive therapy: Basics and beyond.* New York: Guilford.

Bellack, A. S., Morrison, R. L., Mueser, K. T. & Wade, J. (1989). Social competence in schizoaffective disorder, bipolar disorder and negative and non-negative schizophrenia. *Schizophrenia Research*, 2, 391–401.

Benson, R. (1975). The forgotten treatment modality in bipolar illness: Psychotherapy. *Disease of Nervous System*, 36, 634–638.

Bernstein, D. A. & Borkovec, T. D. (1973). *Progressive relaxation training: A manual for therapists*, Research Press.

Blackburn, I. M. & Davidson, K. (1990). *Cognitive therapy for depression and anxiety: A practitioner's guide.* Oxford: Blackwell.

Bowden, C. L., Brugger, A. M., Swann, A. C. et al. (1994). Efficacy of divalproex vs lithium and placebo in the treatment of mania: The Depakote Mania Study Group. *Journal of America Medical Association*, 271, 918–924.

Boyd, J. H., Burke, J. D., Gruenberg, E. et al. (1984). Exclusion criteria of DSM-III: A study of co-occurence of hierarchy-free syndromes. *Archives of General Psychiatry*, 41, 983–989.

Brewin, C. R. (1989). Cognitive change processes in psychotherapy. *Psychological Review*, 96, 379–394.

British National Formulary (1997). British Medical Association and the Royal Pharmaceutical Society of Great Britain.

Brown, G. W. & Harris, T. O. (1989). Depression. In G. Brown and T. Harris (eds), *Life Events and Illness* (pp. 49–93). London: Unwin Hyman.

Burke, K. C., Burke, J. D. Jr., Regier, D. A. & Rae, D. S. (1990). Age at onset of selected mental disorders in five community populations. *Archives of General Psychiatry*, 47, 511–518.

Calabrese, J. R., & Delucchi, G. A. (1990). Spectrum of efficacy of valprote in 55 patients with rapid-cycling bipolar disorder. *American Journal of Psychiatry*, 147, 431–434.

Calabrese, J. R., Fatemi, S. H. & Woyshville, M. J. (1996). Antidepressant effects of lamotrigine in rapid cycling bipolar disorder. *American Journal of Psychiatry*, 153, 1236.

Calabrese, J. R., Markovitz, P. J., Kimmel, S. E. & Wagner, S. C. (1992). Spectrum of efficacy of valproate in 78 rapid-cycling bipolar patients. *Journal of Clinical Psychopharmacology*, 12 (1 suppl.), 53S–56S.

Cannon, M., Jones, P., Gilvarry, C. et al. (1997). Premorbid social functioning in schizophrenia and bipolar disorder: Similarities and differences. *American Journal of Psychiatry*, 154, 1544–1550.

Carlson, G. A., Kotin, J. L., Davenport, Y. B. & Adland, M. (1974). Follow-up of 53 bipolar manic-depressive patients. *British Journal of Psychiatry*, 124, 134–139.

Carney, P. A., Fitzgerald, C. T. & Monaghan, C. E. (1988). Influence of climate on the prevalence of mania. *British Journal of Psychiatry*, 152, 820–823.

Chakrabarti, S., Kulhara, P. & Verma, S. K. (1992). Extent and determinants of burden among families of patients with affective disorders. *Acta Psychiatrica Scandinavica*, 86, 247–252.

Chen, Y-W & Dilsaver, S. C. (1996). Lifetime rates of suicide attempts among subjects with bipolar and unipolar disorders relative to subjects with other axis I disorders. *Biological Psychiatry*, **39**, 896–899.

Clarkin, J. F., Glick, I. D., Haas, G. L. et al. (1990). A randomised clinical trial of inpatient family intervention: V. Results for affective disorders. *Journal of Affective Disorders*, **18**, 17–28.

Cobb, S. (1976). Social support as a moderator of life stress. *Psychosomatic Medicine*, **38**, 100–114.

Cochran, S. D. (1984). Preventing medical noncompliance in the outpatient treatment of bipolar affective disorders. *Journal of Consulting and Clinical Psychology*, **52**, 873–878.

Cohen, M. B., Baker, G., Cohen, R. A. et al. (1954). An intensive study of twelve cases of manic-depressive psychosis. *Psychiatry*, **17**, 103–137.

Cohen, S. & Willis, T. A. (1985). Stress, social support and the buffering hypothesis. *Psychological Bulletin*, **98** (no. 2), 310–357.

Cooper, P., Osborn, M., Gath, D. & Feggetter, G. (1982). Evaluation of a modified self-report measure of social adjustment. *British Journal of Psychiatry*, **141**, 68–75.

Coryell, W., Endicott, J., Keller, M. et al. (1989). Bipolar affective disorder and high achievement: A familial association. *American Journal of Psychiatry*, **146**, 983–988.

Cowdry, R. W., Wehr, T. A., Zis, A. P. and Goodwin, F. K. (1983). Thyroid abnormalities associated with rapid-cycling bipolar illness. *Archives of General Psychiatry*, **40**, 414–420.

Coxhead, N., Silverstone, T. & Cookson, J. (1992). Carbamazepine vs lithium in the prophylaxis of bipolar affective disorder. *Acta Psychiatrica Scandinavica*, **85**, 114–118.

Creer, C. & Wing, J. K. (1974). *Schizophrenia at home*, London: Institute of Psychiatry.

Cumming, E. & Cumming, J. (1957). *Closed ranks: An experiment in mental health education*. Cambridge, Mass.: Harvard.

Davenport, Y. B., Ebert, M. H., Adland, M. L. & Goodwin, F. K. (1977). Couples group therapy as an adjunct to lithium maintenance of the manic patient. *American Journal of Orthopsychiatry*, **47**, 495–502.

David, A. S., Buchanan, A., Reed, A. & Almeida, O. (1992). The assessment of insight in psychosis. *British Journal of Psychiatry*, **161**, 599–602.

Demers, R. G. & Davis, L. S. (1971). The influence of prophylactic lithium treatment on the marital adjustment of manic-depressives and their spouses. *Comprehensive Psychiatry*, **12**, 348–353.

Department of Health Education and Welfare Medical Practice Report (1979). *A State of the Science Report for the Office of the Assistant Secretary for the US Department of Health, Education and Welfare*. Baltimore MD: Policy Research.

Depue, R. A., Krauss, S. P. & Spoont, M. R. (1987). A two-dimensional threshold model of seasonal bipolar affective disorder. In, Magnusson, D. & Ohman, A. (eds), *Psychopathology: An interactionist perspective* (pp. 95–123). New York: Academic Press.

Desforges, D. M., Lord, C. G., Ramsey, S. et al. (1991). Effects of structured cooperative contact on changing negative attitudes toward stigmatized social groups. *Journal of Personality and Social Psychology*, **60**, 531–544.

Dickson, W. E. & Kendell, R. E. (1986). Does maintenance lithium therapy prevent recurrences of mania under ordinary clinical conditions? *Psychological Medicine,* **16**, 521–530.

Dobson, K. S. (1989). A meta-analysis of the efficacy of cognitive therapy for depression. *Journal of Consulting and Clinical Psychology,* **57**, 414–419.

Dunner, D. L. & Fieve, R. R. (1974). Clinical factors in lithium prophylaxis failure. *Archives of General Psychiatry,* **30**, 229–233.

Elkin, I., Shea, M. T., Imber, S. T., Watkins, J. T. et al. (1989). National Institute of Mental Health Treatment of Depression Collaborative Research Program: General effectiveness of treatments. *Archives of General Psychiatry,* **46**, 971–982.

Ellicott, A., Hammen, C., Gitlin, M. et al. (1990). Life events and the course of bipolar disorder. *American Journal of Psychiatry,* **147**, 1194–1198

Emrich, H. M., Dose, M., & von Zerssen, D. (1985). The use of sodium valproate, carbamazepine and oxcarbazepine in patients with affective disorders. *Journal of Affective Disorders,* **8**, 243–250.

Epstein, S. (1994). Integration of the cognitive and psychodynamic unconscious. *American Psychologist,* **49**, 709–724.

Esparon, J., Kolloori, J., Naylor, G. J. et al. (1986). Comparison of the prophylactic action of flupenthixol with placebo in lithium treated manic-depressive patients. *British Journal of Psychiatry,* **148**, 723–725.

Estroff, T. W., Dackis, C. A., Gold, M. S., & Pottash, A. L. C. (1985). Drug abuse and bipolar disorders. *International Journal of Psychiatry in Medicine,* **15**, 37–40.

Fadden, G., Bebbington, P., & Kuipers, L. (1987). Caring and its burdens: A study of the spouses of depressed patients. *British Journal of Psychiatry,* **151**, 660–667.

Faedda, G. L., Tondo, L., Baldessarini, R. J. et al. (1993). Outcome after rapid vs gradual discontinuation of lithium treatment in bipolar disorders. *Archives of General Psychiatry,* **50**, 448–455.

Farina, A. & Felner, R. D. (1973). Employment interviewer reactions to former mental patients. *Journal of Abnormal Psychology,* **82**, 268–272.

Feldman-Naim, S., Turner, E. H. & Leibenluft, E. (1997). Diurnal variation in the direction of mood switches in patients with rapid-cycling bipolar disorder. *Journal of Clinical Psychiatry,* **58**, 79–84.

Fieve, R. R. & Peselow, E. D. (1983). Lithium: Clinical applications. In G. D. Burrows, T. R. Norman & B. Davis (eds) *Antidepressant.* Amsterdam: Elsevier.

Foa, E. B., Rothbaum, B. O., Riggs, D. S. & Murdock, T. B. (1991). Treatment of post-traumatic stress disorder in rape victims: A comparison between cognitive-behavioral procedures and counseling. *Journal of Consulting and Clinical Psychology,* **59**, 715–723.

Foerster, A., Lewis, S., Owen, M. & Murray, R. M. (1991). Pre-morbid adjustment and personality in psychosis: Effects of sex and diagnosis. *British Journal of Psychiatry,* **158**, 171–176.

Fogelson, D. L., Jacobson, S., & Sternbach, H. (1991). A retrospective study of valproate in private psychiatric practice. *Annals of Clinical Psychiatry,* **3**, 315–320.

Fowler, D., Garety, P. & Kuipers, E. (1995). *Cognitive behaviour therapy for psychosis: Theory and practice.* London: Wiley.

Frank, E., Kupfer, D. J., Ehler, C. L. et al. (1994). Interpersonal and social rhythm therapy for bipolar disorder: Integrating interpersonal and behavioural approaches. *Behaviour Therapy,* **17**, 143–149.

Frank, E., Kupfer, D. J., Perel, J. M. et al. (1990). Three year outcomes for maintenance therapies in recurrent depression. *Archives of General Psychiatry*, **47**, 1093–1097.

French, C. C., Richards, A. & Scholfield, E. J. C. (1996). Hypomania, anxiety and the emotional Stroop. *British Journal of Clinical Psychology*, **35**, 617–626.

Fromm-Reichmann, F. (1949). Intensive psychotherapy of manic depressives: A preliminary report. *Confina Neurologica*, **9**, 158–165.

Gaviria, M., Flaherty, J. A. & Val, E. (1982). A comparison of bipolar patients with and without a borderline personality disorder. *Psychiatric Journal of University of Ottawa*, **7**, 190–195.

Gelenberg, A. J., Kane, J. M., Keller, M. B. et al. (1989). Comparison of standard and low serum levels for lithium of maintenance treatment of bipolar disorder. *New England Journal of Medicine*, **321**, 1489–1493.

Gilbert, P. (1992). *Counselling for depression*. London: Sage.

Gilbert, P. (1997). The evolution of social attractiveness and its role in shame, humiliation, guilt and therapy. *British Journal of Medical Psychology*, **70**, 113–147.

Gitlin, M. J., Swendsen, J., Heller, T. L. & Hammen, C., (1995) Relapse and impairment in bipolar disorder. *American Journal of Psychiatry*, **152**, 1635–1640.

Glassner, B. & Haldipur, C. V. (1983). Life events and early and late onset of bipolar disorder. *American Journal of Psychiatry*, **140**, 215–217.

Goddard, G. V., McIntyre, D. C. & Leech, C. K. (1969). A permanent change in brain function resulting from daily electrical stimulation. *Experimental Neurology*, **25**, 295–330.

Goodwin, F. K. & Jamison, K. R. (1990). *Manic-depressive illness*. New York: Oxford University Press.

Gotlib, I. H. & Lee, C. M. (1989). The social functioning of depressed patients: A longitudinal assessment. *Journal of Social and Clinical Psychology*, **8**, 223–237.

Gray, J.A. (1982). *The neuropsychology of anxiety*. Oxford: Oxford University Press.

Greenberger, D. & Padesky, C. A. (1995). *Mind over mood: A cognitive therapy treatment manual for clients*. New York: Guilford.

Greer, S., Morris, T. & Pettingale, K. W. (1979). Psychological response to breast cancer: Effect on outcome. *Lancet*, **2**, 785–787.

Hamilton, M. (1960). A rating scale for depression. *Journal of Neurology and Psychiatry*, **23**, 56–62.

Hammen, C. (1991). *Depression runs in families: The social context of risk and resilence in children of depressed mothers*. New York: Springer-Verlag.

Hammen, C., Ellicott, A., Gitlin, M., & Jamison, K. R. (1989). Sociotropy/autonomy and vulnerability to specific life events in patients with unipolar depression and bipolar disorders. *Journal of Abnormal Psychology*, **98**, 154–160.

Hammen, C. & Gitlin, M. (1997). Stress reactivity in bipolar patients and its relation to prior history of disorder. *American Journal of Psychiatry*, **154**, 856–857.

Harrow, M., Goldberg, J. F., Grossman, L. S., & Meltzer, H. Y. (1990). Outcome in manic disorders. A naturalistic follow-up study. *Archives of General Psychiatry*, **47**, 665–671.

Hatfield, A. B. & Lefley, H. P. (1993). *Surviving mental illness: Stress, coping and adaptation*. New York: Guilford.

Hayward, P. & Bright, J. A. (1997). Stigma and mental illness: A review and critique. *Journal of Mental Health*, **6**, 345–354.

Hayward, P., Chan, N., Kemp, R. et al. (1995). Medication self-management: A preliminary report on an intervention to improve medication compliance. *Journal of Mental Health*, **4**, 511–517.

Hayward, P., Wong, G., Bright, J. & Lam, D.H. (unpublished manuscript). Views on manic depression questionnaire.

Healy, D. & Williams, J. M. G. (1989). Moods, misattributions and mania: An interaction of biological and psychological factors in the pathogenesis of mania. *Psychiatric Developments*, **7**, 49–70.

Henderson, S., Byrne, D. G. & Duncan-Jones, P. (1981). *Neurosis and the social environment.* Sydney: Academic Press.

Himmelhoch, J. M., Thase, M. E., Mallinger, A. G. & Houck, P. (1991). Tranylcypromine versus imipramine in anergic bipolar depression. *American Journal of Psychiatry*, **148**, 910–916.

Hirsch, S. R., Platt, S., Knights, A. & Weyman, A. (1979). Shortening hospital stay for psychiatric care: Effects on patients and their families. *British Medical Journal*, **1**, 442–446.

Hollon, S. D., Shelton, R. C. & Loosen, P. T. (1991). Cognitive therapy and pharmacotherapy for depression. *Journal of Consulting and Clinical Psychology*, **59**, 88–99.

Honig, A., Hofman, A., Rozendaal, N. & Dingemens, P. (1997). Psycho-education in bipolar disorder: Effect on expressed emotion. *Psychiatry Research*, **72**, 17–22.

Hooley, J. M., Richters, J. E., Weintraub, S. & Neale, J. M. (1987). Psychopathology and marital distress: The positive side of positive symptoms. *Journal of Abnormal Psychology*, **96**, 27–33.

Hunt, N., Bruce-Jones, W. & Silverstone, T. (1992). Life events and relapse in bipolar affective disorder. *Journal of Affective Disorders*, **25**, 13–20.

Hurry, J., Sturt, E., Bebbington, P. & Tennant, C. (1983). Socio-demographic associations with social disablement in a community sample. *Social Psychiatry*, **18**, 113–121.

Isometsa, E., Heikkinen, M., Henriksson, M. et al. (1995). Recent life events and completed suicide in bipolar affective disorder. A comparison with major depressive suicides. *Journal of Affective Disorders*, **33**, 99–106.

Jablensky, A. (1981). Symptoms, patterns of course and predictors of outcome in the functional psychoses: Some nosological implications. In G. Tognoni, C. Bellantuono & M. Lader (eds): *Epidemiological impact of psychotropic drugs* (pp. 71–97). Amsterdam: Elsevier.

Jacobson, N. S. & Hollon, S. D. (1996). Cognitive-behavior therapy versus pharmacotherapy: Now that the jury's returned its verdict, it's time to present the rest of the evidence. *Journal of Consulting and Clinical Psychology*, **64**, 74–80.

Jamison, K. R. (1993). *Touched with fire: Manic-depressive illness and the artistic temperament.* New York: Free Press.

Jamison, K. R. (1995). *An unquiet mind: A memoir of moods and madness.* New York: Knopf.

Jamison, K. R., Gerner, R. H. & Goodwin, F. K. (1979). Patient and physician attitudes toward lithium: Relationship to compliance. *Archives of General Psychiatry*, **36**, 866–869.

Janicak P. G., Davis, J. M., Preskorn, S. H. & Ayd, F. J. (1993). *Principles and practice of psychopharmacotherapy.* Baltimore: Williams and Wilkins.

Janowsky, D. S., Leff, M. & Epstein, R. S. (1970). Playing the manic game: Interpersonal maneuvers of the acutely manic patient. *Archives of General Psychiatry*, **22**, 252–261.

Johnson, S. L. & Miller, I. (1997). Negative life events and time to recovery from episodes of bipolar disorder. *Journal of Abnormal Psychology*, **106**, 449–457.

Johnson, S. L. & Roberts, J. E. (1995). Life events and bipolar disorder: Implications from biological theories. *Psychological Bulletin*, **117**, 434–449.

Joyce, P. R. (1984). Age of onset in bipolar affective disorder and misdiagnosis as schizophrenia. *Psychological Medicine*, **14**, 145–149.

Joyce, P. R. (1985). Illness behaviour and rehospitalisation in bipolar affective disorder. *Psychological Medicine*, **15**, 521–525.

Joyce, P. R., Oakley-Browne, M. A., Wells, J. E. et al. (1990). Birth cohort trends in major depression: Increasing rates and earlier onset in New Zealand. *Journal of Affective Disorders*, **18**, 83–89.

Kane, J. M. (1988). The role of neuroleptics in manic-depressive illness. *Journal of Clinical Psychiatry*, **49**, (11, supp), 12–13.

Keck, P. E. (1995). Lithium, the present and the future. *Journal of Clinical Psychiatry*, **56**, 41–48.

Keller, M. B., Lavori, P. W., Kane, J. M. et al. (1992). Subsyndromal symptoms in bipolar disorder: A comparison of standard and low serum levels of lithium. *Archives of General Psychiatry*, **49**, 371–376.

Kemp, R., David, A. & Hayward, P. (1996a). Compliance therapy: An intervention targeting insight and treatment adherence in psychotic patients. *Behavioural and Cognitive Psychotherapy*, **24**, 331–350.

Kemp, R., Hayward, P., Applewhaite, G. et al. (1996b). Compliance therapy in psychotic patients: Randomised controlled trial. *British Medical Journal*, **312**, 345–349.

Kemp, R., Hayward, P. & David, A. (1997). *Compliance therapy manual*. Macclesfield: Gardiner-Caldwell.

Kemp, R., Kirov, G., Everitt, B. et al. (1998). Randomised controlled trial of compliance therapy: 18-month follow-up. *British Journal of Psychiatry*, **172**, 413–419.

Kennedy, S., Thompson, R., Stancer, H. C. et al. (1983). Life events precipitating mania. *British Journal of Psychiatry*, **142**, 398–403.

Kessler, R. C., Rubniow, D. R., Holmes, C. et al. (1997). The epidemiology of DSM-III-R bipolar I disorder in a general population survey. *Psychological Medicine*, **27**, 1079–1089.

Kilbey, M. M. & Ellinwood, E. H. (1977). Reverse tolerance to stimulant-induced abnormal behaviour. *Life Sciences*, **20**, 1063–1076.

Kingdon, D. G. & Turkington, D. (1994). *Cognitive-behavioral therapy of schizophrenia*. Hove: Erlbaum.

Kinsman, R. A., Dirks, J. F. & Jones, N. F. (1982). Psychomaintenance of chronic physical illness. In T. Millon, C. Green & R. Meagher (eds), *Handbook of clinical health psychology* (pp. 435–466). New York: Plenum.

Klein, D. C., Moore, R.Y. & Reppert, S. M. (1991). *Suprachiasmatic nucleus: The mind's clock*. New York: Oxford University Press.

Kraepelin, E. (1913) *Psychiatrie. Ein lehrbuch fur studirende und aerzte*. Leipzig: J. A. Barth, 1896. 8th edn. Reprinted 1976, New York: Arno Press.

Krauss, S. S., Depue, R. A. Arbisi, P. A. & Spoont, M. (1992). Behavioral engagement level, variability, and diurnal rhythm as a function of bright light in bipolar II seasonal affective disorder: An exploratory study. *Psychiatry Research*, **43**, 147–160.

Kripke, D.F. & Robinson, D. (1985). Ten years with a lithium group. *McLean Hospital Journal*, **10**, 1–11.

Krupnick, J. L., Sotsky, S. M., Elkin, I. et al. (1996). The role of the therapeutic alliance in psychotherapy and pharmacotherapy outcome: Findings in the National Institute of Mental Health treatment of depression collaborative research program. *Journal of Consulting and Clinical Psychology*, **64**, 532–539.

Kuipers, L., Leff, J., & Lam, D. (1992). *Family work for schizophrenia: A practical guide*. London: Gaskell.

Kupfer, D. J., Frank, E. F., Perel, J. M. et al. (1992). Five-year outcome for maintenance therapies in recurrent depression. *Archives of General Psychiatry*, **49**, 769–773.

Lam, D. (1991). Psychosocial family intervention in schizophrenia: A review of empirical studies. *Psychological Medicine*, **21**, 423–441.

Lam, D. H., Bright, J., Jones, S. et al. (in press). Cognitive therapy for bipolar illness — a pilot study of relapse prevention. *Cognitive Therapy and Research*.

Lam, D. H. & Wong, G. (1997). Prodromes, coping strategies, insight and social functioning in bipolar affective disorders. *Psychological Medicine*, **27**, 1091–1100.

Lambert, P. A. & Venaud, G. (1992). Comparative study of valproate vs lithium in treatment of affective disorders. *Nervure*, **5**, 57–65.

Leonhard, K. (1957). *Aufteilung der Endogenen Psychosen*. Berlin: Akademie-Verlag. [*The Classification of Endogenous Psychoses*. 5th edn. Translated by Russell Berman. Edited by Eli Robins. New York: Irvington (1979)].

Lerner, M. J. & Miller, D. T. (1978). Just world research and the attribution process: Looking back and ahead. *Psychological Bulletin*, **85**, 1030–1051.

Linehan, M. M. (1993). *Cognitive-behavioral treatment of borderline personality disorder*. New York: Guilford.

Link, B. G. (1987). Understanding labeling effects in the area of mental disorders: An assessment of the effects of expectations of rejection. *American Sociological Review*, **52**, 96–112.

Link, B. G., Cullen, F. T., Struening, E. et al. (1989). A modified labeling theory approach to mental disorder: an empirical assessment. *American Sociological Review*, **54**, 400–423.

Link, B. G., Mirotznik, J. & Cullen, F. T. (1991). The effectiveness of stigma coping orientations: Can negative consequences of mental illness labeling be avoided? *Journal of Health and Social Behavior*, **32**, 302–320.

Linkowski, P., Kerkhofs, M., Van Onderbergen, A. et al. (1994). The 24-hour profiles of cortisol, prolactin and growth hormone secretion in mania. *Archives of General Psychiatry*, **51**, 616–624.

Loeb, F. F. & Loeb, L. R. (1987). Psychoanalytic observations on the effect of lithium on manic attacks. *Journal of American Psychoanalytic Association*, **35**, 877–902.

Lovejoy, M. C. & Steuerwald, B. L. (1995). Subsyndromal, unipolar and bipolar disorders: comparisons on positive and negative affect. *Journal of Abnormal Psychology*, **104**, 381–384.

Luborsky, L. B., McLellan, A. T., Woody, G. E. et al. (1985). Therapist success and its determinants. *Archives of General Psychiatry*, 42, 602–611.

Lusznat, R.M., Murphy, D.P. & Nunn, C.M.H. (1988). Carbamazepine vs lithium in the treatment and prophylaxis of mania. *British Journal of Psychiatry*, 153, 198–204.

Lyon, H., Startup, M. & Bentall, R. P. (submitted for publication). Social cognition and the manic defense: Attributions, selective attention and self-schema in bipolar affective disorder.

McElroy, S. L., Keck, P. E. Jr., Pope, H. G. Jr., & Hudson, J. I. (1988). Valpraote in the treatment of rapid-cycling bipolar disorder. *Journal of Clinical Psychopharmacology*, 8, 275–279.

McFarlane, A. H., Neale, K. A., Norman, G. R. et al. (1981). Methodological issues in developing a scale to measure social support. *Schizophrenia Bulletin*, 7, 73–81.

Maj, M., Del Vecchio, M., Starace, F. et al. (1984). Prediction of affective psychosis response to lithium prophylaxis. *Acta Psychiatrica Scandinavica*, 69, 37–44.

Marker, H. R. & Mander, A. J. (1989). Efficacy of lithium prophylaxis in clinical practice. *British Journal of Psychiatry*, 155, 496–500.

Marshall, M. H., Neumann, C. P. & Robinson, M. (1970). Lithium, creativity, and manic-depressive illness: Review and prospectus. *Psychosomatics*, 11, 406–488.

Mathew, M. R., Chandrasekaran, R. & Sivakumar, V. (1994). A study of life events in mania. *Journal of Affective Disorders*, 32, 157–161.

Miklowitz, D. J., Goldstein, M. J., Nuechterlein, K. H. et al. (1988). Family factors and the course of bipolar affective disorder. *Archives of General Psychiatry*, 45, 225–231.

Miller, F. T., Busch, F. & Tanebaum, J. H. (1989). Drug abuse in schizophrenia and bipolar disorder. *American Journal of Drug and Alcohol Abuse*, 15, 291–295.

Miller, I. W., Keitner, G. I., Epstein N. B. et al. (1991). Families of bipolar patients: Dysfunction, course of illness and pilot treatment study. Presented at the annual meeting of the Association for the Advancement of Behaviour Therapy; November, 1991, New York, NY.

Minors, D. S. & Waterhouse, J. M. (1986). Circadian rhythms and their mechanisms. *Experientia*, 42, 1–13.

Molnar, G. J., Feeney, M. G., & Fava, G. A. (1988). Duration and symptoms of bipolar prodomes. *American Journal of Psychiatry*, 145, 1576–1578.

Moncrieff, J. (1995). Lithium revisited: A re-examination of the placebo-controlled trials of lithium prophylaxis in Manic-Depressive Disorder. *British Journal of Psychiatry*, 167, 569–574.

Monk, T. H., Flaherty, J. F., Frank, E. et al. (1990). The Social Rhythm Metric: An instrument to quantify daily rhythms of life. *Journal of Nervous and Mental Disease*, 178, 120–126.

Moorey, S. (1996). When bad things happen to rational people: Cognitive therapy in adverse life circumstances. In P. Salkovskis (ed.), *Frontiers of cognitive therapy* (pp. 450–469). New York: Guilford.

Mueser, K. T., Webb, C., Pfeiffer, M. et al. (1996). Family burden of schizophrenia and bipolar disorder: Perceptions of relatives and professionals. *Psychiatric Services*, 47, 507–511.

Murray-Parkes, C. (1972). *Bereavement: Studies of grief in adult life*. London: Tavistock.

Myers, D. H. & Davies, P. (1978). The seasonal incidence of mania and its relationship to climatic variables. *Psychological Medicine*, **8**, 433–440.

Newman, C. F. & Beck, A. T. (unpublished manuscript). Cognitive therapy for rapid cycling bipolar affective disorder—treatment manual.

Novaco, R. W. (1976). Treatment of chronic anger through cognitive and relaxation controls. *Journal of Consulting and Clinical Psychology*, **44**, 681.

O'Connell, R. A., Mayo, J. A., Flatow, L. et al. (1991). Outcome of bipolar disorder on long-term treatment with lithium. *British Journal of Psychiatry*, **159**, 122–129.

Okuma, T., Inanaga, K., Otsuki, S. et al. (1981). A preliminary double-blind study on the efficacy of carbamazepine in prophylaxis of manic-depressive illness. *Psychopharmacology* (Berlin), **73**, 95–96.

Oomen, H. A., Schipperijn, A. J. & Drexhage, H. A. (1996). The prevalence of affective disorder and in particular of a rapid cycling of bipolar disorder in patients with abnormal thyroid function tests. *Clinical Endocrinology* (Oxford), **45**, 215–223.

Padesky, C. A. (1994). Schema change processes in cognitive therapy. *Clinical Psychology and Psychotherapy*, **1**, 267–278.

Padesky, C. A. & Greenberger, D. (1995). *Clinician's guide to mind over mood*. New York: Guilford.

Page, S. (1977). Effects of the mental illness label in attempts to obtain accommodation. *Canadian Journal of Behavioural Science*, **9**, 85–90.

Pai, S. & Kapur, R. L. (1981). The burden on the family of a psychiatric patient: Development of an assessment scale. *British Journal of Psychiatry*, **138**, 332–335.

Palmer, A. G., Williams, H. & Adams, M. (1995). CBT in a group format for bipolar affective disorder. *Behavioural and Cognitive Psychotherapy*, **23**, 153–168.

Paykel, E. S. (1979). Recent life events in the development of depressive disorders. In R. A. Depue (ed.), *The psychobiology of the depressive disorders*. New York: Academic Press.

Paykel, E.S. & Weissman, M. (1973). Social adjustment and depression: A longitudinal study. *Archives of General Psychiatry*, **28**, 659–663.

Peet, M. & Pratt, J. P. (1993). Lithium: Current status in psychiatric disorders. *Drug*, **46**, 7–17.

Pennebaker, J. W. (1993). Putting stress into words: Health, linguitic and therapeutic implications. *Behaviour Research and Therapy*, **31**, 539–548.

Pennebaker, J. W. (1997). *Opening up: The healing power of expressing emotions*. New York: Guilford.

Perry, A., Tarrier, N., Morriss, R. et al. (1998). Randomised controlled trial of efficacy of teaching patients with bipolar disorder to identify early symptoms of relapse and obtain treatment. *British Medical Journal*, **318**, 139–153.

Platt, S., Weyman, A., Hirsch, S. & Hewett, S. (1980). The Social Behaviour Assessment Schedule (SBAS): Rationale, contents, scoring and reliability of a new interview schedule. *Social Psychiatry*, **15**, 43–55.

Pollack, L. E. (1990). Improving relationships: Groups for inpatients with bipolar disorder. *Journal of Psychosocial Nursing*, **28**, 17–22.

Pope, H. G. Jr., McElroy, S. L., Keck, P. E. Jr. & Hudson, J. I. (1991). Valproate in the treatment of acute mania: A placebo-controlled study. *Archives of General Psychiatry*, **48**, 62–68.

Post, R. M., Kennedy, E., Shinohara, M. et al. (1984). Metabolic and behavioral consequences of lidocaine-kindled seizures. *Brain Research*, **324**, 295–303.

Post, R. M, Rubinow, D. R. & Ballenger, J. C. (1986a). Conditioning and sensitisation in the longitudinal course of affective illness. *British Journal of Psychiatry*, **149**, 191–201.

Post, R. M., Uhde, T. W., Putnam, F. W. et al. (1982). Kindling and carbamazepine in affective illness. *Journal of Nervous and Mental Disease*, **170**, 717–731.

Post, R. M., Uhde, T. W., Putnam, F. W. & Weiss, S. R. B. (1986b). Antimanic effects of carbamazepine: mechanisms of action and implications for the biochemistry of manic depressive illness. In A. Swan (ed.) *Mania: New research and treatment*. Washington, DC: American Psychiatric Association Press.

Post R. M. & Weiss, S. R. (1989). Sensitisation, kindling, and anticonvulsants in mania. *Journal of Clinical Psychiatry*, 50 Suppl 23–30.

Post, R. M., Weiss, S. R. B., Pert, A. & Uhde, T. W. (1985). Chronic cocaine administration: Sensitisation and kindling effects. In S. Fisher et al. (eds) *Cocaine: Clinical and biobehavioural aspects* (pp. 109–173). New York: Oxford University Press.

Power, M. J., Champion, L. A. & Aris, S. J. (1988). The development of a measure of social support: The Significant Others (SOS) Scale. *British Journal of Clinical Psychology*, **27**, 349–358.

Power, M. J., Katz, R., McGuffin, P. et al. (1994). The Dysfunctional Attitude Scale (DAS): A comparison of forms A and B and proposal for a new sub-scaled version. *Journal of Research in Personality*, **28**, 263–276.

Priebe, S., Wildgrube, C. & Muller-Oerlinghausen, B. (1989). Lithium prophylaxis and expressed emotion. *British Journal of Psychiatry*, **154**, 396–399.

Prien, R. F., Caffey, E. M. Jr. & Klett, C. J. (1972). Comparison of lithium carbonate and chlorpromazine in the treatment of mania: Report of the Veterans Administration and National Institute of Mental Health Collaborative Study Group. *Archives of General Psychiatry*, **26**, 146–153.

Prien, R. F., Kupfer, D. J., Mansky, P. A. et al. (1984). Drug therapy in the prevention of recurrences in unipolar and bipolar affective disorders: Report of the NIMH Collaborative Study Group comparing lithium carbonate, imipramine, and a lithium carbonate–imipramine combination. *Archives of General Psychiatry*, **41**, 1096–1104.

Prien, R. F. & Potter, W. Z. (1990). NIMH workshop report on treatment of bipolar disorder. *Psychopharmacology Bulletin*. **26**, 409–427.

Prochaska, J. O., & DiClemente, C. C. (1986). Toward a comprehensive model of change. In W. R. Miller & N. Heather (eds), *Treating addictive behaviors: Processes of change* (pp. 3–27). New York: Plenum.

Prochaska, J. O., DiClemente, C. C. & Norcross, J. C. (1992). In search of how people change: Applications to addictive behaviors. *American Psychologist*, **47**, 1102–1114.

Quitkin, F. M., Kane, J., Rifkin, A. et al. (1981). Prophylactic lithium carbonate with and without imipramine for bipolar I patients: a double-blind study. *Archives of General Psychiatry*, **38**, 902–907.

Rachman, S. J. (1980). Emotional processing. *Behaviour Research and Therapy*, **18**, 51–60.

Radke-Yarrow, M., Cummings, E. M., Kuczynski, L. & Chapman, M. (1985).

Patterns of attachment in two- and three-year-olds in normal families and families with parental depression. *Child Development,* **56,** 884–893.

Ramana, R. & Bebbington, P. (1995). Social influences on bipolar affective disorders. *Social Psychiatry and Psychiatric Epidemiology,* **30,** 152–160.

Raue, P. J., Goldfried, M. R. & Barkham, M. (1997). The therapeutic alliance in psychodynamic-interpersonal and cognitive-behavioral therapy. *Journal of Consulting and Clinical Psychology,* **65,** 582–587.

Regier, D. A., Farmer, M. E., Raye, D. S. et al. (1990). Comorbidity of mental disorders with drug and alcohol abuse: Results from the Epidemiological Catchment Area (ECA) study. Cited in Goodwin and Jamison, 1990.

Regier, D. A., Hirschfeld, R. M. A., Goodwin, F. K. et al. (1988). The NIMH depression awareness, recognition and treatment program: Structure, aims and scientific basis. *American Journal of Psychiatry,* **145,** 1351–1357.

Richards, D. A. & Rose, J. S. (1991). Exposure therapy for post-traumatic stress disorder. *British Journal of Psychiatry,* **58,** 836–840.

Robins, C. J., Hayes, A. M., Block, P. et al. (1995). Interpersonal and achievement concerns and the depressive vulnerability and symptom specificity hypotheses: A prospective study. *Cognitive Therapy and Research,* **19,** 1–20.

Robins, L. N., Hezler, J. E., Weissman, M. M. et al. (1984). Lifetime prevalence of specific psychiatric disorders in three sites. *Archives of General Psychiatry,* **41,** 949–958.

Rogers, C. R. (1957). The necessary and sufficient conditions of therapeutic personality change. *Journal of Consulting and Clinical Psychology,* **21,** 95–103.

Rollnick, S., Heather, N. & Bell, A. (1992). Negotiating behaviour change in medical settings: The development of brief motivational interviewing. *Journal of Mental Health,* **1,** 25–37.

Romans, S. E. & McPherson, H. M. (1992). The social networks of bipolar affective disorder patients. *Journal of Affective Disorders,* **25,** 221–228.

Rosenbaum, M. (1980). A schedule for assessing self-control behaviors: Preliminary findings. *Behavior Therapy,* **11,** 109–121.

Rounsaville, B. J., Anton, S. F., Carroll, K. et al. (1991). Psychiatric diagnoses of treatment-seeking cocaine abusers. *Archives of General Psychiatry,* **48,** 43–51.

Sachs, G. S., Lafer, B., Stoll, A. L. et al. (1994). A double-blind trial of bupropion versus disipramine for bipolar depression. *Journal of Clinical Psychiatry,* **55,** 391–393.

Safran, J. D. & Segal, Z. V. (1996). *Interpersonal processes in cognitive therapy.* Northvale, NJ: Aronson.

Sarason, I. G., Levine, H. M., Basham, R. B. & Sarason, B. R. (1982). Assessing social support: the social support questionnaire. *Journal of Personality and Social Psychology,* **44,** 127–139.

Schou, M. (1968). Lithium in psychiatric therapy and prophylaxis. *Journal of Psychiatric Research,* **6,** 67–95.

Schou, M. (1979). Artistic productivity and lithium prophylaxis in manic-depressive illness. *British Journal of Psychiatry,* **135,** 97–103.

Scott, J. (1996). Cognitive therapy for clients with bipolar disorder. *Cognitive and Behavioral Practice,* **3,** 29–51.

Seggie, J., Werstiuk, E. S. & Gorta, L. (1987). Lithium and circadian patterns of melatonin in the retina, hypothalamus, pineal and serum. *Progress in Neuropsychopharmacology and Biological Psychiatry,* **11,** 325–334.

Shakir, S. A., Volkmar, F. R., Bacon, S. & Pfefferbaum, A. (1979). Group psychotherapy as an adjunct to lithium maintenance. *American Journal of Psychiatry*, **136**, 455–456.

Small, J. G. (1990). Antidepressants in affective disorders. *Psychopharmacology Bulletin*, **26**, 25–36.

Small, J. G., Klapper, M. H., Milstein, V. et. al. (1991). Carbamazepine compared with lithium in the treatment of mania. *Archives of General Psychiatry*, **48**, 915–921.

Smith, J. A. & Tarrier, N. (1992). Prodromal symptoms in manic depressive psychosis. *Social Psychiatry and Psychiatric Epidemiology*, **27**, 245–248.

Solomon, D. A., Keitner, G. I., Miller, I. W. et al. (1995). Course of illness and maintenance treatments for patients with bipolar disorders. *Journal of Clinical Psychiatry*, **56**, 5–13.

Sonne, S. C., Brady, K. T. & Morton, W. A. (1994). Substance abuse and bipolar affective disorder. *Journal of Nervous and Mental Disease*, **182**, 349–352.

Souetre, E., Salvati, E., Pringuey, D. et al. (1986). The circadian rhythm of plasma thyrotropin in depression and recovery. *Chronobiology International*, **3**, 197–205.

Speer, D. C. (1992). Differences in social resources and treatment history among diagnostic groups of older adults. *Hospital and Community Psychiatry*, **43**, 270–274.

Stancer, H. C., & Persad, E. (1982) Treatment of intractable rapid-cycling manic-depressive disorder with levothyroxine: Clinical outcomes. *Archives of General Psychiatry*, **39**, 311–312.

Strakowski, S. M., McElroy, S. L., Keck, P. E., Jr. & West, S. A. (1996). The effects of antecedent substance abuse on the development of first episode psychotic mania. *Journal of Psychiatric Research*, **30**, 59–68.

Strupp, H. H. & Hadley, S. W. (1979). Specific versus nonspecific factors in psychotherapy. *Archives of General Psychiatry*, **36**, 1125–1136.

Suppes, T., McElroy, S. L., Gilbert, J. et al. (1992). Clozapine in the treatment of dysphoric mania. *Biological Psychiatry*, **32**, 270–280.

Surtees, P. G. (1980). Social support, residual adversity and depressive outcome. *Social Psychiatry*, **15**, 71–81.

Surwit, R. S. & Schneider, M. S. (1993). Role of stress in the etiology and treatment of diabetes mellitus. *Psychosomatic Medicine*, **55**, 380–393.

Symonds, R. L. & Williams, P. (1981). Lithium and the changing incidence of mania. *Psychological Medicine*, **11**, 193–196.

Targum, S. D., Dibble, E. D., Davenport, Y. B. & Gershon, E. S. (1981). The Family Attitudes Questionnaire: Patients' and spouses' views of bipolar illness. *Archives of General Psychiatry*, **38**, 562–568.

Teasdale, J. D. (1993). Emotion and two kinds of meaning: Cognitive therapy and applied cognitive science. *Behaviour Research and Therapy*, **31**, 339–354.

Tohen, M., Waternaux, C. M. & Tsuang, M. T. (1990a). Outcome in mania: A 4-year prospective follow-up of 75 patients utilizing survival analysis. *Archives of General Psychiatry*, **47**, 1106–1111.

Tohen, M., Waternaux, C. M., Tsuang, M. T. & Hunt, A. T. (1990b). Four-year follow-up of twenty four first episode manic patients. *Journal of Affective Disorders*, **19**, 79–86.

Torrey, E. F. (1986). *Witchdoctors and psychiatrists: The common roots of psychotherapy and its future.* New York: Harper & Row.

Tsujimoto, T., Yamada, N., Shimoda, K. et al. (1990). Circadian rhythms in depression: II. Circadian rhythms in inpatients with various mental disorders. *Journal of Affective Disorders*, **18**, 199–210.

Volkmar, F. R., Shakir, S. A., Bacon, S. & Pfefferbaum, A. (1981). Group therapy in the management of manic-depressive illness. *American Journal of Psychotherapy*, **35**, 226–234.

Walden, J., Hesslinger, B., van-Calker, D. & Berger, M. (1996). Addition of lamotrigine to valproate may enhance efficacy in the treatment of bipolar affective disorder. *Pharmacopsychiatry*, **29**, 193–195.

Warner, R. (1997). *Recovery from schizophrenia: Psychiatry and political economy*. London: Routledge.

Wehr, T. A., Sack, D. A. & Rosenthal, N. E. (1987). Sleep reduction as a final common pathway in the genesis of mania. *American Journal of Psychiatry*, **144**, 201–204.

Wehr, T. A., Sack, D. A., Rosenthal, N. E. et al. (1983). Circadian rhythm disturbances in manic-depressive illness. *Federation Proceedings*, **42**, 2809–2814.

Weissman, M. (1975). The assessment of social adjustment. *Archives of General Psychiatry*, **32**, 357–365.

Weissman, M. (1979). The psychological treatment of depression. *Archives of General Psychiatry*, **36**, 1261–1269.

Weissman, M. & Bothwell, S. (1976). Assessment of social adjustment by patient self-report, *Archives of General Psychiatry*, **33**, 1111–1115.

Weissmann, M. M., Leaf, P. J., Tischler, G. L. et al. (1988). Affective disorders in five United States communities. *Psychological Medicine*, **18**, 141–153.

Weissman, M. M. & Myers, J. K. (1978). Affective disorders in a US urban community: The use of Research Diagnostic Criteria in an epidemiological survey. *Archives of General Psychiatry*, **35**, 1304–1311.

Weissman, M. M. & Paykel, E. S. (1974). *The depressed woman: A study of social relationships*. London: University of Chicago Press.

Weissman, M. M, Paykel, E. S., Seigel, R. & Klerman, G. L. (1971). The social role performance of depressed women: Comparisons with a normal group. *American Journal of Orthopsychiatry*, **41**, 390–405.

Welsh, D. K. & Moore-Ede, M. C. (1990). Lithium lengthens circadian period in a diurnal primate, Saimiri sciureus. *Biological Psychiatry*, **15**, 117–126.

Wever, R. A. (1980). Circadian rhythms of finches under bright light: Is self sustainment a precondition of rhythmicity? *Journal of Comparative Psychology*, **139**, 49–58.

Winokur, G., Clayton, P. J. & Reich, T. (1969). *Manic depressive illness*. St Louis: CV Mosby.

Winokur, G., Coryell, W., Keller, M. et al. (1993). A prospective follow-up of patients with bipolar and primary unipolar affective disorder. *Archives of General Psychiatry*, **50**, 457–465.

Winokur, G. & Kadrmas, A. (1989). A polyepisodic course in bipolar illness: Possible clinical relationships. *Comprehensive Psychiatry*, **30**, 121–127.

Winokur, G., & Tsuang, M. (1975). The Iowa 500: Suicide in mania, depression and schizophrenia. *American Journal of Psychiatry*, **132**, 650–651.

Wolff, G., Pathare, S., Craig, T. & Leff, J. (1996). Public education for community care: A new approach. *British Journal of Psychiatry*, **168**, 441–447.

Wolpe, J. (1973). *Practice of behaviour therapy* (2nd edn). New York: Pergamon Press.

World Health Organisation (1993). *Manual of the International Statistical Classification of Disease, Injuries and Causes of Death,* 10th revision. Geneva: WHO.

Wulsin, L., Bachop, M., & Hoffman, D. (1988). Group therapy in manic depressive illness. *American Journal of Psychotherapy,* **42,** 263–271.

Young, D. M. (1995). Psychiatric morbidity in travelers to Honolulu, Hawaii. *Comprehensive Psychiatry,* **36,** 224–228.

Zahn-Waxler, C., Mayfield, A., Radke-Yarrow, M. et al. (1988). A follow-up investigation of offspring of parents with bipolar disorder. *American Journal of Psychiatry,* **145,** 506–509.

Zis, A. P., Grof, P. & Goodwin, F. K. (1979). The natural course of affective disorders: Implications for lithium prophylaxis. In: T. B. Cooper, S. Gershon, N. S. Kline & M. Schou (eds) *Lithium: Controversies and unresolved issues* (pp. 381–398). Amsterdam: Excerpta Medica.

Zis, A. P., Grof, P., Webster, M., & Goodwin, F. K. (1980). Prediction of relapse in recurrent affective disorder. *Psychopharmacology Bulletin,* **16,** 47–49.

Zornberg, G. L. & Pope, H. G. Jr. (1993). Treatment of depression in bipolar disorder: New directions for research. *Journal of Clinical Psychopharmacology,* **13,** 397–408.

INDEX

Notes. The abbreviation 'CBT' stands for cognitive behavioural therapy; page references in **bold** are to figures, those in *italics* are to appendices.

see also cognitive behavioural
    intervention model; cognitive
    techniques
cognitive triad 113–14
collaboration in therapy 24, 56–7
    coping with prodromes 166–8
    information sheets 80–3, *273–80*
    introducing the model 80–93
    see also client–therapist relationship
comorbid pathology 30–1
compliance with medication 34, 36–7,
        39, 40, 230–2
    goal setting 96–8
    introducing CBT 87–9, 90–1
    pre-therapy assessment 70
    and stigma 192
    within CBT 63
compliance therapy 232
conditioning 42, 47–8
continuum technique 190–2, 193–4
coping strategies
    information sheet *276*
    irritability 229–30
    prodromes 15–18, 54–5, 160–1
        depression 175–81, **180**
        mania 166–70, **171**
        pre-therapy assessment 71–2,
            243–5
    stigma 189–92
cost–benefit analysis of hypomania
        128–30
couple relationships 22, 55, 207–11
    changes in libido 211–14
    couple therapy 38, 39, 210
    goal setting 99–100
    guilt 196–7
    partner involvement in therapy
        209–10, 213–14
    pre-therapy assessment 79, *270–2*
    social stigma 193
course of bipolar disorder 6–11, 17–18
creativity 20, 88–9, 187
    collecting automatic thoughts 118–19
    denial of illness 90–1
    therapeutic alliance 224, 227

crisis avoidance 146–7
    time allocation 147, 148
criticism of others 114, 228–30
cycle length (duration of episodes) 8,
        44
cyclothymia 1–2, 18–20, 46
cyclothymic disorder 5
cyclothymic personality 18–19

daily living routines *see* routines for
        daily living
delaying excessive activity 130–2,
        153–4, 182
delusions
    identifying prodromes 173–4
    Insight Interview *237–8*
    neuroleptics *280*
denial of illness 90–1, 187
depression, DSM-IV criteria 3, 4
desipramine 29
diagnostic criteria 2–5
diathesis–stress models 42, 46–51, 54–5
    and CBT 52–5, 56
    information sheet *273–6*
    life events and relapse 43–6
    patient acceptance of 89–93
    pharmacotherapy 25
divorce rates 22
drug abuse
    cyclothymia 19
    as factor in relapses 9
    stimulus control 155
drug therapy *see* pharmacotherapy
DSM-IV criteria 3–5
duration of episodes (cycle length) 8
    life events 44
Dysfunctional Attitudes Scale 71,
        239–41
dysfunctional beliefs 62, 70–1, 132–5
    patient education pamphlet *274–5*,
        276
    pre-therapy assessment 70–1, *237–8*,
        239–41
    stigma 189–90
dysregulation, biological 42, 46

repairing damage 183, 200
see also support services
sociotropy–autonomy 70–1, *239–41*
sociotropy–autonomy scale (SAS) 44–5,
71
Socratic questioning 120, 121–5, 134
spouses *see* couple relationships
stigma, sense of 185–6, 188–93, 194
families 206
pre-therapy assessment 71, *242*
stimulus control 154–6
stress
buffering hypothesis 219
circadian rhythm instability 52–4, 56
coping with 182–3
diathesis–stress models 42, 46–51, 54–5
and CBT 52–5, 56
information sheet *273–6*
life events and relapse 43–6
patient acceptance of 89–93
pharmacotherapy 25
on families 205–7
family therapy 38
interpersonal and social rhythm
therapy 37
minimisation 184
regenerating relapse 55
substance abuse
affective disorder predating 9
cyclothymia 19
as factor in relapses 8–9
stimulus control 155
subsyndromal symptoms 9–10
suicide risk 10, 74–6
support groups 206–7
support services 219–20, 233–4
child care 216
coping with prodromes 179, 181
depression 178–9
mania 170
for families 206–7
goals for use of 102–4
patient management of 183
team working 233–4
symptom history 60, 66–9

symptom reduction goals 94–6
symptoms, reframing thoughts as 125,
126–8

task assignment 151–3, 168
therapeutic alliance 221
autonomy 232–3
grandiose ideas 225–7
irritability 228–30
rapport 224–5
trust 222–4
thought records 118
thoughts 84
challenging 62, 101–2, 120–5
changes with mood states 113–15
collection 115–19
delaying 130–2
in depression prodromes 173
grandiose 85–6
client–therapist relationship 225–7
cognitive techniques 126–8, 131–2
goal setting 102–4
in mania prodromes 163, 168–9
monitoring 61–2
pre-therapy assessment 71, *239–42*
patient education pamphlet *274–5*
reframing as symptoms 125, 126–8
self-critical 84–5
thyroid, lithium prophylaxis 31
time delaying tactics 130–2, 153–4, 182
time prioritisation 147, 148
time of year 6, 49
timing of therapy 58–9
tranylcypromine 29
tricyclic antidepressants 29, 51, *279*
trust, client–therapist 222–4

unipolar depression 2

valproate
acute depression 29
acute mania 28, 30
prophylactic 31, 32
side effects 27, 28
views of illness *see* mental illness

Index compiled by Liz Granger

The Wiley Series in

CLINICAL PSYCHOLOGY

Ronald Blackburn	The Psychology of Criminal Conduct: Theory, Research and Practice
Ian H. Gotlib and Constance L. Hammen	Psychological Aspects of Depression: Toward a Cognitive-Interpersonal Integration
Max Birchwood and Nicholas Tarrier (Editors)	Innovations in the Psychological Management of Schizophrenia: Assessment, Treatment and Services
Robert J. Edelmann	Anxiety: Theory, Research and Intervention in Clinical and Health Psychology
Alastair Agar (Editor)	Microcomputers and Clinical Psychology: Issues, Applications and Future Developments
Bob Remington (Editor)	The Challenge of Severe Mental Handicap: A Behaviour Analytic Approach
Colin A. Espie	The Psychological Treatment of Insomnia
David Peck and C.M. Shapiro (Editors)	Measuring Human Problems: A Practical Guide
Roger Baker (Editor)	Panic Disorder: Theory, Research and Therapy
Friedrich Försterling	Attribution Theory in Clinical Psychology
Anthony Lavender and Frank Holloway (Editors)	Community Care in Practice: Services for the Continuing Care Client
John Clements	Severe Learning Disability and Psychological Handicap